Gene Hackman

ALSO BY PETER SHELLEY
AND FROM MCFARLAND

Anne Bancroft: The Life and Work (2017)

Philip Seymour Hoffman: The Life and Work (2017)

Gwen Verdon: A Life on Stage and Screen (2015)

*Neil Simon on Screen: Adaptations and
Original Scripts for Film and Television* (2015)

Sandy Dennis: The Life and Films (2014)

Australian Horror Films, 1973–2010 (2012)

Frances Farmer: The Life and Films of a Troubled Star (2011)

Jules Dassin: The Life and Films (2011)

*Grande Dame Guignol Cinema:
A History of Hag Horror from* Baby Jane *to* Mother (2009)

Gene Hackman
The Life and Work

PETER SHELLEY

McFarland & Company, Inc., Publishers
Jefferson, North Carolina

ACKNOWLEDGMENTS: Thanks are offered to Barry Lowe and Kath Perry for their continued support.

LIBRARY OF CONGRESS CATALOGUING-IN-PUBLICATION DATA

Names: Shelley, Peter, 1962– author.
Title: Gene Hackman : the life and work / Peter Shelley.
Description: Jefferson, North Carolina : McFarland & Company, Inc., Publishers, 2019 | Includes bibliographical references and index.
Identifiers: LCCN 2018053637 | ISBN 9781476670478 (softcover : acid free paper) ∞
Subjects: LCSH: Hackman, Gene. | Actors—United States—Biography.
Classification: LCC PN2287.H16 S54 2019 | DDC 791.4302/8092 [B] — dc23
LC record available at https://lccn.loc.gov/2018053637

BRITISH LIBRARY CATALOGUING DATA ARE AVAILABLE

ISBN (print) 978-1-4766-7047-8
ISBN (ebook) 978-1-4766-3369-5

© 2019 Peter Shelley. All rights reserved

No part of this book may be reproduced or transmitted in any form or by any means, electronic or mechanical, including photocopying or recording, or by any information storage and retrieval system, without permission in writing from the publisher.

Front cover: Gene Hackman, 2001 (Bravo/Photofest)

Printed in the United States of America

McFarland & Company, Inc., Publishers
  Box 611, Jefferson, North Carolina 28640
  www.mcfarlandpub.com

Table of Contents

Acknowledgments   iv
Preface   1

1. Beginning   3
2. *Bonnie and Clyde*   22
3. *The Poseidon Adventure*   46
4. *The French Connection II*   59
5. Semi-Retirement   74
6. *Twice in a Lifetime*   86
7. *Superman IV: The Quest for Peace*   97
8. *Narrow Margin*   113
9. A Second Academy Award   125
10. *Extreme Measures*   139
11. *Heist*   151
12. Retirement   164

Appendix   169
Bibliography   174
Index   191

Preface

I think I first saw Gene Hackman in the action adventure *The Poseidon Adventure* (1972) where he played a priest but not a conventional one. He was a man who had a violent temper, and even though he turned out to be right about what to do in the situation as opposed to Arthur O'Connell's priest who was passive (and who drowned), there was something frightening about his intensity. Hackman played what was described as a modern priest and the actor gave his character heroic and anti-heroic qualities.

This ambivalence was perhaps indicative of the heroes in 1970s cinema, a genre in which Hackman became a star. But he was an unconventional star, unlike his contemporaries Robert Redford, Al Pacino, Dustin Hoffman and Jack Nicholson. Although at this time he played leading man roles, Hackman rarely was a romantic figure despite his masculine appearance. He had begun acting at a relatively late age and, being tall with a double chin and paunch and a receding hairline, he described himself as a "big lummox." According to American playwright John Logan, talent agent Sue Mengers saw Hackman as an "ugly potato head." Pauline Kael wrote that he didn't have the sexiness of a movie star. While she admitted that Hackman was a superlative actor with an interesting expressive face, she felt that he was more like a character actor. His characters might have female sexual partners but his roles were more often violent ones, which is ironic since he said he hated violence. There was a rage in the actor that could be easily summoned, and it wasn't until later in his career that he began to also finesse that anger to comedic ends. Perhaps the turning point for Hackman was that at the height of his career in the 1970s he decided to retire, and it was when he returned to films with *All Night Long* (1981) that he was able to play a comic and romantic role opposite Barbra Streisand. This shift in perception led to an even greater period of leading man roles. Though in the 1990s he was playing a lot of supporting ones, he managed to end his career back in leading ones.

Hackman had mannerisms but they were not as distracting as those of others. He could overuse his hands in gesturing, had self-conscious self-touching, and laughed when sometimes there was no context for it. Some directors photographed him to conceal these mannerisms, but others seemed to allow them. Hackman could employ the misguided actor notion that one had to have an activity as they spoke, which proved to be untrue in his case since often the greatest moments were ones of stillness.

He also wasn't big on disguise. Hackman could wear a mustache or a beard, glasses and outlandish costumes, have his hair colored or shortened or shaven, and use an accent, but he was always recognizably himself. The roles in which Hackman came closest to completely transforming include his blind man scene in *Young Frankenstein* (1974), his appearance with false teeth in *Get Shorty* (1995), then in drag in *The Birdcage* (1996), and in *Heartbreakers* (2001) where he wore yellowed dentures and a red nose. The December 16, 2001, *New York Times* featured an insightful analysis of his acting, describing it as occupying a middle ground between character acting and movie stardom that had earned him the bland appellation "Everyman." He didn't disappear into his roles to effect a dazzling transformation like Gary Oldman or Meryl Streep, didn't make his roles disappear into him like Brando or Jack Nicholson, didn't project any charismatic ease with himself like Paul Newman, and didn't give off live-wire Method sparks like Al Pacino or Robert Duvall. Kael wrote that Hackman had an instant audience rapport perhaps *because* he looked dull and ordinary, but unlike other actors who played mediocre men, Hackman illuminated mediocrity and that's what made him a star.

This is the first book to span his entire career to date. There have been two previous biographies of him, one by Allan Hunter (1987) and the other by Michael Munn (1997). The present book cannot be considered the definitive coverage of Hackman's career since some of his television work is not available for viewing. In these cases, as much information as possible has been provided. In my research, I reviewed interviews that he gave to newspapers and magazines, with the archives of *The New York Times*, the Internet Movie Database's Related News, and the Getty Images website being particularly helpful.

The book is written as a biography, with Hackman's career presented in the context of his life. I have not made new chapters for each film, television appearances or stage show. They are mixed into the biography, with work listed in the order they were made as opposed to when they were opened or were released or broadcast. I analyze the work when possible, positioning Hackman's place in the project, commenting on his look and performance, and quoting any comments I have found by the actor as well as comments *about* him by his director and co-stars. I have also given the critical reaction that the work received and information about any awards it earned.

An appendix lists his performances onstage, in films, in featurettes/video, and on television; his five books are also listed.

1

Beginning

Gene Hackman was born Eugene Hackman on January 30, 1930, in San Bernardino, California. Some sources give his middle name as Alden, others Alda, and the California Birth Index gives it as Allen. His father was Eugene Ezra (born May 24, 1903), a journalist, and his mother, Anna Lyda Elizabeth *née* Gray (born May 13, 1904). Their second son Richard was born in 1942.

During the Great Depression, Eugene Sr. moved around the country to where the work was, taking his family with him. This led them to the small Midwestern town of Danville, Illinois, when Gene was three. The quiet backwater town was in the Corn Belt, about 120 miles south of Chicago and very close to the Indiana border, with a population of around 10,000. It was the hometown of Bobby Short and Dick and Jerry Van Dyke. Danville provided an apple-pie existence, with the highlight of the week being a Saturday night parade down Main Street. Because of their unsettled circumstances, the Hackmans rented and never owned their own home, and the boy's education was undertaken at four high schools, meaning he was always behind his classmates in learning.

The young boy and his brother were taken to the neighborhood movie theater by their mother, a great film fan. She told her son one day she would see him act, though she never did. He liked Errol Flynn, Tyrone Power and Douglas Fairbanks in their swashbuckling adventure roles, and also Edward G. Robinson, but his favorite was James Cagney. Cagney was different from anything he had ever seen: a New York-y, tough-looking, cocky wise guy who was also the consummate actor. After seeing one of his films, the boy would look at himself in a mirror in the lobby and be stunned that he wasn't him, and a period of depression would follow. Movie stars and movies provided a fantasy life and he prepared an Academy Award acceptance speech when he was 12. Too scared to try the Glee Club, the chorus or the community players, the boy decided to wait a while before pursuing acting. Another factor that held him back was his weight. He was plump and self-conscious about it so never dated in high school or went to a dance. At home in the basement, the boy used a cardboard house next to the coal bin as a place to hide. He called it his "own spot" though the basement itself terrified him: It was the place where his father doled out punishment if Gene was rude to him.

When the boy was 13, his parents divorced and Eugene Sr., no longer able to find work in Danville, left the town. The boy had no warning of the break between his parents. He was playing at a friend's house on a Saturday and saw his father drive by and wave, and knew from that wave that his father wasn't coming back. The two had a complicated relationship, with Gene fearing him and dreading his mother's cry of "Wait till your father gets home" after he had committed some offense; Eugene Sr. was "always going too far" and "laying it on pretty heavy." But his father also tried to spend Saturdays with his son, doing something together, except this Saturday that didn't happen. The boy ran home and his mother confirmed that his father had left for good. Hackman said he doubted he would have become an actor and so sensitive to human behavior if his father had not left in the way he did. It was that wave that meant so much: a small gesture but so precise. The actor later tried to have a relationship with him, and though they could never resolve their differences, it was important to make the effort. It took him a long time to understand his father's leaving and to come to grips with it, and the memory would stay with him, so much so that Hackman's recalling it on his *Inside the Actors Studio* episode saw him still visibly upset over it. He said that the experience was a good one for an actor to draw on and get in touch with his feelings.

The family now lived with Anna's mother Beatrice, an unyielding woman who had perhaps contributed to the rift between Eugene Sr. and Anna. She had come to North America from England and had spent hard winters in northern Canada before settling in Danville. Beatrice considered her son-in-law weak, and told Anna that she had married beneath her. Being somewhat infirm, Hackman spent time alone with her, and they became very close as she was a great storyteller. Money was scarce but the family wasn't so poor as to go hungry. Perhaps because of his father's absence, the boy was withdrawn and rebellious, getting into trouble at home and at school. He would lose his temper and lash out at authority figures. He also stole, spending one night in jail for taking candy and a soda.

He lived briefly in Storm Lake, Iowa, and spent his sophomore year at Storm Lake High School. In December 1946, there was an incident with his school basketball coach. The 16-year-old got into a shouting match and left school to go home, passing the Marine recruitment center he had passed many time before. This day, the teenager decided to enlist out of pique. He was underage and needed parental consent. He was going to leave home one way or another and if he was in the Marines, his mother would at least know where he was. She surprised him by giving her consent. Hackman figured his mother did so because she had had enough of his acting-out and thought that a spell in the Marines might do him good, or she believed he would hate the rigors of boot camp and be back in a week.

1. Beginning

Hackman entered the Marines in January 1947, right after his seventeenth birthday. His mother was right that he hated it but the teenager stayed on because of what came with the training: the opportunity for freedom and travel. Hackman had no desire to stay in Danville, particularly after having worked at a steel mill in a summer job. The experience affirmed that he could not be satisfied in such a mundane blue-collar environment.

After training at Camp Lejeune, North Carolina, Hackman attended the Field Wire Telephone School. He submitted to the authority of his superiors and found that the discipline both toughened him up and helped him lose weight. He rose to the rank of corporal. He was also busted for fighting. He traveled, serving in Hawaii, Japan, the Western Pacific island of Okinawa and Tsingtao in China. In China, he joined the Armed Forces Radio Service as a volunteer all-round disc jockey and broadcaster.

Standing six feet two inches might have made Hackman a stereotypical Marine except that he was shy. His work for the radio station helped him to overcome it. His style of presentation was faltering and he would often dry up when reading the news. The teenager saw the job as performing, and his drying up was classic stage fright, but it served to make him more determined to succeed. He overcame his fear and gradually acquired a taste for the work, despite the fact that it didn't much matter what he said as 90 percent of his audience was Chinese who couldn't understand a word of it.

The Korean War escalated and American troops were sent into the battle zone. Hackman's battalion received orders to go to Korea but a twist of fate kept him away. Late on night during training, he was on his motorcycle when he slammed into a tractor that had no lights. Hackman broke his right leg, left knee and right shoulder, which made him unfit for active service. (The injuries later caused discomfort when the actor was called upon to do action scenes or chases.) He resented not going with his battalion but the accident ironically also saved Hackman's life: Of those who went to Korea, only one in ten survived.

Gene was shipped to Camp Pendleton, near Oceanside, California, where he recovered and completed the four years of his Marine service. Two days before he was to be discharged, an officer asked him why his hair was so long. The officer gave him a choice: cut his hair or join the Reserves. Preferring the longer hair, he joined the Reserves. Two months later, he was called back into the Marines. After serving for four and a half years, the 20-year-old was discharged as disabled in 1950, with his left knee held together with plastic and metal joints.

The G.I. Bill entitled Hackman to $150 a month as a wounded veteran and he enrolled at the University of Illinois. The Bill required that what was studied would lead to a job, so he chose commercial drawing and journalism over acting classes. But, lacking the concentration and patience required, he had no aptitude for writing.

He dropped out after six months and decided instead to try for a career in radio. In 1951, he relocated in order to attend the School of Radio Technique in Manhattan. He lived at the YMCA and studied to become a professional broadcaster. He also indulged his hobby for painting at the Arts Student League for a year, believing he had a little bit of talent, and naively hoping this would feed him while waiting to be an actor. Painting and drawing relaxed Hackman, though he described it as unshowable. Running out of money, he was unable to pay his rent so the YMCA locked him out of his room until the debt was paid.

He decided to attend a YMCA dance in his casual day clothes. There he met a pretty, dark-haired Italian New Yorker, Chemical Bank secretary Faye Philippa Maltese, who said she couldn't help notice him because he wasn't wearing socks. Hackman asked her to dance and she agreed because she liked him immediately. They began seeing each other regularly. Hackman felt it was a case of opposites attracting, with he being the hick and Faye the big city girl from a large family. Their relationship developed into a romance and Hackman found a second family. She encouraged him in everything he did.

Graduating from the School of Radio Technique, Hackman moved into television as a floor manager and assistant director, traveling to stations in his home town of Danville, as well as Florida and California. He grew bored with the work and missed Faye. So he decided at the age of 26 to be an actor.

Acting would help Hackman overcome his shyness, but shyness wasn't the only problem. He said his face suggested middle age, describing it as "your everyday mine worker," despite the fact that he had a cleft in his chin like Kirk Douglas and Cary Grant. He called himself a "big lummox kind of person." His ordinary looks made him no Errol Flynn, so he didn't imagine ever becoming a leading man. And there was the issue of his age in an industry that favored those who were younger and better-looking than he. Hackman's family and friends thought it was a mistake but Faye remained supportive. In 1986, Hackman said he didn't know why he became an actor. It was an unsolved mystery and a decision never examined closely. On another occasion, he said that the reason was Marlon Brando, who he had seen in the film dramas *The Men* (1950) and *A Streetcar Named Desire* (1951). Hackman felt a kinssship with Brando, because although he was good-looking, he played "common man" roles. The young actor told himself, perhaps naïvely, that he could do what Brando did because he made it look so easy. But every young actor in New York was imitating Brando, and Hackman didn't want to be just another imitator.

He married Faye on New Year's Day 1956 and decided to go to California to pursue his new career. He was accepted at the Pasadena Playhouse of Theater Arts, whose motto was "Work with the stars, become a star." Hackman's fellow students were all five years younger than he, having come right out of high school, and this made him feel like a fish out of water. They were also better looking, as he feared.

1. Beginning

Described by Hackman as "walking surfboards," they were tall and blonde and wore fake guns to practice quick-draws for the hit television westerns of the time. His experience was chastening and he was cruelly dubbed by the Playhouse alumni as one of the two students least likely to succeed, the other being 19-year-old Dustin Hoffman who would become one of Hackman's closest friends. They were in a couple of classes together, and did a scene from *Of Mice and Men*, and an improvisation on Uncle Remus, with Hackman playing the title character. The pair found solace in each other's company, playing bongos on the roof of the Playhouse building. The Hackmans lived in the apartment next to the one Hoffman shared with another budding actor, Steve Ihnat. The dubbing of Hackman and Hoffman as failures proved to be a minor irritant to both actors and an incentive to prove the alumni wrong. Hackman didn't last one year in the program—he was kicked out after three months "for having no talent." The students were graded on a scale of one to ten for movement, characterization, gestures, articulation and makeup. He scored a 1.3; Hoffman said Hackman's work was so natural that the alumni didn't think it was acting. But he was selected for a production at the Playhouse's main stage, picked because an older cast member was needed. Another source says that Hackman was cast before he was asked to leave the school when the principal was not impressed by his performance in it. The play was *The Curious Miss Caraway* with Zasu Pitts in the title role. She had difficulty remembering her lines so they were written on the back of couches and chairs on the set.

In the July 21, 2000, issue of *The Guardian*, the actor recalled a reunion with one of the other Playhouse students 10 or 12 years after was let go. He was in California, brought out to do a little part in a television show, and while driving he saw a man on the street he recognized. Hackman yelled out his window, "Hey, Steve, I saw you on *Blue Light*," which was an ABC television show that aired in 1966. Steve responded with an "oh," apparently not remembering the actor, who then drove off. In his rear-view mirror, Hackman saw a car behind him, trying to catch up. When the two cars were side by side, Hackman recognized the driver was Steve, who yelled out, "It's gonna be repeated," and then drove away.

The Hackmans moved back to New York by bus and lived in a sixth-floor cold water walk-up apartment on 26th Street and Second Avenue. It had one bedroom and a living room-kitchenette and the rent was $22 a month. Faye found work again as a bank secretary and assumed the role of breadwinner. Their plans for a family would have to wait until they both had healthy incomes. Hackman took whatever short-term work he could get to allow him to be available for auditions and do the rounds of the offices of agents and producers. Finding acting jobs difficult to come by, Hackman worked as a soda jerk, a relief counterman at Whelan Drugs (where he said the customers treated him like "crapola"), a truck driver and a women's shoe salesman at Saks 34th Street. His customers in the latter job were annoyingly fussy women. He said the worst job he had was working nights at the Chrysler Building as part of a crew that polished the leather furniture. Hackman worked moving furniture for Greenwich Village Moving Company, hauling refrigerators into walk-up apartments. He included Dustin Hoffman on one job—Hoffman only lasted an hour. Another time, he and another actor were moving a valuable art collection, including a Picasso lithograph, which accidently got a tossed broom through it. Hackman was working as a doorman at Howard Johnson's, wearing a white uniform with green piping, when he was spotted by his first Marine sergeant wearing dress blues. Hackman said he just wanted to die but gave the sergeant a snappy salute and a big grin, to which he responded with "You're a sorry-looking son of a bitch" before walking on. On the job, Hackman also ran into a despised Pasadena Playhouse instructor who once told him he was not good enough to be an actor. Reinforcing "The Least Likely to Succeed" vote, the man said, "See, Hackman, I told you you wouldn't amount to anything."

He made his professional theatrical debut as an unpaid intern in summer stock at Bellport, Long Island, where he built sets, scavenged for props and set up lights. In a two-week production of Arthur Miller's *A View from the Bridge*, there happened to be one uncast role: Marco, the strong, silent Italian workman. The director, Ulu Grosbard, from the Yale School of Drama, picked Hackman. Grosbard said that the actor was a complex guy—very intelligent, with a generosity of spirit and socially charming—but he was tormented with ghosts from the past. The director felt Hackman brought this torment to his work. Hackman said Grosbard was the first theater person to encourage him. Robert Duvall was the lead in the play and Hackman was impressed with him from the first rehearsal. In addition to their desire to be actors, the pair also had military service in common.

Hackman began to study with George Morrison, an alumnus of Lee Strasberg's Actors Studio, with its Method internalized style of acting. Morrison taught him that acting was a matter of making choices, of finding what was real, what was appropriate, and how you were like and unlike a character. He was also trained in effective memory, to use what he had chosen to wear that day, and what he had seen and heard and smelled and tasted and touched. At the same time, Hackman was still moving furniture. The turning point came when Morrison included him in an improvisational troupe he directed, The Premise. In a tiny theater on Bleecker Street in Greenwich Village, the company did a revue show with skits, eight or nine times a week and two on the weekend. Hackman learned the technical skills to comedy: timing, delivery, voice. Morrison said the experience helped bring him out of his shell. Hackman studied with him for eight years and said that Morrison had the most influence on him of anybody in the business and he was eternally grateful. Morrison had a way of finding something in his pupil, something that other people had not seen, that he was then able to use, and which gave him great confidence. Hackman continued to do the full-body relaxation exercise that Morrison taught him the first week.

When he finally got an interview, Hackman was caught with a lie on his résumé: The interviewer had been in a production that Hackman said he was *also* in. He hated auditioning and said being at the bottom in the theater was a very ugly place, reading with the stage manager in front of two or three people you couldn't see sitting in the fifteenth row of a dark theater or being asked to wait for 30 minutes to read with someone else and then never being called back. Sometimes Hackman went to open cattle calls, where there were no appointments and hopefuls showed up by the hundreds, where people asked to jump the queue if they had to go to work or just ask to go ahead of him to get it over with. Gene Kelly once held one for a musical he was directing; Hackman stood in line and sang, and Kelly told him, "Nice try. Musicals are hard." He and his friends did not do what other actors did, immediately giving a full-out performance, thinking the producers and directors wanted to see what you would be like on opening night. Their philosophy was that they gave very little at first, waiting for the character to be discovered internally in rehearsal. This, plus their lack of leading-man looks, made them hard to cast.

Hackman reacted to rejection as if it was psychological warfare and he "wasn't going to let those fuckers get him down." But though some actors said they liked the struggle to get an audition or a job, Hackman saw that it made you a little crazy. You were trained to do the work and then nobody would let you do it so all the disappointment and rejection and the menial jobs brought out a simmering, suppressed anger. This could be helpful in exploring the dangerous edge of characters; Hackman later used this when playing mean-guy roles, as he used his shy kindness to play vulnerability. But the unpredictable and violent component to his personality found a cathartic expression when after a movie or dinner with friends he would leave to go to a bar to get in a fight. Hackman didn't want to get hit but he also didn't want to "take any shit."

In 1958, Dustin Hoffman turned up at the Hackmans' apartment, having finished his studies at the Pasadena Playhouse. He needed a place to stay and they let him sleep on their kitchen floor, by the fridge. Hoffman would take a bath while the couple was having breakfast. The two days Hoffman had asked to stay turned into three weeks. He wanted to go out and find his own apartment but the city was cold and lonely and he was too scared to leave. To him, the Hackmans were more than just his friends—they were his family.

In his October 19, 1988, appearance on *Late Night with David Letterman*, Hackman reported that Hoffman was the worst housemate and they had to hose the rooms down and sweep them out.

Hackman introduced Hoffman to Robert Duvall and the three men soon became inseparable, and looked out for each other. Hoffman finally moved out of the apartment and into one in Hell's Kitchen with Duvall and three others. He admired the way his two friends could talk to girls, since he was shy and awkward with them. Hackman knew how to talk to people and Hoffman said he could have picked up any girl he wanted.

With other struggling actors like Elliott Gould, James Caan and Jon Voight, play-reading parties were organized. They also played musical instruments and sang and took great delight in acting out dirty jokes. Another actor, Robert Redford, joined the group, and they wandered the streets of New York. What helped them survive was a sense of humor: They would meet for coffee and crack jokes to keep from crying. Hoffman said Hackman won the award for unflagging good humor. There was a feeling of Jack Kerouac at that time: kids just wanting to have a good time and experience things that didn't have anything to do with being successful. Hackman's wife Faye held parties with cooked pots of spaghetti for a crowd of actors. One night after dinner, they all lay down on the floor and went to sleep, then woke up for dessert. But Hoffman knew his friend would make it as an actor just by the way he walked into a room. The man had a presence that was unmistakable.

Despite his occupational frustrations, Hackman was hypersensitive and compulsively preoccupied with human behavior. He would spend time observing people as part of his studies, getting up in the morning and wanting to be out in the streets watching. Hackman would go alone to some of 42nd Street's cheap, seedy movie theaters that doubled as flophouses, and came away with oral dramas he had heard in the darkness. One was from a man who yelled in a heavy New York accent, "You're sorry! You piss all over my wife and you say you're sorry?" Hackman even turned his boring menial jobs into acting exercises. At Howard Johnson's, a crippled man came in every day and seemed to enjoy being difficult. He would leave a quarter or 15-cent tip and say, "Gene, to the bank. To the bank!"

Hackman sometimes went for weeks without seeing his friends. Duvall remembered him as a tormented guy, always into his own space, his own thing.

In time, Hackman landed roles in Off Broadway plays. A three-hour drama, *Chaparral* was written and directed by Valgrem Massey and produced at the Sheridan Square Playhouse. It ran from September 10 to 20, 1958, and centered on a decadent and incestuous Texas family. The production was lambasted by the *New York Times'* Brooks Atkinson, who made no mention of Hackman. *The Saintliness of Margery Kempe* was a comedy-drama by John Wulp based on the 15th century autobiography *The Book of Margery Kemp*. It was produced by New Drama Productions at the York Playhouse from February 2, 1959, and was directed by James Price. Hackman played the part of John Kempe, the mild and helpless husband of Margery (Frances Sternhagen), a woman who attempted to achieve notoriety by conversion to the faith and a pilgrimage to the Holy Land. The show was praised by the *Times'* Atkinson, who also said that Hackman's performance was one of a

1. Beginning

number of interesting performances in the production. The show was not a box office success.

Hackman made his TV debut in the April 22, 1959, episode of CBS's live anthology series *The United States Steel Hour*, "The Little Tin God." This was filmed in New York, had a teleplay by Joe Palmer, Jr., and was directed by Tom Donovan. It centered on the patients and staff of a tuberculosis sanitarium. Hackman played Joey Carlton. The show was praised by John P. Shanley in *The New York Times*, who called Hackman a first-rate source of comedy.

At this time, Faye was pregnant and would soon have to give up work, so they were reliant upon what work Gene could get. They were not leading roles but they were enough to keep up his spirits. Hackman said he was lucky because he would find that just when he was at his lowest ebb, a small job would come along and that was really encouraging.

He returned to *The United States Steel Hour* for the July 15, 1959, episode "The Pink Burro," directed by Paul Bogart. The teleplay was by Kay Arthur, based on a play by Jean Riley which had been produced at the Palm Springs Playhouse in 1958. June Havoc starred as former vaudeville singer Lil Anders, and Hackman played the part of Steve.

The actor next made the first of three uncredited appearances on the CBS crime drama *Brenner*, which was also filmed in New York. The July 25, 1959, episode "The Bluff" had a teleplay by George Bellak and was directed by Herman Hoffman. The story had Detective Brenner (Edward Binns) trying to find a policeman who reportedly abandoned a woman needing help. Hackman played the part of Officer Richard Clayburn. He was back on *The United States Steel Hour* for the November 4, 1959, episode "Big Doc's Girl." The teleplay was by Leonard Moran from a story by Mary Medearis, and it starred Margaret O'Brien as Mary Clayborne, a farmer's daughter with musical ambitions. Hackman played Reverend MacCreighton.

The actor said he enjoyed doing live television. It was exciting because things would happen and you had to get through it. Hackman recalled how one time one actor was really funny in rehearsal telling great stories rather than working. In the live performance, he went so dry that he couldn't have told you his name. The scene was set around a card table so the other actors started taking this actor's lines until he finally, after about three or four minutes, came back. Hackman said the experience taught him a great lesson: don't fool around in rehearsal. There was another incident involving props. In some shows, actors weren't allowed to handle them (that was the job of a union prop man), so the actors pantomimed using them. In one scene there was a telephone at a desk and it rang. Instead of reaching for it, Hackman reached over it and started talking to this imaginary phone piece. In the middle of the conversation he realized what he had done and then slowly lowered his hand with the imaginary piece and grabbed the real one.

By this time, the Hackmans had moved to a 27th Street apartment where the rent was $33 a month. In 1960, they had a son they named Christopher Allen. Once Hackman had children, his friends noticed a change in him. Now a family man, Hackman had spectacular pride. One noted that they had never seen a father as happy as he was. Hackman wanted a big family, and he and Faye achieved that.

He was back on *The United States Steel Hour* for the August 24, 1960, episode "Bride of the Fox," written by Bud Fishel and Barry Hyams and directed by Don Medford. It was based on a true event from the life of Tom Hines (played by Richard Kiley), whose success at spying and sabotage during the Civil War made him a Confederate hero. The actor's part is unknown.

Hackman made his film debut in the crime drama *Mad Dog Coll* (1961). The film was shot on location in New York from October 1960 with interiors lensed at Baltimore Studios. It had a screenplay by Edward Schreiber based on material by Leo Lieberman and was directed by Burt Balaban. The title character, kill-crazy 23-year-old Vincent Coll (John Chandler), leads a New York gang in the 1920s and declares war against Dutch Schultz (Vincent Gardenia). Hackman, uncredited, appears in one scene as a uniformed policeman who, with 16th Precinct Detective Darro (Telly Savalas), stakes out Coll's garage. Darro has scenes with other uniformed policeman but none of them appear to be Hackman again, although in one scene, one policeman's face is not shown.

The film was released on May 12, 1961, with the taglines "The Blistering Exposé of the Roaring Twenties!" and "His Own Raging Story…A Maniac with a Machine Gun!" The story of Coll was re-told on television in the July 28 and August 4, 1961, episodes of *The Lawless Years*, "The Mad Dog Coll Story." A 1992 film with the same title was directed by Greydon Clark and Ken Stein.

Hackman made an appearance on the crime drama *Tallahassee 7000*, a TV show that was shot in Florida. The May 16, 1961, episode "The Fugitive" was written by M.L. Davenport and Max Ehrlich from a story by George Lefferts and the director was Harmon Jones. The story had police pursuing an escaped prisoner, and Hackman played Joe Lawson. He was next on the CBS drama *The Defenders*, shot at the Filmways Studio in New York. The September 16, 1961, episode "Quality of Mercy," written by Reginald Rose and directed by Buzz Kulik, had lawyers Lawrence Preston (E.G. Marshall) and Kenneth Preston (Robert Reed) defending a doctor, and Hackman played the part of Jerry Warner.

The actor returned to *The United States Steel Hour* for the John Vlahos–scripted October 4, 1961, episode "Brandenburg Gate." The story was set on the eve of the closing of the Brandenburg Gate between East and West Germany. Richard Kiley plays an East German underground leader and an American newspaper man, but Hackman's part is unknown.

The actor made his last *United States Steel Hour* appearance in the January

1. Beginning

10, 1962, episode "Far from the Shade Tree," written by Joe Palmer, Jr., and directed by Tom Donovan. The story cecntered on Don McCabe (Keir Dullea), and Hackman played the part of Ed. Hackman was on the February 10, 1963, episode of CBS's religious anthology series *Look Up and Live*, "The End of the Story." He played the part of Frank Collins.

Hackman's mother died on December 30, 1962, at the age of 59, as a result of a fire she accidentally set while smoking in bed.

Hackman next appeared on the February 13, 1963, episode of CBS's crime drama–thriller series *Naked City*, "Prime of Life." It was written by Stirling Silliphant and directed by Walter E. Grauman. The plot had 32-year-old Detective Adam Flint (Paul Burke) present at the electric chair execution of Phillip Hames (Richard Hamilton), a murderer he captured in New York. Seventh-billed, Hackman played the part of Mr. Jasper, a reporter witnessing the execution. We see Jasper fidgety and repeatedly bringing his handkerchief to his mouth; he is also shown sketching the chair as he waits in the death chamber. (This recalls Hackman's own interest in drawing.) Hackman has a couple of lines, asking the prison desk guard (Maxwell Glanville) about the "wall" that exists between the prisoner and the audience in the death chamber, and says to himself, "Don't let me be sick in front of these men" at the execution. During the execution scene, Hackman gets his only closeup in the show and he is sweating in his fear. Director Grauman also gives him many solo medium reaction shots and a long-ish one after the execution.

The actor appeared in the Broadway production of Irwin Shaw's comedy *Children from Their Games* at the Morosco Theater. After two previews, the show opened on April 11, 1963, and closed on April 14. Directed by Sam Wanamaker and set in a New York brownstone, it centered on misanthropic Melvin Peabody (Martin Gabel) and his friends and relatives. Hackman played the part of Charles Widgin Rochambeau, a New York Giants tackle who courts Melvin's daughter-in-law Melissa (Brenda Vaccaro). In *The New York Times*, Howard Taubman wrote that Hackman played it droll and with stolid simplicity. The actor commented that his role in the play was flashy and he had a great time with it. On April 17, 1963, Hackman was one of the winners of the Clarence Derwent Awards, which were given for the best performances in a non-featured role by an actor or actress on or off Broadway. He won for his performance in *Children from Their Games* and he was to receive $500 at the Actors Equity meeting in June.

He returned to *The Defenders* in the April 20, 1963, episode "Judgment Eve," written by Reginald Rose and directed by David Greene. Contract bricklayer Frank Thorpe (Arch Johnson) is on trial for hiring Herbert Jaffe (Michael Conrad) to murder a competitor. Eighth-billed Hackman played Stanley McGuirk, who guards Frank in prison. He appears in two scenes, speaking to Frank; both times, his face is obscured by the cell bars.

Hackman had made his film debut in *Mad Dog Coll* but he preferred to say that *Lilith* was his first film. Shot in 1963, the drama was scripted by Robert Rossen based on the novel by J.R. Salamanca, and directed by Rossen. It went into production in late April or on May 6 (sources differ); it was shot on Long Island, in Maryland and Virginia, and at the Filmways Studios. Lilith Arthur (Jean Seberg), a patient at the Stonemont Poplar Lodge, a private asylum, has a romance with the novice occupational therapist Vincent Bruce (Warren Beatty). Hackman played Norman, the husband of Vincent's ex-girlfriend Laura (Jessica Walter). Norman works with the electric company and attends meetings of the United Citizens' Council. Hackman, sixth-billed, appears in one extended scene where Norman meets Vincent who visits his house, eating chocolates and drinking coffee. The actor speaks with a Southern accent and his directness can be contrasted to the acting of Beatty, which is self-conscious with pauses and stuttering. Hackman gets a laugh with a joke about Norman's brother working in the female garment industry and how Norman never expected to see him in ladies' underwear. One senses that Laura's marriage in an unhappy one, in the way Norman shouts to her when she is the kitchen, how he tells Vincent that working in an asylum must allow him to see pretty funny stuff going on, and how Laura drinks alcohol.

The film premiered at the New York Film Festival on September 19, 1964, and then opened on October 1 with the taglines "Powerful Shocker About Love!," "You will understand Lilith more than anyone!," "Perhaps women will understand Lilith better than anyone!" and "Before Eve there was Evil...and her name was Lilith!" Lambasted by *Variety* and Pauline Kael in "5001 Nights at the Movies," the film was a box office failure.

Robert Rossen reportedly saw Hackman in *Children from Their Games* when he was engaged in casting smaller roles for the film. Beatty commented that the best thing about the film was Hackman. He said he enjoyed working with the actor because he talked and listened, which is what acting was meant to be. Beatty felt that Hackman made him better in their scenes and said, "I gotta not lose this guy." This would lead to their reunion in *Bonnie and Clyde* (1967).

Jean Seberg said that she liked Hackman but she never thought he had a chance of making it as a star because he just didn't look like Warren Beatty or any of the other Hollywood handsome men. Seberg found him to be handsome because he had such character in that face and that's what made an actor interesting. But men were expected to have that heartthrob image and she said Hackman was never going to be a heartthrob. But she knew he was a really good actor. He didn't question the director about his motivation or ask to have his lines changed or go for any of that method acting. Hackman was just professional, nervous and willing to do his best.

After these film experiences, Hackman fell in line with the attitude of most

1. Beginning

New York stage actors. Movie work was little more than a way to make money, to spend a little time in California and get your hotel expenses paid, and then get back home again. Real acting was to be done on the stage. Hackman felt that most films were hardly seen because only a handful of films were successful and a bad film didn't make a difference to a stage actor. He said he didn't know anything about the technique of film acting and he really didn't care that much.

Hackman made an appearance on the May 10, 1963, episode of the CBS adventure television series *Route 66*, "Who Will Cheer My Bonnie Bride," which was shot in Cape Coral, Florida. It was written by Shimon Wincelberg and directed by James Goldstone. The story has Tod Stiles (Martin Milner) and Linc Case (Glenn Corbett) in Cape Coral, where they meet two men who involve them in a stick-up and shooting. Hackman played a motorist.

The actor was back on Broadway in the Howard Teichmann comedy *A Rainy Day in Newark*, produced at the Belasco Theater and directed by Albert Marre. The play concerned a session of the International Transport Union Local 821 in Endicott, New Jersey, and Hackman played the part of Sidney Rice. It ran from October 22 to 26, 1963.

Hackman's friend Robert Redford had a success on Broadway in the Neil Simon comedy *Barefoot in the Park*. The show, directed by Mike Nichols at the Biltmore Theatre, opened on October 23, 1963, and ran until June 25, 1967. Hackman was said to have joined the cast in a supporting role though which one is unknown. The actor is not listed in the opening night credits and neither is his name given as a replacement on the Internet Broadway Database. The actor said doing the brief run provided him with an opportunity to hone his comedy technique before an audience, and to explore a character at greater length than ever before. Hackman began to feel that he really had a future, and the nightly audience response served to reinforce his hopes. It never occurred to him to play the lead—that was for glamorous types like Redford—but he considered a career as a character actor something that seemed perfect for him.

Around October 1963, Hackman auditioned for the Muriel Resnik comedy *Any Wednesday*. It was scheduled to open on Broadway on February 12, 1964, after tryouts from January 22 in New Haven and from January 27 in Boston. Resnik wrote a book about the experience of mounting the play, *Son of Any Wednesday*. The book features photographs of Hackman by Wallace Litwin, auditioning, in rehearsal in New York, in New Haven, and on stage in the play.

Resnik wrote that she got an enormous charge out of hearing her lines read properly by Hackman when he auditioned, saying she was beside herself with pleasure. She felt he was so good and so right that she wanted him straight away, despite the fact that the others on the team told her to not make up her mind before they saw others' auditions. But she knew then that no one could have been better no matter how many they read. She went to see Hackman in his show *A Rainy Day in Newark*, which once again convinced her that he was the actor to play Cass. Hackman went to Resnik's apartment to read for John Newland, who was possibly going to direct. But she said the actor read badly because he was in a hurry: He was due to rehearse an episode of the television show *That Was the Week That Was*. (In that episode, aired on November 10, 1963, he played a reverend of Treeville, New York, who is interviewed and who talks about how big sin in his town has fallen off, but they're having a record year for little sin.)

Newland did not want Hackman for the play and neither did Sandy Dennis, its star, as she found him repulsive. One source claims that the actress' objection was because Hackman resembled Gerard O'Loughlin, with whom she had just broken up. Since Resnik insisted on the actor's casting and her contract had given her casting approval, George Morrison replaced Newland as director.

When President John F. Kennedy was assassinated on November 22, 1963, Hackman felt a sense of immense loss. He loved Kennedy, who was bright and sophisticated and seemed to care about people.

Hackman appeared in another television anthology series, NBC's *DuPont Show of the Week*, in the December 1, 1963, episode "Ride with Terror." Written by Nicholas E. Baehr and directed by Ron Winston, it told the story of 12 people held captive by hoodlums Connors (Gregory Rosakis) and Ferrone (Tony Musante) on a New York City subway train. He played the part of Douglas McCann. The show was remade as the feature *The Incident* (1967) by director Larry Pearce.

On December 10, 1963, the actor appeared in a special performance of three one-act plays by Michael Shurtleff. Entitled *Come to the Place of Sin*, it ran at the Off Broadway Theatre de Lys. The plays were "A Baker's Dozen," "The Lady Is a Tramp, Geraldine" and "So It's all so Rashoman." Directed by Milton Katselas, the show was part of the American National Theater's Matinee Series.

"Creeps Live Here," the December 23, 1963, episode of the CBS drama *East Side/West Side*, was shot at the Biograph Studios in New York and on location. It was written by Philip Reisman, Jr., and directed by Water Grauman. Community Welfare Service social worker Neil Brock (George C. Scott) tries to stop the demolishment of the Ivory Tower, a residential house in the Bronx, to make room for a supermarket. Tenth-billed Hackman played a 31-year-old uniformed policeman.

For *Any Wednesday*, Dick York was cast and rehearsals were scheduled to begin on December 30, 1963, at the New Amsterdam Roof and Riviera Gardens. But on December 29, York withdrew due to a sudden illness, so Hackman was hired. George Morrison said he would be able to cope with the actor's wounded ego since Hackman knew that the producers didn't want him, though Resnik wasn't sure if knew Dennis didn't want him either. Morrison told Dennis of the casting and she accepted it as a *fait accompli*, and the actor went on a diet.

1. Beginning

In 1963, the Hackmans had a daughter, Elizabeth Jean. Hackman was determined to do a good job as a father, perhaps because he had been raised largely without one of his own. The actor's marriage was a success, unlike that of his parents, and he said that without Faye, his life would have been unbearable. To come home every night and find her there made him want to go on and his children gave him the sense of belonging that he thought all men needed.

Any Wednesday was scheduled to open at the Music Box on Broadway. It centered on married businessman Don Cleves (Don Porter), who keeps a mistress, Ellen Gordon (Sandy Dennis), in an executive suite. Hackman played Cass Henderson, a visitor from Akron who wangles his way into the apartment to settle a business score with Cleves.

A Hackman portrait from Broadway's *Poor Richard* (1964–65).

On January 14, during rehearsals in New York and a week before the show was due to go to New Haven, George Morrison quit. He wanted the new ending for the play that he had made Resnik write and the producers wanted the script that had gone into rehearsal. Hackman feared that he would be fired but he wasn't and the show moved to the Shubert Theater in New Haven for tryouts from January 21, 1964. A possible new director, Richard Altman, felt that Hackman was miscast and knew nothing about playing comedy. Mike Nichols said he could help as a friend and come to New Haven and Boston as much as he could.

The cast traveled from New York to New Haven on a Greyhound bus and stayed at the Hotel Taft. The show's new director was Howard Erskine, one of its producers, but Resnik wrote this was only temporary since someone was needed to bring the show to New Haven. It was praised by F.R.J. in the *New Haven Journal-Courier*, who wrote that Hackman gave a forceful presentation. Henry Kaplan became the new director. Resnik noted that while Hackman had been withdrawn, vague and anxious all during rehearsals, he really delivered before an audience. She wrote that he was a superb actor and that it was possible to watch him growing and developing in his part each time he played it. And the audiences loved him.

The company moved to Boston on the same Greyhound bus on January 26.

17

They rehearsed at the Colonial Theater for the show was to be produced at the Wilbur. Hackman's trick knee went out. He had had an operation on it some years previously and usually, if it went out of joint, he was able to put it back. A doctor was called, and the problem seemed to be solved. The show opened on January 27 and was praised by Alta Maloney in the *Boston Traveler.* According to *Variety,* Hackman brought a pleasing personality and a good sense of comedy. Elinor Hughes in the *Boston Herald* said that it was a pleasure to have Hackman around, and *The Boston Globe* said that he was good. Elliot Norton in the *Boston Record American* wrote that Hackman played with a surprising amount of cool control, as though by sheer will power he was able to believe in his lines.

The company traveled back to New York by train. The show had four previews from February 14, 1964. It opened on February 18. It was praised by Howard Taubman in *The New York Times,* who wrote that Hackman brought youthful vigor and intelligence to his role. The show was a hit and ran until June 26, 1966, transferring to the George Abbot Theatre from February 15, 1966. Sandy Dennis won the Best Actress Tony Award for her performance.

A September 1, 1967, *Time* magazine article on Dennis commented that the actress' antics in the show caused problems and antagonized the other actors. She was said to improvise "to an indulgent and irresponsible extreme." One night in the middle of a love scene, someone in the audience sneezed and instantly she called out "God bless you." On other nights she would get into coughing matches with the audiences or wave goodbye to those she saw leaving early. Dennis jiggered with the script and some nights the play would finish 30 minutes earlier than usual because of her "revisions." The show's best known props were balloons and the actress used an air rifle to shoot those that had floated to the ceiling. Co-stars Rosemary Murphy and Hackman refused to speak to her offstage. In a June 19, 1966, *New York Times* interview, Dennis commented that she and Hackman did not speak for a month, though they worked well onstage. She said he behaved totally professionally and later, after he won Oscars and become a star, she was embarrassed that she had refused to work with him. The actress didn't know if he ever forgave her for the treatment.

Hackman was not cast in the Warner Bros. film version of the play. It was directed by Robert Ellis Miller and released on October 13, 1966. Dean Jones played Cass.

Hackman said that he hadn't really been aware until his last two years in New York how much more expertise and judgment it took to do comedy as opposed to drama. In comedy, if the laugh didn't come, there was no way you could defend that—you did it wrong.

The actor returned to the CBS crime drama *Brenner* for the May 24, 1964, episode "Laney's Boy," written by Peter Stone and directed by James Sheldon. Several

1. Beginning

police officers are charged with covering up crimes committed by a juvenile because his father was a veteran, well-respected police sergeant. Hackman played an uncredited police officer in the squad room. He made his third appearance on the show in the July 5, 1964, episode "Unwritten Law," written by George Bellak and directed by Dick Gaye. The show had the police investigating a mob murder, with Roy Brenner (Edward Binns) focusing on a police officer who may have aided and abetted the dead man's missing chauffeur. Hackman was again uncredited, as Officer Richard Clayburn.

On August 31, 1964, *The New York Times* reported the actor was to get his first starring role on Broadway in the Jean Kerr comedy *Poor Richard*. The show was scheduled to open on December 2 at the Helen Hayes Theatre. Hackman was to leave *Any Wednesday* on October 28, 1964. The actor became bored with the grind of repeat performances, despite the security that a long-running play offered. But having scored a Broadway success, he was now more entrenched and this made it easier to land other parts.

Staged by Peter Wood and presented by Stevens Productions, *Poor Richard* was set in Greenwich Village. The title character was the English poet Richard Ford (Alan Bates) and the play focused on his romance with his secretary Catherine Shaw (Joanna Pettet). Hackman played Sydney Carroll, Richard's editor. After two previews, it opened as scheduled and ran until March 13, 1965. Howard Taubman of *The New York Times* commented that the role of Sydney gave Hackman little to do except an amusing bit at the end about the fate of being indistinguishably ordinary. (The March 5, 1965, *New York Times* reported that Warner Bros had acquired the film rights to *Poor Richard*. However, the film was not made.)

The actor was seen by film producer Walter Mirisch in the play, and this led to his being cast in the drama *Hawaii* (1966). This had a screenplay by Dalton Trumbo and Daniel Taradash, based on the novel by James A. Michener. The director was George Roy Hill. Some sources claim the production was shot from February 1965 to September 1965 and others say it was from March to October 1965. Interiors were done at the Goldwyn Studios in Hollywood and exteriors on location in Hawaii, French Polynesia, Norway and Massachusetts. The plot: Nineteenth century Calvinist missionary Abner Hale (Max von Sydow) travels from New England with his wife Jerusha (Julie Andrews) to bring Christianity to the heathen natives of Lahaina. Fourth-billed Hackman was cast as Abner's friend, doctor-missionary John Whipple, who goes with him to Hawaii. Dressed in period clothes by Dorothy Jeakins, he sports long sideburns and has gray streaks in his hair to suggest his aging over time. In Hackman's best scene, he talks about the negative impact white men have had on the population of the island. The actor brings anger and some emotion to the scene, no doubt aided by the fact that he holds the dead measles-infected body of the islander Keoki (Manu Tupou) as he speaks to Abner.

The film was released on October 10, 1966, with the tagline "James Michener's novel reaches the screen." It was praised by *Variety* and Pauline Kael and lambasted by Vincent Canby in *The New York Times*. A box office success, it received Academy Award nominations for Best Supporting Actress (Jocelyne LaGarde), Best Color Cinematography, Color Costume Design, Best Special Visual Effects, Best Score, Best Original Song and Best Sound. The sequel *The Hawaiians* (1970) was directed by Tom Gries.

The actor reportedly worked on the movie for seven weeks, joining the cast on location in Hawaii in June 1965. He also appears to be in some of the scenes shot in Massachusetts. Away from filming, he attended gatherings held by Julie Andrews at her house in Kahala where she showed movies. Hackman discovered that idyllic Hawaii was also hot and uncomfortable. Returning to New York, Hackman learned that Faye was pregnant again.

On January 6, 1966, Hackman co-starred in a WNDT-TV production of the Arkady Leokum one-act play *Neighbors*. The play about race relations depicts what happens when a white couple in a New York suburban community decides to sell their home to a black couple. Glenn Jordan was the director and Hackman played the white male Chuck Robinson. On January 8, the *Times* reported that the broadcast had been postponed. On January 31, the decision was made not to reschedule. The station's president John Kiermaier believed that the material was too controversial to show.

Hackman made an appearance on the March 18, 1966, episode of the CBS drama *The Trials of O'Brien*: "The Only Game in Town," shot at New York's Filmways Studio, was written by Robert Van Scoyk and Gene Wang. Daniel O'Brien (Peter Falk), an interim judge on the New York Supreme Court, handles the case of Seaman Francisco Perez (Alejandro Rey), accused of murdering a co-worker with a longshoreman's hook. Hackman played Roger Nathan, the prosecutor in the case. Hackman then appeared in "Marriage," the June 5, 1966, episode of the ABC family drama *Directions*.

The New York Times reported on June 23, 1966, that Hackman was to appear in a triple-bill of short plays by Murray Schisgal, to be produced at the Berkshire Theater Festival in Stockbridge, Massachusetts. The director was Martin Fried. The plays were *Fragments* (which was also the overall title), *Reverberations* and *The Old Jew*.

The actor next appeared on the September 8, 1966, episode of the ABC crime drama *Hawk*, "Do Not Mutilate or Spindle," shot at the Filmways Studios in New York. It was written by Allan Sloane and directed by Sam Wanamaker. The story centered on New York Detective John Hawk's (Burt Reynolds) search for the killer of computer technician Catherine Delancey (Toni Darnay). The killer is a former New York Hospital elevator man (Hackman) who lost his job because of automation.

1. Beginning

A psychotic religious fanatic, he makes threatening phone calls to his next victim (Eliane Nadeau). According to the show's end credits, fifth-billed Hackman's character name is Houston Worth, but it's never used in the narrative. Sporting glasses, Hackman displays some frightening rage. His best moment: After his climactic fight with Hawk, he thanks Hawk for returning the glasses that have fallen off him.

2

Bonnie and Clyde

The actor received a call from Warren Beatty, his *Lilith* co-star, about a new role. Beatty was producing the biographical crime actioner *Bonnie and Clyde* (1967), shot in Texas and California from October to November 1966. The screenplay was by David Newman and Robert Benton, and the director was Arthur Penn. The title characters were café waitress Bonnie Parker and ex-con Clyde Barrow, who in 1931 began a violent crime spree, robbing cars and banks. Their story had been previously portrayed in *The Bonnie Parker Story* (1958) where Clyde was called Guy. Hackman played Clyde's ex-con brother Buck, who joins the Barrow Gang. Buck is described by Bonnie as an "ignorant, uneducated hillbilly" but the only thing that Hackman does to suggest this, apart from his use of a Southern accent, is speak loudly. He sometimes stammers in his dialogue, presenting a laughing familiarity with his co-star. Hackman makes Buck funny and he gets some funny lines. He comments about his wife Blanche (Estelle Parsons), "It's the face powder that gets a man interested but it's the baking powder that keeps him home," and he states, "I believe I lost my shoes" after he is fatally shot by the police. In his best scene, he tells Clyde the story of the teetotaling sick mother who is fed brandy in her milk, a story he repeats to undertaker Eugene Grizzard (Gene Wilder). The film also features the actor's first film death scene.

It premiered at the Montreal Film Festival on August 4, 1967, and then opened on August 13 with the taglines "The strangest damned gang you ever heard of. They're young. They're in love. They rob banks" and "They're young… they're in love… and they kill people." Pauline Kael of *The New Yorker* wrote that Hackman gave a beautifully controlled performance. *Variety*'s Dave Kaufman wrote that Hackman was more a clown than a baddie.

The film was a box office success and earned Academy Award nominations for Best Picture, Best Director, Best Original Screenplay, Best Actor, Best Actress, Best Supporting Actor (Hackman), Best Supporting Actress for Parsons, Best Cinematography for Burnett Guffey, and Best Costume Design. Parsons and Guffey were winners.

One of Hackman' scenes was reduced or altered to keep the running time down. This was the scene of the arrival of Buck and Blanche, which was originally longer, with Buck singing Bible hymns and Blanche scolding him for bringing her to see Clyde.

One source claims that Jack Nicholson was Beatty's first choice for the role of Buck, but Nicholson was unavailable or unwilling. Another source says that Nicholson was also considered for the role of C.W. Moss (who was played by Michael J. Pollard) before it was deemed that the actor was too similar to Beatty.

Hackman claims that when he had been ill in hospital in New York for six weeks with blood poisoning, Beatty came to see him and mentioned the part. Elsewhere he said that Arthur Penn came to see him when he was doing a Broadway play to talk about the film. In a 1971 *New York Times*, Hackman said that he was in California doing a TV show and his wife told him that Beatty had called for him. Another source has Beatty driving around Hollywood when he spotted Hackman standing on the corner of Hollywood and Vine and remembered him from *Lilith*. Estelle Parsons claims that she suggested the actor to Beatty. Another source says that she only alerted Hackman to the film and suggested he inquire after the part. Arthur Penn said Beatty suggested Hackman to him. Penn reported that Beatty screened a *Lilith* scene featuring Hackman, and the director thought it was wonderful. He had seen the actor in the Murray Schisgal plays in the Berkshires with Parsons, and he thought they would be great together. On his *Inside the Actors Studio* episode, Hackman says he thinks it was Beatty who requested that Penn go see the actor. However, Penn was in attendance at the *Actors Studio* show and said that Hackman's memory was wrong, and that Beatty only suggested Penn watch *Lilith*. The director reported that there was opposition to the casting of Hackman because it was thought he didn't have the right look. However, Beatty told Penn that he was a hell of an actor.

Hackman spoke about the difficulty Beatty had in interesting a Hollywood studio in backing the film. No one but Beatty saw the potential of the material. Hackman just hoped it would get made and that he would

Hackman in *Bonnie and Clyde* (1967).

be paid well, and hoped the film might be successful enough to get him more work. Hackman felt that Beatty had this image of being a playboy, but he was really a shrewd filmmaker. Hackman was quoted in Peter Biskind's book *Star: How Warren Beatty Seduced America* about the trouble Beatty had during the film's shooting. In Suzanne Finstead's book *Warren Beatty: A Private Man*, she says that Hackman observed this when he first arrived for shooting. She adds to Hackman's story that it was because Beatty was such a tremendously good-looking guy that the crew just figured he was a Hollywood dilettante. But he overcame that and as it turned out, Beatty was a lot better at his job that they ever were at theirs. Hackman remained full of admiration for the way Beatty handled the production work while simultaneously delivering his performance in the film. Despite Hackman being 37, Beatty believed a strength of the cast was their comparative youth which would appeal to the youth of the time. Finstead also reports that Hackman used the accent of Bill Stokes, the Texan whose company built the soundstage, as a model for Buck's.

The film gave the actor more screen time that he had previously had but he still felt he didn't have enough experience in film acting. Beatty insisted that Penn shoot everything 30 times, and while Hackman could improvise for the first and second takes, after that he had trouble. Penn proved helpful in teaching Hackman the difference between stage and film acting and he advised him how to adjust his performance so he could underplay and react more internally. In time, the actor could make repeated takes seem as fresh and spontaneous as the first. Hackman admitted that he grew bored playing the character, partly because of Buck's lazy drawl, which he grew tired of using. He said it was so heavy that it depressed him. He had been working for several years in New York, working to try to say his -ing sounds, and now he had to go back to saying goin' and comin'.

In Peter Biskind's book, Estelle Parsons said that Hackman made her cry. She said he was a beginning movie star and wanted to get somewhere with it. But it was beyond her comprehension that anybody could be as good an actor as Hackman was on the stage and want to be a movie star. Parsons thought he was in some sort of competition with Beatty and he wanted to be noticed.

Hackman later said that he believed one of the reasons the film worked was that it was released while the country was deep into the Vietnam War, when every day the public saw body bags coming back home. What he took away from the film was that if moviemaking or acting in general was like this, then he was in for the duration, because he loved it. He loved the ensemble and to him it was the ultimate acting experience. The release of the film came just after Hackman had been fired from *The Graduate,* when he was quite depressed. The success of *Bonnie and Clyde* gave him some hope of maybe sticking around as an actor.

On *Inside the Actors Studio*, Hackman said he remembered thinking early on that acting was great because there were all these wonderful people bouncing around and he thought it would always be like that. Later, he admitted, his experiences were not always like that. What he came to believe after *Bonnie and Clyde* was that, to get a great performance, the director had to create an atmosphere that you could work in. Somebody like Penn was capable of making him feel as if he was part of their movie. And that's why the movie worked.

In 1966, Hackman appeared in the 16mm short *Community Shelter Planning*, written and directed by Marc Isaacs. It was produced by the Army Pictorial Center for the Office of Civil Defense Staff College, Battle Creek, Michigan, and shot in Bucks County, Pennsylvania. Its purpose was to identify fallout shelter space for all of the citizens of the community. Hackman, uncredited, plays the supporting role of Donald Ross, a Regional Civil Defense official who attempts to convince John, a skeptical county commissioner (played by an unseen Arnold Moss), to adopt a Community Shelter Planning program. The film premiered at the Bucks County Courthouse on June 6, 1967. Also in 1966, the Hackmans had their third child, a daughter they named Leslie Anne.

He made an appearance on the January 15, 1967, episode of the ABC crime drama *The F.B.I.* "The Courier," shot at Warner Bros., was written by Charles Larson (based on a story by Robert C. Dennis) and directed by Ralph Senensky. The episode had the F.B.I. investigating the theft of plans for a new cobalt bomb and Hackman played the part of Herb Kenyon.

The actor's next film role was in the World War II drama *First to Fight* (1967), shot in California and Florida. The film had a screenplay by Gene L. Coon and was directed by Christian Nyby. Marine Sgt. Jack "Shanghai" Connell (Chad Everett), a Medal of Honor hero at Guadalcanal in 1942, later trains recruits at Camp Pendleton and is the platoon leader during a battle at Maui, Hawaii. Hackman, billed sixth, played the supporting role of Marine Sgt. Tweed, who is second in command at the battle. He's at his best in a scene where he angrily confronts Jack about retreating from the first stage of the battle. It premiered in Charlotte, North Carolina, on January 25, 1967, with the tagline "The blockbusting story of a fighting marine that comes mortar-screaming out of green hells and jungles!" Hackman said the role allowed him to recall his life as a Marine and to pretend that he was very brave.

Hackman's next film, the drama *A Covenant with Death* (1967), was shot in Mexico. One source claims that it went into production before *First to Fight* and that the actor was rehired by William Conrad, who produced both titles. The screenplay was by Lawrence Marcus and Saul Levitt based on the novel by Stephen Becker, and the film directed by Lamont Johnson. Set in Soledad County in 1923, it focused on a 29-year-old novice judge (George Maharis) presiding over the murder trial of Bryan Talbot (Earl Holliman). Hackman, who played the police chief, was billed sixth. His hair is streaked with gray and he speaks with a Southern accent (no one else heard in the movie uses one). In his best scene, he attempts to articulate to the judge the strange desire he felt for the murdered Mexican woman, Louise Talbot (Jadine Vaughan). The film was released on February 15, 1967, with the taglines "The bristling best seller comes to angry life," "The line between lust and love and murder is sometimes as fragile as Louise Talbot's lovely neck" and "Never talk too big. Never beat your wife. One night she could get strangled. And who would believe the hands weren't yours?" It was lambasted by Clive Hirschhorn in "The Warner Bros. Story."

Hackman commented that his main function in the film was to find a suicide note from the real murderer, which didn't take much emoting. This comment diminishes Hackman's performance since he also expresses the police chief's disturbance at the murder scene, his black humor at Bryan's hanging, and his anger in other scenes. He would remark of his last two films that he couldn't say he was any good in them because he hadn't learned how to do movie acting. But it didn't matter because they were not much better than his acting.

Hackman was back on the stage for the Lee Thuna comedy *The Natural Look*, in which he played a dermatologist married to Brenda Vaccaro, advertising director in a cosmetics firm; the pressures of her job create domestic problems. After 18 previews from February 23, 1967, the show opened on schedule on March 11 but it closed the same night. Walter Kerr in *The New York Times* wrote that Hackman was funny.

The actor's friendship with Dustin Hoffman paid off when Hoffman secured for him the role of Mr. Robinson in *The Graduate* (1967). At the rehearsal stage in March 1967, director Mike Nichols persevered with Hackman for a while, seeing that he was floundering opposite Anne Bancroft who played Mrs. Robinson. The actor realized he just wasn't capable of giving the director what he wanted. In the third week of rehearsal, Hackman told Hoffman in the men's rest room of his fear of being fired (which he was). It was painful but the actor knew it was his own fault. At the time, it seemed to Hackman it was the end of his career but the release of *Bonnie and Clyde* changed all that.

He next appeared in the romance *Banning* (1967) which was shot on location at the Riviera Country Club in Los Angeles and at Universal. This had a screenplay by James Lee based on a story by Hamilton Maule, and was directed by Ron Winston. Mike Banning (Robert Wagner) uses his past associations to become the new assistant golf pro at the Arizona El Presidente Country Club. Ninth-billed Hackman played Tommy Del Gaddo, the club's golf pro, who is said to be a drunken has-been (which is presumably why we never see him play golf). He appears in only three scenes, including one where he is semi-naked in a steam room. His hair has gray streaks. In Hackman's best scene, Tommy apologizes to Mike, speaking of his backstory in vague terms. The film premiered in Nashville, Tennessee, on June 30, 1967, and was then given a wide release on December 13, 1967, with the taglines "The

2. Bonnie and Clyde

truth about the women who go all out ... when they go for a man!" and "The action begins ... when the auction ends!" It received an Academy Award nomination for Best Original Song.

Hackman appeared on the October 17, 1967, episode of the ABC science fiction series *The Invaders.* "The Spores," shot at the Sam Goldwyn Studios in Hollywood, was written by Ellis Kadison and Joel Kane, based on a story by Al Ramrus, John Shaner, Kadison and Kane, and directed by William Hale. In Phillipsburg, Colorado, David Vincent (Roy Thinnes) is in pursuit of alien courier Tom Jessup (Hackman). Tom has a case of experimental cargo—two dozen spores that are to be taken to an incubation point so they will grow into aliens. The actor, top-billed among the episode's guest stars, plays an alien who is violent—getting into a fight with David and roughing up teenagers (James Gammon and Kevin Coughlin) who steal his case. Tom is killed in a climactic fire at a hop house.

"Leopards Try, But Leopards Can't," the October 28, 1967, episode of the ABC western *Iron Horse*, was written by Jeri Emmett and Norman Katkov and directed by Leo Penn: The town of Scalplock gets a new sheriff, former bounty hunter Harry Wadsworth (Hackman), who becomes a romantic rival to railway owner Ben Calhoun (Dale Robertson) for the affections of storekeeper Julie Parsons (Ellen Burstyn). Hackman has a sizable part and a character with depth, described as having "courtly manners and explosive violence." He uses a Southern accent and spends his pre-sheriff time unshaven. In the course of the episode, he gets in two fistfights and two gunfights and repeatedly slaps Julie, with Hackman showing Harry's anger to be terrifying. He gets a funny line after Dan Barrington (Roy Barcroft) tells him to leave town: "Subtracting me won't subtract the burrs from your bed-blanket." Hackman's best scene is perhaps when he tells Lloyd Barrington (Sam Melville) about his dead mother's infidelity just to be provocative. In her memoir *Lessons in Becoming Myself*, Burstyn said that the actor really scared her in the episode and she made a point of remembering his name.

The September 10 *New York Times* featured a photograph of the actor with Tresa Hughes, in rehearsals as a scientist and his wife in Murray Schisgal's short plays due October 2 at the Off Broadway Cherry Lane Theater. On October 1 there was a photograph of Hackman with Humbert Allen Astrado, who were said to play two parts of a single human being split into three parts in Schisgal's comedy of manners. Staged by Larry Arrick, the show *Fragments* was two one-act plays entitled "The Basement" and "Fragments." Hackman played Zach in the first and Baxter in the second. Clive Barnes in the *Times* wrote that the actor in both was stylish and true. It ran from October 2 to 22, 1967.

"My Father and My Mother," a *CBS Playhouse* drama broadcast on February 13, 1968, was set in Indiana Falls, Massachusetts, and focused on magazine editor Ned Piper (Hackman) and his relationship with his parents and children. It was written by Robert Crean and directed by George Schaefer. The show was filmed at CBS Television City Studio in Hollywood. Jack Gould of the *Times* wrote that Hackman did a resourceful straightforward job.

On January 13, 1968, Hackman was named as the Best Supporting Actor for *Bonnie and Clyde* by the National Society of Film Critics. A reception was held at the Algonquin Hotel in New York.

In January, Hackman was in California shooting his next film, the crime drama *The Split* (1968). It had a screenplay by Robert Sabaroff based on the novel *The Seventh* by Richard Stark, and was directed by Gordon Flemyng. Jim Brown starred as McClain who, with a group of ex-cons, steals $548,000 from the Los Angeles Memorial Coliseum during a football game. Fourth-billed Hackman is Detective Lt. Walter Brill, called in when McClain's ex-wife Ellie (Diahann Carroll) is murdered. Sporting a brown suit, Hackman appears in the last 20 minutes. He has little of interest to do, with his actions of killing Ellie's killer and taking the money occurring off-screen. During the climax, which is set at night, Brill tells McClain to go ahead of him: "You'd be harder to see first." This presumably refers to Brown's skin color, despite the fact that McClain's clothes are a lighter color than Brill's.

The film premiered in Chicago in October 1968 and then opened on November 4 with the taglines "Crime is our business" and "The money was easy to steal ... but hard to split!" The *Times*' Renata Adler wrote that Hackman's acting was solid and lean. It was reportedly a box office success.

Hackman appeared in the February 26, 1968, episode of NBC's comic action-adventure series *I Spy*, "Happy Birthday Everybody," which was shot at Paramount Studios. Written by Morton Fine and David Friedkin and directed by Earl Bellamy, it had Kelly Robinson (Robert Culp) and Alexander Scott (Bill Cosby) in Mexico, where they meet escaped mental patient Frank Hunter (Hackman).

On April 10, 1968, Hackman attended the 40th Annual Academy Awards ceremony at the Santa Monica Civic Auditorium. He was nominated for Best Supporting Actor for *Bonnie and Clyde*. The award was presented by Patty Duke to winner George Kennedy (for *Cool Hand Luke*). When Bobby Kennedy was assassinated in Los Angeles on June 6, the actor felt his loss deeply: He had met him at Sardi's a couple of months before.

His next film, the romantic actioner *The Gypsy Moths* (1969), was shot on location in Kansas and at MGM from July 1968. Written by William Hanley (based on the James Drought novel) and directed by John Frankenheimer, it centered on Mike Rettig (Burt Lancaster), Joe Browdy (Hackman) and Malcolm Webson (Scott Wilson), parachute stunt jumpers who visit Bridgeville, Kansas on a Fourth of July. Hackman sings "The U.S. Air Force" and rotates in the air in a visual effect. The film was released on August 28, 1969, with the taglines "When you turn on by falling free ... when jumping is not only a way to live, but a way to die, too ... you're

2. Bonnie and Clyde

a Gypsy Moth" and "The Gypsy Moths fall fast. They can't stop risking their lives—not even for their down-to-earth women." According to *Variety*, Hackman was forceful and gave an excellent account of himself; Roger Ebert said that the actor was particularly good at capturing the speech rhythms of an unhurried man. The film was not a box office success. Hackman was offered the film after *Bonnie and Clyde*, when it was known as *The Fall Guys*, but since it wasn't scheduled to go into production until the summer of 1968, he did *The Split* and *Riot* in the interim. His freefalling shots were done with him rotating on a spindle against a rear-projection screen in the studio. He did none of the stunt jumping but the aerial work thrilled him so much that he learned to be a pilot and took up stunt-flying as a hobby. Flying was to become one of his great passions—an expensive one—but he could now afford it with the kind of money he was making. This more affluent lifestyle also led the Hackmans to buy a house in Hollywood.

The actor observed how people deferred to Burt Lancaster. He admitted that Lancaster was a bright guy and it seemed, since he had reached a certain level, people were frightened of his money or his power. This worried Hackman because he felt it was a bad thing to have yes-men, but despite this, the actor learned a great deal about how an important actor handled himself on the set.

What John Frankenheimer remembered most about the movie was Hackman, whom he considered one of the greatest movie actors who ever lived. According to Frankenheimer, you could see from his performance that he was going to become the star he became. The director augmented his part and called him the engine that made the movie work; he felt that Hackman had the ability to project the truth. He made any director look good, and Frankenheimer said he would work with him on anything he wanted to do. The director felt Hackman's character's talk about the time he did the cape jump was the best scene in the film because Hackman was so brilliant.

Hackman returned to TV for ABC's, science fiction actioner *Shadow on the Land*, broadcast on November 4, 1968. This had a teleplay by Nedrick Young and was directed by Richard C. Sarafian. Set at Christmas in Los Angeles, the story focussed on Major Shepherd McCloud (Marc Strange), a member of the emergency government's Internal Security Forces. He is assigned to find Lt. Col. Andrew Davis (Jackie Cooper), who is in league with the Society of Man, a group of underground freedom fighters. Fourth-billed, Hackman played Reverend Tom Davis, who works at the Midnight Mission and is the brother of Andrew and childhood friend of Shepherd. The actor has the sensitivity to be believable as a priest with self-righteous passion and he scores a laugh from the way Tom prays as Shepherd insults him. Hackman's best scene is perhaps Tom's quiet reaction to having shot and killed I.S.F. agent Falting (Scott Thomas) in the film's climax.

His next film was the science fiction adventure *Marooned* (1969), which began filming on November 14, 1968. It was shot on location in Florida and at the Sunset Gower Studios in Hollywood. It had a screenplay by Mayo Simon based on the novel by Martin Caidin, and was directed by John Sturges. The film told the story of three American astronauts, Commander Jim Pruett (Richard Crenna), Science Systems Astronaut Clayton Stone (James Franciscus) and Apollo Guidance Pilot Buzz Lloyd (Hackman), whose spacecraft *Ironman One* malfunctions during a five-month mission, stranding them in space. Hackman, billed fifth, is seen unshaven after we are told the ship's electric razor is broken. The actor gets only one costume, a yellow and white spacesuit with a red helmet, designed by Seth Banks. He gets to do some aerial acrobatics as Buzz floats inside the spaceship and in space, shows dying of oxygen deprivation in a subtle way, and cries in a child-like manner because he blames himself for the malfunction. Hackman's best scene is perhaps when he yells in anger "Get us out of here!" to Mission Control.

The film premiered in Washington, D.C., on November 10, 1969, and was then given a wide release on November 11 with the taglines "Three marooned astronauts. Only 55 minutes left to rescue them. While the whole world watches and waits..." and "The Saga of Ironman One." Roger Ebert who wrote that Hackman was particularly good. The film was not a box office success but it won the Best Special Visual Effects Academy Award for Robie Robinson, and was also nominated for Best Cinematography and Best Sound.

John Sturges cast Hackman for believability and because he didn't see the actor as a star, since he figured that if he cast stars as the astronauts, the audience would know they would get back and the studio would have insisted on them surviving.

Hackman's next film was the crime drama *Riot* (1969) shot on location at the Arizona State Prison. This had a screenplay by James Poe based on the novel *The Riot* by Frank Elli, and was directed by Buzz Kulik. A riot that breaks out in a state prison is actually the cover-up for an escape attempt. Hackman played "Red" Fraker, leader of the escape attempt by the inmates of the isolation section. Hackman is billed second behind Jim Brown, who plays prisoner Cully Bristol. He appears to have his hair dyed red (hence his nickname). Hackman presents Red as a sensitive, intelligent and funny man. His best scene is his death scene, simply because having his throat cut by fellow escapee Surefoot (Ben Carruthers) is such a shock and more interesting than anything else he is called upon to do. Since the film was made with real prison inmates, he and the rest of the cast and crew had to carry identity cards which they needed to produce every time they left the compound.

The film premiered at Arizona State Prison in December 1968; Hackman was unable to attend because by that time he was filming *Marooned*. It was released on January 15, 1969, with the tagline "Freedom ... by any means necessary." According to *Variety*, Hackman gave the best performance in the film. Roger Ebert said that the actor gave a competent performance without really coming up to potential.

2. Bonnie and Clyde

Riot producer William Castle said he believed Hackman would work for the rest of his life because he had versatility but he would never be a leading man. Castle equated the actor with Jim Brown, who was only a star for a short time, and he felt Hackman was never going to be Jim Brown. Castle suggested that the actor continue his career as a star heavy, like Ernest Borgnine.

Hackman's next film, the sports drama *Downhill Racer* (1969), was shot around April 1969 with location work in Austria, France, Switzerland and Colorado, and interiors at Paramount in Hollywood. The screenplay was by James Salter and the director was Michael Ritchie. It centered on skier David Chappellet (Robert Redford) from Idaho Springs, Colorado, who joins the U.S. ski team in Europe as a downhill racer and competes in the Winter Olympics. Second-billed Hackman played team coach Claire. He has an interesting moment when the coach and a helmeted David touch heads when conferring before the climactic race. Hackman's best scene is perhaps the one where he tells David that nobody races unless he says so, after a fun race between David and Creech (Jim McMullan) sees a teammate plow into a stone wall.

The film premiered in Reno, Nevada, on October 28, 1969; Hackman was part of an October 29 press conference in Reno. It then opened on November 6 with the tagline "How fast must a man go to get from where he's at?" *Variety* called Hackman's characterization virile and thoroughly human. Roger Ebert said that the actor's performance was superb. The film was not a box office success.

Hackman was approached by Michael Ritchie about *Downhill Racer* while he was shooting *Marooned*. Ritchie found the character only half-formed in the script and he felt he needed an extraordinary actor to bring it to life, with his decision approved by Redford, Hackman's old friend. On the set of *Marooned*, the director and the actor discussed their knowledge of skiing, which was virtually non-existent, and some of the planned script rewrites. Ritchie said Hackman quickly breathed life into his character and brought such strength and authority to the part that the only problem they had was when Redford was called upon to leave the coach bewildered. In Michael Feeney Callan's Robert Redford biography, Ritchie said the actor had no ego and didn't care how he was photographed, and although Hackman liked Redford, he was dismayed and appalled that the star did his own skiing. He said, "Does that idiot know about insurance liabilities? If he falls, we're all on our way home."

The actor compared the film's limited budget with that of the James Bond action adventure *On Her Majesty's Secret Service* (1969) which was filming simultaneously in Switzerland. They would see crates of champagne hauled up the mountain for the 007 VIPs, but in the end, Hackman thought their film did well out of the competition. He later admitted that during the film's production he often felt like a high-priced extra. He said he still wanted to be a romantic leading man who got the girl even though he felt it was unlikely to ever happen. Ritchie commented that Hackman's frustration in this regard was the key to understanding his career. The director felt the coach's ambiguity and even outright duplicity was seldom found in parts for the leading men roles that the actor wanted. But it was very human and Ritchie believed it was at the core of Hackman's greatest performances.

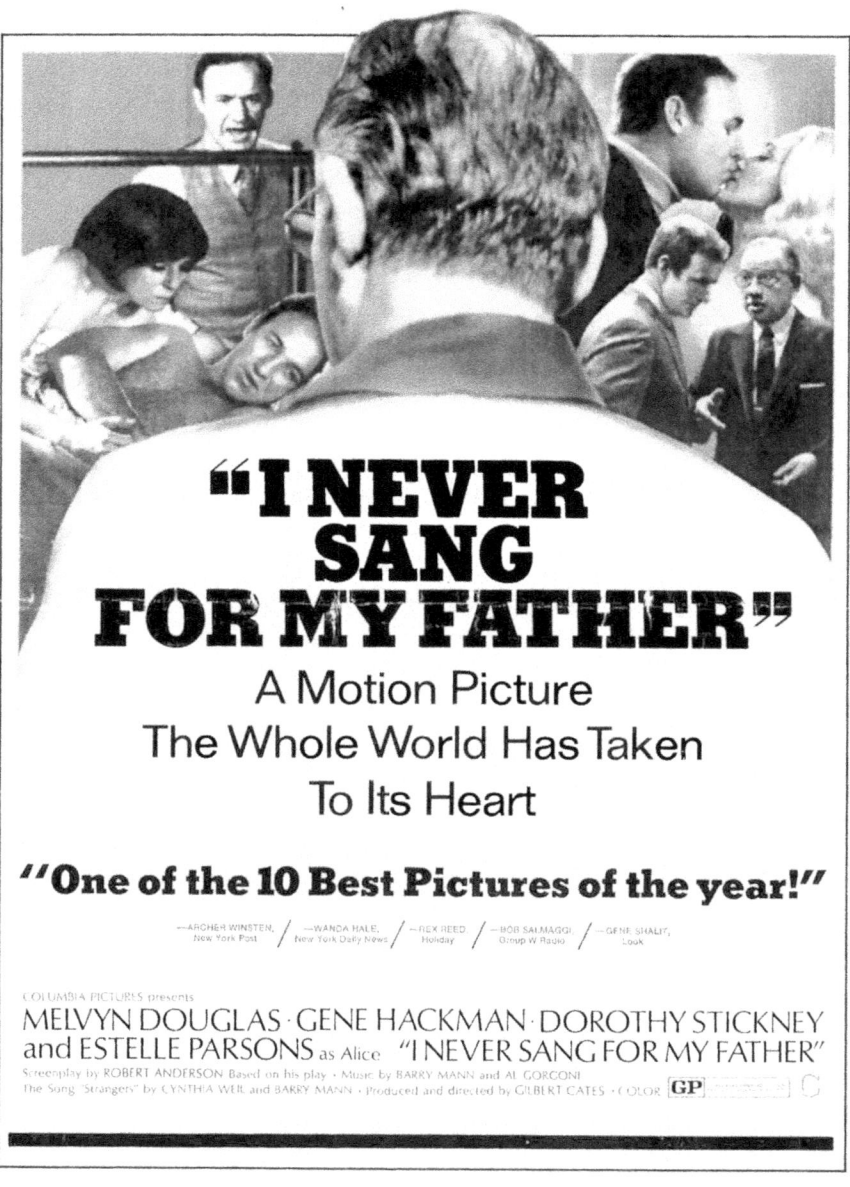

Poster for *I Never Sang for My Father* (1970).

2. Bonnie and Clyde

On January 5, 1969, *The New York Times* had reported that Hackman was set for the film version of the Robert Anderson play *I Never Sang for My Father*. Gilbert Cates, co-producer of the play, was set to produce and direct the film for Columbia. The drama was about troubled family relationships, with Melvyn Douglas cast as the elderly, ill-tempered father and Hackman as his son Gene, who tries desperately to establish a bond with him. The play had run on Broadway at the Longacre Theatre from January 25 to May 11, 1968. Directed by Alan Schneider, it had starred Hal Holbrook as Gene.

I Never Sang for My Father had a rehearsal period of one week prior to the beginning of shooting. Location filming took place at Kennedy Airport and a house in New York, with interiors done at the Biograph Studios in the Bronx. Hackman played widowed New York teacher and published short story writer Gene Garrison, who plans to get married to gynecologist Peggy Thayer (Elizabeth Hubbard) and move to California. He reconsiders when his suburban New York mother Margaret (Dorothy Stickney) dies and then must deal with his controlling father, 80-year-old Tom (Melvyn Douglas). Gene is seen semi-naked in bed with artist Norma (Lovelady Powell) and director Cates gives him an extreme closeup so we see the actor's dark blue eyes. Hackman cannot make some of Robert Anderson's bad lines work, but he is to be admired for playing a weak, dominated man who eventually asserts himself to his father. The 14-minute climax where Gene gets angry at Tom is perhaps Hackman's best scene since it allows him to express a range of emotions. But his efforts cannot compare to Douglas' dynamic performance.

The film was released on October 18, 1970. Roger Ebert wrote that Hackman was magnificent, and *Variety* called him superb. Pauline Kael (*The New Yorker*) said Hackman was believable and compelling in what could have been a drag of a role, and that the film gave him his best screen role thus far. But Vincent Canby in *The New York Times* said that Hackman left him cheerless. It was not a box office success but it earned Academy Award nominations for Best Actor for Douglas, Best Supporting Actor for Hackman, and Best Screenplay Based on Material from Another Medium. When Hackman heard that his nomination was for Best Supporting Actor rather than Best Actor, he told Michael Ritchie, "I think the Academy is trying to tell me something." The film was remade by the *American Playhouse* television series in an episode broadcast on June 15, 1988. It was directed by Jack O'Brien and Daniel J. Travanti played Gene Garrison.

Hackman said that at first he didn't think a lot of the project and was taking it very lightly. Then Melvyn Douglas told him that he would never have what he wanted with the way he was behaving himself. Douglas taught him not to use his reservations as an excuse for not doing the work. Hackman confessed that he loved the film, which he called beautiful, and he loved working with Douglas.

Bonnie and Clyde's enormous success had made him a sought-after supporting actor with a healthy looking future. For the first time, Hackman could see his life mapped out in front of him and he should have been delighted but in fact he went through a very depressing period. He said he subsisted on a day-to-day level for so long that he had found he quite liked the idea of not knowing what he would do next. Suddenly he had a good salary and firm jobs, and he found it surprisingly tough to adjust. One day he was walking through Greenwich Village and a group of people started shouting to him, calling him "Buck." It was startling to Hackman because he had never realized the true power of films until that moment. So he grabbed everything that came along, terrified that the bubble was going to burst. He was also gloomy about his looks, especially his double chin. He knew he was not a leading man but he still worried.

Hackman nearly accepted the role of Mike Brady in the ABC-TV family comedy *The Brady Bunch*, but declined. Series creator Sherwood Schwartz wrote in his book *Brady, Brady, Brady: The Complete Story of The Brady Bunch as Told by the Father/Son Team Who Really Know* that he had wanted to interview the actor but Paramount wouldn't okay him because he had a very low TVQ. TVQ was a survey that executives used to determine the audience's familiarity with performers. Robert Reed got the part. Hackman guested on the December 30, 1969, episode of *The David Frost Show*, a talk show filmed in New York.

The New York Times of July 25, 1971, reported that in 1969, Hackman had been approached about doing the John Guare play *The House of Blue Leaves* on Broadway. It said that he seemed intrigued but then became evasive and finally said no. The play opened Off Broadway at the Truck and Warehouse Theatre on February 10, 1971.

The drama *Doctors' Wives* (1971), written by Daniel Taradash based on the novel by Frank G. Slaughter, and was directed by George Schaefer. It involved the marriages and romantic entanglements of doctors at the Weston Clinic of the Stella Porter Memorial Hospital. Hackman played mustached psychiatrist Dave Randolph, married to golfer Nella (Rachel Roberts). His best scene is when Nella confesses to him about her lesbian affair with Lorrie Dellman (Dyan Cannon). At first Hackman listens with his head down and his interlocked hands to his face, and then he suddenly hits Nella repeatedly on the face with a newspaper. The capper is that, as Dave then hugs her, he delivers straight the funny line, "You can't hit people with newspapers. I'll have to see someone about it. It's a bad habit."

The film was released on February 3, 1971, with the taglines "It started out as five love stories. It didn't end that way," "Doctors' Wives have everything. Except husbands," "Meet the women behind the men. Each was a wife and a lover. But not always to the same man" and "And Forgive Them Their Trespasses." Hackman said he never saw the film.

Hackman appeared on the May 29, 1970, episode of the CBS religious-themed anthology drama *Insight*, "Confrontation," scripted by John T. Dugan and filmed in Hollywood. He was sought by director Richard C. Sarafian for the role of car delivery driver Kowalski in the action crime thriller *Vanishing Point* (1971), but Fox studio executive Richard Zanuck insisted on casting the relatively unknown actor Barry Newman in the role.

Hackman's next film role was the western actioner *The Hunting Party* (1971), shot on location in Spain with interiors at the Moro Studios in Madrid from June 22 to September 5, 1970. It was written by William H. Norton, Gilbert Alexander and Lou Morheim, based on a story by Alexander and Morheim, and directed by Don Medford. Ruger County cattle rancher Brandt Ruger (Hackman) pursues Frank Calder (Oliver Reed) and his gang of gunfighters, who were hired to kidnap Brandt's wife (Candice Bergen). He wears a mustache and his hair is wavier and longer than in his previous films. He gets to ride a horse and fire a Sharps Borchardt telescope rifle, new cinematic feats for Hackman. Brandt is a sexual sadist who rapes Melissa, tortures a prostitute (Francesca Tu) and stares with silent fascination at the body of one of the men he has shot. Hackman provides a poetic physicality in Brandt's exhausted walk around Frank as he watches him die in the desert climax. According to a December 1968 *Daily Variety*, Rod Steiger was initially to play the part of Frank Calder, and his wife Claire Bloom was to appear as Melissa. The May 1969 *Hollywood Reporter* noted that the impending Steiger-Bloom divorce necessitated recasting the film.

The film was released on July 16, 1971, with the taglines "They Hunted The Biggest Game of All–Man and Woman!," "A Rich Man's Sport" and "In the west revenge is a deadly game." Roger Greenspun in *The New York Times* wrote that Hackman looked as if he were someplace else.

Hackman hated the film's blood-letting and vowed never to get involved in another project which had gratuitous violence. He also got in trouble over the film from his wife. In the film was an actor who looked like Hackman, and a magazine used a photo of that actor with half-nude girls on his knee. Everyone, including Faye, thought it was Hackman. He had to convinced her that this was not him.

But the time the actor was spending away from home was causing a strain in their relationship. Faye was unable to have the family join Hackman on-location shooting, since she didn't want to disrupt their children's schooling. He agreed with her about this but he had to keep working.

In their book *A Little Solitaire: John Frankenheimer and American Film*, Murray Pomerance and R. Barton Palmer wrote that Frankenheimer wanted Hackman for the part of Sheriff Tawes in *I Walk the Line* (1970). However the studio hired Gregory Peck since he was under contract to them. Hackman believed the role would have been a heaven-sent opportunity and a crucial career move because it was a romantic leading role (the sheriff falls in love with a moonshiner's daughter). He

Poster for *The French Connection* (1971).

felt he couldn't become a really big star unless he played a romantic hero and, after he had, he could do anything and the public would accept it. But Columbia went with Peck.

The actor was happy that his next film would be shot on location in California as this would allow him to patch things up between himself and Faye. The drama *Cisco Pike* (1972) went into production under the title *Dealer* (it had also been known as *Silver Tongued Devil*). Shot in the autumn of 1970, it was written and directed by B.L. Norton. The title character (Kris Kristofferson), a Venice musician and former drug dealer, is hired by crooked 17-year Los Angeles Police Department Narcotics Sergeant Officer Leo Holland (Hackman) to sell 100 keys of confiscated marijuana in 59 hours. Hackman's best scene is perhaps when Holland brutally confronts Pike with a gun to ensure he will succeed in the drug sale but then changes tone to a seemingly earnest and funny concern for Pike's health because of his smoking. Hackman breathes heavily in the scene, and ends on a pause and a silent smile to Pike.

The film was released on January 14, 1972, with the taglines "Gene Hackman and Kris Kristofferson and Karen Black and Viva and a footrace … a crooked cop … a lot of money and so little time," "A Has-Been Rock Star. A Crooked Cop. And a Lot of Money" and "A Powerhouse of a Picture!" It was not a box office success.

Hackman next appeared in the action-crime drama *The French Connection* (1971), shot on location in France, Washington and New York from November 30, 1970, to February 1971 (or March 1971; sources differ). The Ernst Tidyman screenplay was based on the book by Robin Moore, and the director was William Friedkin. It tells the story of Jimmy "Popeye" Doyle (Hackman) and Buddy "Cloudy" Russo (Roy Scheider), Brooklyn Narcotics Bureau detectives who discover $32 million of uncut heroin being shipped into the country from Marseilles under the watchful eye of Alain Charnier (Fernando Rey). Hackman is clean-shaven, and his wardrobe by Joseph Fretwell III includes a distinctive porkpie hat. The role requires him to do a lot of walking, running and driving. The film's most famous sequence has Popeye driving through Brooklyn streets trying to keep up with an elevated running train that has been hijacked by hitman Pierre Nikoli (Marcel Bozzuffi). In this sequence, Friedkin provides some extreme closeups of Hackman. He fails to make the single-minded Popeye likable, which is highlighted by his lack of reaction at having accidentally shot FBI agent Mulderig (Bill Hickman) in the film's climax. In Hackman's best dramatic scene, he tries to persuade his lieutenant (Eddie Egan) that luncheonette owner Sal Boca (Tony Lo Bianco) is linked to Charnier.

The film was released on October 7, 1971, with the taglines "The time is just right for an out and out thriller like this," "In the great tradition of American thrillers," "Doyle is bad news—but a good cop," "A $32,000,000 chase turns into the American thriller of the year!" and "There are no rules and no holds barred when Popeye cuts loose!" In *The New York Times*, Roger Greenspun wrote that Hackman's characterization was one of the most successful of his career. Roger Ebert said that the actor generated an almost frightening single-mindedness and a cold determination to win at all costs. A box office success, it received Oscar nominations for Best Picture, Best Director, Best Actor for Hackman, Best Supporting Actor, Best Adapted Screenplay, Best Film Editing for Gerald B. Greenberg, Best Cinematography and Best Sound. Producer Philip D'Antoni, Hackman, Friedkin, Tidyman and Greenberg all won. The sequel *French Connection II* (1975), directed by John Frankenheimer, also starred Hackman. Ed O'Neill starred as Popeye in the made-for-TV movie *Popeye Doyle* (1986). The Popeye character did not appear in the made-for-TV movie *N.Y.-70* (2005), another version of the film.

In a deleted scene, Nikoli is whipped by a leather-clad prostitute; some sources erroneously report that Popeye is the one being whipped. His taste for such sadomasochism was suggested by the scene where Cloudy finds him with his legs handcuffed to his bed after sex with the Bicycle Girl (Maureen Mooney). Another deleted scene had Popeye picking up a black streetwalker and inviting her into his car; the sex was implied, not shown. A deleted scene at the Westbury Hotel reception had Popeye talking to the desk clerk about Charnier, and there were two scenes at Mutchie's Bar. One had him drawing on coasters and speaking to a group of ex-cons about Willie Mays, and the other had him speaking alone to Mutchie (Fat Thomas). Popeye was also seen pretending to arrest the Bicycle Girl in order to get her into his car, and at Dan's Lunch donut shop where he frisks Hector and finds a switchblade.

Twentieth Century–Fox didn't think that the leading roles should be played by stars, which pleased Friedkin and D'Antoni who felt the same way. However, inevitably, stars were initially considered because they would be box office insurance. Friedkin first considered Paul Newman who was out of their budget range, then Jackie Gleason, Peter Boyle and New York columnist Jimmy Breslin, who had never acted before. It was thought that Gleason would not have been able to do the physical work the role required. Boyle declined because he disapproved of the violent theme of the film; Friedkin said that the actor wanted to play romantic leads. Breslin refused to get behind the wheel of a car, which was required for the integral car chase scene. Turner Classic Movies claims that Breslin was hired briefly but then fired because his acting was below par and because he could not drive. Friedkin reported that Breslin completed three weeks of rehearsals with Roy Scheider before being fired. He said that it was clear that Breslin couldn't sustain from one day to the next. But in his memoir *The Friedkin Connection*, he wrote that Breslin only worked for a week, which included one day when he was late and another when he failed to show up. The director also said that Breslin's refusal to drive was the result of a deathbed promise to his mother.

2. Bonnie and Clyde

Steve McQueen was also considered, but he did not want to do another police film after *Bullitt* (1968) and his fee would have exceeded the movie's budget. Other actors considered were Charles Bronson, Robert Mitchum (who hated the story), Lee Marvin (who hated cops), James Caan and Adam West. Friedkin almost went with Rod Taylor; Hackman said that Taylor had actively pursued the role, was another choice the studio approved, and was the choice of Eddie Egan, the man Popeye was based on. When Hackman's name came up, the director was against it, but he feared that the studio would lose interest in backing the film.

The actor found Popeye to be a wonderful chance for his career and a departure from anything he had done before. Hackman was not known for playing heroes of any kind, feeling he was usually cast as the heavy. He said he wasn't sure if he would have cast himself in the part but he was damned glad somebody did. His agent Sue Mengers was instrumental in getting him interviewed. She had told him about the project but that it was probably unlikely he would get it. Friedkin wanted an unknown and the studio wanted a name star—and Hackman was neither.

Mengers had attended a dinner party where she sat next to Breslin and condemned him for taking a job that should have gone to a real actor. After Freidkin let Breslin go, Mengers lobbied hard for Hackman. Friedkin and D'Antoni agreed to meet him though neither was excited. Friedkin had seen the actor in *Bonnie and Clyde* and *I Never Sang for My Father*. Hackman flew from California to meet with them at New York's Plaza Hotel over a meal. He said it was an interesting meeting because they looked him over and must have seen he was very eager. The actor found Friedkin to be funny and engaging and D'Antoni to be quiet and a terrific guy. They didn't ask Hackman to test or audition or read for the part. D'Antoni noted that the actor had apparently lost weight and, sporting a mustache, looked like Errol Flynn. But Friedkin found Hackman to be humorless. The director and the producer had reservations about Hackman: This teddy bear of a man seemed too nice to play a brutal, ruthless, street-wise cop. But Fox needed an answer and Hackman was both available and cheap. They kept the actor waiting over a weekend until Friedkin acquiesced. He had time off from the three-month shoot on location in New York when Friedkin concentrated on scenes with Charnier. This allowed Hackman to fly back to California to spend Christmas 1970 with his family.

It seemed like a chance to do all those things he watched Jimmy Cagney do as a kid, but the violence was a great problem. He did quite a bit of research, probably more than he had ever done before. This included working with Eddie Egan and Sonny Grosso, the two policemen who were the inspiration for the film (and credited as technical consultants). Hackman and Roy Scheider went on patrol with them at night in their police car, with the provision that the policemen not hurt anybody. The actors watched the policemen break into crack houses and shooting galleries in Harlem, where Hackman saw a pregnant woman shooting up with her husband.

They also went into bars, with Egan hollering. He behaved like a drill instructor—flat and unemotional and very authoritative. If anyone talked back, his voice would go a pitch higher. No one got the better of him.

Hackman was disgusted at what he saw. One time he had to help restrain a suspect in the squad car and he worried that he would be sued for impersonating a policeman. When Grosso met Hackman, he said the actor was big enough and looked strong enough, but he just didn't seem like he could become Eddie Egan, the most outlandish, flamboyant extrovert Grosso had met in his life. For the first week they did the raids and the actors watched. Hackman said for the first four or five days, neither he nor Scheider got out of the car, but in the second week they went in with the policemen. By the third week, *they* went in and the policemen were watching *them*. For Hackman, the time was an education.

Hackman felt that Egan was everyone's idea of what a New York cop should look like—big, tough, loud, vulgar in many ways, and extremely successful in terms of the number of felony arrests he made. At first Hackman found him difficult to play. He didn't want to do an imitation—he couldn't have done one anyway, as he wasn't that kind of actor. He wanted to get to the essence of him. Concerned about finding Popeye's humanity and compassionate side, Hackman, Friedkin and D'Antoni went to lunch without Scheider for the first weeks of filming, and they argued about the character. Friedkin felt that Popeye had no human or compassionate side—he found him to be a monster. Since Popeye was a racist, Hackman wanted to show an explanation for it, but Friedkin refused. The director said that Hackman hated Popeye and didn't identify with him. The actor would eventually play him the way the director wanted. Hackman knew that there wasn't a lot of Popeye in him, and one of the real problems he had early in the shooting was pushing around the street hustler (Alan Weeks). After an unsuccessful day, Hackman went to Friedkin and told him that he feared that what was required was beyond him. He wanted to quit but Fox pointed out he had signed a contract and if he quit, they would sue him. He went back to work, trying to come to terms with the violence by approaching it as a simple acting problem that had to be resolved.

Friedkin decided to re-shoot the scene with the hustler (Weeks) at the end of the schedule. Hackman said he found it difficult to be brutal and it took a lot out of him, regardless of how easy it looked to an audience. Hackman's uneasiness had made them initially try the scene 32 times, and by this time blood was coming from Weeks' face because of the slaps he was getting. Weeks encouraged the actor to hit him but this made it harder for Hackman. Hackman had never known that kind of New York intenseness, the push, the competitiveness. Even though he had lived in New York for 17 years, he never allowed it to rub off on him. He had observed Egan but all the violence the man had inside him scared Hackman. He had gone into the film with the usual attitudes about policemen and he didn't have any sympathy with

2. Bonnie and Clyde

Egan at all. The policeman was on the set all the time and one day, after observing Hackman perform a violent scene, he told the actor that he "was more me than me." This remark horrified Hackman, who feared what he was becoming in playing the part.

However, after three months of working in the streets and taking all the guff from people, he changed. He would come out of the film experience saying it was all too easy to criticize police violence and the Popeye character. The police had to go into the streets alone and fight against drug racketeers, and to Hackman, Popeye was a product of his environment. Being around policemen changed his mind about them. They couldn't play Mr. Nice Guy and get people's attention. It was an enormously difficult job because they had so much to contend with and they were working in sometimes dangerous circumstances. Hackman was all for them and felt more people should know the kind of work they did and respect them a great deal more.

He found Roy Scheider very supportive and helpful. Scheider lived in New York and was more used to the streets whereas Hackman had been away from the city for quite some time. Something else that helped the actor was that off-duty policemen were used in the bar raid scene as drug pushers so he overcame his initial fear that he would be unable to handle these big, tough-looking individuals.

Hackman didn't see the film until after it had opened at a Saturday night screening where he stood at the back. He wasn't surprised that it was Oscar-nominated, despite the fact that action films generally were not, because it covered enough new ground to be considered something special. Ultimately Hackman saw it as a great experience that changed his life. Roles like that didn't come along very often, and with Friedkin as the director he felt extremely lucky. But Hackman didn't think that he had anything to do with the quality of the film since that was the director's job. He said anybody would have been good in the role, even Jimmy Breslin, because of Friedkin, who probably could have guided *him* to win the Oscar. If the film was considered a success because of Hackman, that was because audiences saw him as the working guy doing what they wanted to do.

The actor said Friedkin was a terrific director for him because he was very specific about what he wanted. He had great energy and a positive attitude which went a long way to make everyone comfortable despite the sometimes tough filmmaking experience. Hackman loved working with him, and loved the choice of using hand-held camerawork and "stolen" footage, which added to the realism and provided a documentary tone.

Friedkin said Hackman had a hard time using Doyle's racist language, which he thought would be cut because of censorship anyway (it wasn't). Hackman and Freidkin argued about the scene where Popeye stood in the cold street watching Charnier eating inside a French restaurant, since Hackman repeatedly failed to convey how cold his hands were. The director finally demonstrated what he wanted, which made the actor resentfully walk off the shoot for the rest of the day. Friedkin reported that Hackman did some of the driving in the famous car chase sequence, with Bill Hickman as the main stunt driver. It took 21 days to shoot. The actor was involved in an accident: There was a siren on top of the car to help divert traffic, with a police car proceeding and following along the blocked streets. One civilian car made it through and drove into Hackman, pushing his car into a big steel pillar. Luckily, no one was hurt.

Roy Scheider said that he felt he worked well with Hackman because they were both from the theater. His co-star told him that when he heard that the actor was to appear in a play, he knew to get tickets fast because the play would close early. This wasn't because of Hackman's casting but because he chose envelope-pushing experimental plays that were not commercial but had interesting characters.

Hackman found that his injury from his Marine days, which had resulted in the placement of a plastic and steel knee in his left leg, made the running in the film painful. Time off from work gave him time to recover. He spent time with his family and indulged in his hobbies of painting and dirt-track riding, and piloting a rented plane. Being home helped to heal some of the rifts in his marriage, but unemployment made him restless.

In Burt Reynolds' memoir *But Enough About Me*, he wrote that it was rumored that Hackman wanted to play the part of Lewis Medlock in the adventure-thriller *Deliverance* (1972). Reynolds said that director John Boorman passed on the actor because he wanted him to do his own stunts in the film and Hackman wanted to use a double. This idea seems dubious given Hackman's preference to doing his own stunt work. The part was played by Reynolds.

Hackman attended the 43rd Annual Academy Awards ceremony, held on April 15, 1971, at the Dorothy Chandler Pavilion and televised by NBC. He was nominated for Best Supporting Actor for *I Never Sang for My Father* but the award was won by John Mills for *Ryan's Daughter* (1970). Late that summer, he began work on a new film for his *Downhill Racer* director Michael Ritchie. Originally titled *Kansas City Prime*, the action-crime drama *Prime Cut* was shot on location in Chicago, Kansas, Missouri and Canada. Robert Dillon's script focussed Chicago enforcer Nick Devlin (Lee Marvin), who is called in to recover $500,000 owed by the Kansas City Mary Ann Meats butchers. Hackman played Mary Ann, an odd character name that is never explained. He sports a mustache and longer-than-usual hair. In his death scene, director Ritchie cuts to Marvin watching rather than letting Hackman have his final moment. Hackman's best scene is Mary Ann's funny roughhouse fight with his brother Weenie (Gregory Walcott).

The film was released on June 28, 1972, with the tagline "Any way they slice it, it's going to be murder." According to *Variety*, no serious dramatic demands were

2. Bonnie and Clyde

made on Hackman. The film was not a box office success, though Ritchie claimed that his version was only shown in Minneapolis where it was a success. The director's original ending had Devlin and Mary Ann in a mock-samurai confrontation, after which Devlin stepped out into the vast field of sunflowers.

Hackman was six weeks on the production and said he took the job because he hadn't worked for five months. He said it turned out not to be terribly exciting or especially rewarding, though he felt the film worked on a certain level.

Ritchie said Hackman was a fine character actor who was professional and conscientious. Marvin clashed with the director, due to the actor's reported drinking problem, and commented that he felt a little left out of the "Gene Hackman Appreciation Society." Marvin said Hackman was a great actor and a great guy but he wasn't the only one in the film. In his biography *Lee Marvin: Point Blank*, Dwayne Epstein wrote of an incident that occurred early in the filming. Marvin had invited Hackman to drive out with him on location, and commented that he hadn't seen his film *I Never Sang for My Father*, calling it "I Never Sucked My Father's Cock." The actor stayed silent as Marvin spoke about the alienated relationship he had with his own father, a man that he had heard had died. Marvin claimed that his father had died on his birthday and that he had ruined *his* day. Hackman seemed to wonder whether he should take the star seriously since Marvin liked to shock people.

Sissy Spacek played Poppy in the film and in her memoir *My Extraordinary Ordinary Life* wrote about the actor. She was surprised that Hackman was such a normal, humble person. He would knock on the door of her dressing room where Spacek would make collages and ask if he could also work on them. She said he was such a nice guy and a good artist that she always let him.

Hackman was interviewed in the November 21, 1971, *New York Times*. He had formed his own production company, Chelly Ltd., named after his children Christopher, Elizabeth and Leslie. He believed that he had yet to be typecast and didn't want to do only tough guy parts because they were not enjoyable. The actor really wanted to play a combination of people who were strong yet sensitive, attuned to a better world, like the character he played in *I Never Sang for My Father*. At this time, the Hackmans lived in a ranch-style home in Beverly Hills.

Hackman was a guest on the January 7, 1972, episode of the NBC talk show *Late Night with Johnny Carson* and the January 27, 1972, episode of the British television documentary series *Cinema*. Next he guested on the February 28, 1972, episode of the NBC comedy show *Laugh-In*, filmed at the NBC studios in Hollywood. He played three characters: a blotto proponent of the drinking man's diet, an escaping P.O.W. and a mercenary sheriff. Dick Martin recalled the P.O.W. skit where he and Hackman were two convicts digging their way out of prison with teaspoons *à la The Great Escape* who never progressed in their escape.

On February 6, 1972, *The New York Times* reported that Hackman was to play a hard-drinking driver in his next film entitled *Sprinter*. Filming was to start in the spring in the Midwest and on the West Coast. The project centered on drivers who raced in specially built cars on small tracks, with the actor as a happy, gregarious man who kept racing, completely unaware that he was never going to be a winner. Hackman was to co-produce with Norman Twain. The script, based on an original story by Richard Monaco, was being written by Paul Sylbert, who was also to direct the movie for Twentieth Century-Fox. The project was also known as *Dunn*. Hackman later declared that the film had been shelved indefinitely.

On February 6, Hackman attended the 29th Annual Golden Globes Awards, held at the Beverly Hilton Hotel in Hollywood. He was nominated for Best Actor in Drama for *The French Connection* and won the award. The *Times* reported on February 27 that Hackman would star in *Badge 373*, based on the further experiences of Eddie Egan. Hackman returned to *Laugh-In* on March 13.

The actor attended the 44th Annual Academy Awards, held April 10, 1972, at the Dorothy Chandler Pavilion. He and Raquel Welch were presenters of the Best Supporting Actress award, which was won by Cloris Leachman for *The Last Picture Show* (1971). He was also a nominee for the Best Actor award for *The French Connection*, which he won. When Hackman came to the stage, he checked the envelope and said "This is what it says." He commented that sitting in the audience with Barbara Harris reminded him of his first acting scene ever, which was in New York, and the teacher was George Morrison, whom he wanted to thank. He also thanked William Friedkin, Eddie Egan, Phil D'Antoni, Roy Scheider, and his wife. At the after-show party he was photographed on the dance floor with "tight elbowed, fists clenched and a single damp curl on his forehead."

Hackman said that night was like a dream, like he was standing in back of the theater and watching it through a lot of smoke. On the *Inside the Actors Studio* episode, the actor commented that the experience of winning the award was startling. People could say that the awards were commercial or self-serving but when they called your name, it was like a lifetime dream coming true. He thought he would say something clever or erudite but it came out all mush. At the time of his win, Hackman felt the award didn't mean that much to him. He observed that the award could be a blessing or a jinx to its winner. Many Oscar winners priced themselves out of work so the actor instructed his agent to not ask for the world when film offers came in, though his fee shot up from the typical $200,000 to $500,000.

Film stardom and success had arrived at the relatively late age of 42. He was being sought for starring roles and Hackman suddenly had the option to pick what he wanted and have a say over scripts and casting. He tried to focus on the work which had got him where he was, but as he had observed with Burt Lancaster, people's attitude toward him changed: They deferred to him. Hackman said the han-

2. Bonnie and Clyde

dling of power was a fascinating process and a dangerous situation. You could use it to get what you wanted or to feed your ego and become a monster. He now had the authority to ensure that any director would have to take account of his feelings and his working methods. Hackman found it challenging to come on the set unprepared and he knew some wouldn't like this but he preferred to work that way. He rarely wanted to discuss the character but he did want to talk about how to make his part or the film better. He was very concerned with how a director operated, whether he gave an actor a lot of freedom or whether he was very rigid, and he needed to know before he committed to the project.

He said that fame made him paranoid. He wondered if people wanted him for himself or what they could get. Another downside: Friends he hadn't seen in years, some of whom had turned their backs on him during tough times, began reappearing. They asked for money or wanted Hackman to read their scripts. He loaned an actor $3000 so that the bank would not foreclose on his mortgage. The actor was supposed to repay in 30 days, but didn't. on the set of *The Poseidon Adventure*, another friend needed $8000 right away. Hackman's reply was, "Don't we all?" He never saw that friend again.

The most immediate and apparent danger was the effect of his new power on his home life. He was now separated from Faye but he wanted to persuade her to give him another chance.

3

The Poseidon Adventure

The action adventure *The Poseidon Adventure* (1972) was shot on the RMS *Queen Mary* in California and at 20th Century-Fox from April 4 to July 1972. The film had a screenplay by Stirling Silliphant and Wendell Mayes based on the novel by Paul Gallico. It told the story of ten passengers who struggle to survive when their ocean liner, the S.S. *Poseidon,* en route from New York to Athens, is hit by a tidal wave at midnight on New Year's Eve and capsizes. Playing Reverend Scott, an unorthodox priest who is being banished to Africa by his bishop, top-billed Hackman leads the passengers to their eventual escape. Hackman does a lot of his own stunts which involve climbing to great heights, swimming and going through fire and steam. He does have a stunt double when he falls as the ship overturns. His mannerism of over-gesturing perhaps has a context in Scott's excitability, since he is self-righteous but also has leadership qualities and is compassionate. While the actor matches Ernest Borgnine who plays Rogo in yelling arguments, his best scene is perhaps his silent reaction to the trapped passengers who he sees drowning in the ship's Grand Salon.

The film premiered in New York on December 12, 1972, and opened on December 13 with the taglines "Hell, Upside Down," "Who will survive—in one of the greatest escape adventures ever!" and "Combining the talents of fifteen Academy Award Winners." In *The New York Times*, A.H. Weiler wrote that Hackman was fairly convincing.

The film was a box office success. Hackman challenged the negative reviews by saying that in the final analysis, you had to trust the box office grosses, since a film only worked if the public liked it. (Incidentally, he never saw the completed film.) It received Academy Awards for Best Original Song and a Special Achievement Award for Visual Effects, and nominations for Supporting Actress for Shelley Winters, Original Score, Costume Design, Art Direction–Set Decoration, Sound, Cinematography and Film Editing. During Hackman's March 21, 1974, appearance on *The Tonight Show with Johnny Carson,* he spoke about being offered a role in a sequel, despite the fact that his character had died in the original. He said the filmmakers told him they would get around that problem by showing him appearing at

3. The Poseidon Adventure

the cockpit of the helicopter that held the survivors and asking, "Did my brother make it?"

George C. Scott and Burt Lancaster were considered for the role of Scott. Hackman took the film for the money. He described Scott as somewhat rebellious and a very strong man. More like a Unitarian minister, he believes in the will of one's soul, making progress in life, as opposed to prayer. With a garland around him, he proceeds to become a leader when the ship meets the disaster. The role gave Hackman a quality of leadership which was also true in his role in real life because he had the responsibility of the film on him. The actor was more interested in the film as a project than the character, though the fact that he changed in the circumstances made it a challenge. Hackman wanted the experience of a major film shot at a major studio, and he was also attracted to the physicality of the part. But he also had contempt for the film, feeling it was beneath him, because he could have been doing better work. Hackman later said that it didn't do any harm to go off and do an action film once in a while, as something that would stretch you in a different way. He confessed that being on the set of a big action film was the dullest in his experience, being really boring standing around all day long watching the stuntmen work. He also hated the way they had his hair lacquered—poufed up at the end and slicked over, the way the movie's producer Irwin Allen wore it. It was designed by Allen's own hairdresser. Hackman reportedly complained about it every day.

For the scene where Scott drops 25 feet into water surrounded by flames, director Ronald Neame refused to allow Hackman to do the fall for safety reasons. They argued about it, with a stuntman eventually used. The original script also called for Scott to send Belle Rosen (Shelley Winters) on her underwater mission and for her to be trapped and needing rescue by him. According to Neame's auto-

Hackman in *The Poseidon Adventure* **(1972).**

biography *Straight from the Horse's Mouth*, before the scene was shot Hackman told him that it didn't work. He said it was just not believable that he would have let her dive in first and asked that their characters' situations be reversed. Neame found it to be an excellent idea and producer Irwin Allen agreed. However, Winters did not, saying that the scene was the only reason she agreed to do the film. The four argued, and after Neame remarked, "This is the worst morning I've had since I worked with Judy Garland!" Winters walked off the set. She went to the Fox company directors and complained they her part was being destroyed. Allen contacted her agent and an hour later, the actress returned, saying she was ready to do the scene.

Neame commented that they were fortunate to have Hackman because he would do anything, refusing to have a double under any circumstances. The director felt this was due to the actor's awareness that a double would have been filmed from behind and Hackman would be shot doing the stunt in close shots. Neame was aware that the actor thought he was a serious actor slumming, and he agreed, though Neame regretted not toning down Hackman in Scott's arguments with Borgnine's Rogo and his crying over the dead Belle. For another scene, Borgnine suggested an amusing bit of business but Hackman exclaimed, "What are we making here, a comedy?" (Neame did want a few laughs in the narrative to relieve the continuous tension.)

In his memoir, Borgnine recalled before they shot a scene on the *Queen Mary*, he and Hackman rehearsed their lines. When Hackman stumbled a bit, Borgnine asked if everything was okay. Hackman asked, "Are we supposed to know this stuff?" Borgnine replied that that was the general idea and said that Hackman looked at him rather oddly, saying "Really" as if that was a divine revelation. The younger actor commented he had just made *The French Connection* where they made up the lines as they went along, and he assumed it would be the same on this film. After Borgnine informed him that Irwin Allen really liked the script as written, he said the actor never spoke to him again except when they had dialogue in the film. Borgnine wasn't trying to offend Hackman, who he thought was excellent in his part and a great guy to work with, but also someone who never said much to anybody.

Actress Pamela Sue Martin was nervous about a scene where she had to scream at the sight of a body. Hackman took her off to another sound stage and had her practice, taking her under his wing and giving her a sense of confidence. The cast said Hackman received his Oscar during the filming period and to celebrate, there was a big cake. They also said that he had been unnerved by the sequence where he had to go underwater, despite the fact that they had all had received deep breathing training to cope with the experience.

While he was making the film, Fox also spoke to him about their planned sequel

3. The Poseidon Adventure

to *The French Connection.* Hackman said it seemed like a good idea. He was given a choice of cast or director approval and he chose director approval.

Now being an Oscar winner placed new demands on Hackman's time. He had to give more interviews and was expected to attend industry functions and socialize with the Hollywood set. Being someone who cherished his privacy, Hackman was ill at ease at parties where the talk circled endlessly around who was hot, who was cold, and how much a film grossed in its opening weekend. Hackman did his best. He also had to be concerned with his new status. Hackman considered himself a character actor first and a star second. He preferred to present a character with his own personality, with his (Hackman's) personality completely submerged. He wanted to choose the most demanding and testing parts that would win the respect of his peers and critics without alienating the public and forfeiting his position as a bankable leading man. He didn't want to straitjacket his talents into a succession of conventional star roles, relying on his presence alone for their validity, because he knew he would become bored with the business and lose his self-respect. He also aspired to direct and return to the stage. And he also learned that just because he had an Oscar, not everything he wanted to do would come to fruition. He played in the 2nd Annual RFK Pro-Celebrity Tennis Tournament at Forest Hills Stadium in New York on August 5, 1973.

Hackman was offered the script of *Scarecrow*, in which there was a role he was anxious to play. Shot beginning in September 1972 in California, Denver and Detroit, the drama was scripted by Gary Michael White and directed by Jerry Schatzberg. An ex-convict, Max (Hackman), and a sailor, Lion (Al Pacino), meet while hitchhiking and plan to become partners in a car wash business in Pittsburgh. Hackman is clean-shaven, wears glasses, and his hair is in a wavy collar-length style. His one costume is a layered combination of gray coat with black beret, black and white scarf, purple pants, a colored shirt and a red and a white jacket. The screenplay gives him some funny lines. Max tells Lion that he can "tear the ass out of a goddamn elephant." The role is unusual for Hackman in that Max is sexually desirable to *two* women, Darlene (Eileen Brennan) and Frenchy (Ann Wedgeworth), and he gets to play drunk. The drunk scene and the comic striptease he does in a bar are both undermined: Max's face is covered in food in the former, and there are cutaways to Lion and other bar patrons in the latter. In his best scene, he attempts to seduce Frenchy as Lion repeatedly interrupts. Hackman's line to the waitress at the diner, "Is this your first day?" was an ad-lib since he was annoyed with the actress (an uncredited June Dixon).

The film was released on April 11, 1973, with the taglines "The road leads itself to somewhere" and "John D. Rockefeller. J.P. Morgan. Andrew Carnegie. Max and Lion." In "The Warner Bros. Story," Clive Hirschhorn wrote that Hackman gave a tremendously affecting performance. *Variety* said that Hackman was excellent, Vincent Canby in *The New York Times* wrote that he was fine, and Roger Ebert said that he was nicely realistic. A sequel was developed by Schatzberg and Seth Cohen showing the characters 30 years later. Max and Lion's car wash is very successful, he has married Frenchy, adopted a Chinese baby who is now a girl in her twenties, and Lion's son is reunited with Lion in Detroit. It has not yet been made and the

Poster for *Scarecrow* (1973).

3. The Poseidon Adventure

director felt it was unlikely that Hackman would be involved since he has retired from acting.

Hackman said that the role of Max was one of his favorites of the 1970s. He described the story as a mixture of *Midnight Cowboy* and *Of Mice and Men*. It was a very exciting role for him because it had comedic elements, and they were always a challenge. It was the only film that Hackman made totally in sequence, which was helpful in understanding the character development. For him, it was a coming back to the time of *Bonnie and Clyde*, a gritty relationship film that he felt he was trained to do and most at home doing. The fact that he got to work with Pacino, who in Hackman's mind was a great actor, was icing on the cake. He and Pacino prepared for their roles by dressing in cast-off clothes and bumming around San Francisco asking for change (they were both recognized). On the February 10, 1986, *Late Night with David Letterman*, Hackman said that one day in San Francisco they asked a man where the Salvation Army soup kitchen was. After he told them, the man was talking to himself and the actor wondered if he was thinking how fleeting show business was. Despite the film's box office failure, Hackman said that a lot of people came up to him and told him it was one of their favorite films.

The actor said he got along with Jerry Schatzberg, pleased that he allowed for improvisation, but he was not happy how he cast non-actors in some roles. Schatzberg found Hackman difficult to deal with. In the first week of rehearsal, Hackman was quite paranoid because the director had worked with Pacino before. Schatzberg said that Hackman intimidated Pacino as part of his method, and the director let it happen since it seemed to be the way Max treated Lion. The actor argued with everyone on the set including his brother Richard, who was working as his stand-in. To get back at Hackman, Schatzberg gave Richard a part in the film, but Gene was delighted about it.

Pacino also said it wasn't easy working with Hackman, who he loved as an actor. They were dissimilar people, and he didn't think they were as connected as they should have been to play a very close relationship. They didn't hate each other but they were thrown together, and under normal circumstances they would never have cavorted or been friends. Pacino admitted that he was as much to blame as Hackman.

On October 8, 1972, *The New York Times* reported that he had signed up for *The Big Wild Red*. The script by Franklin Coen was described as a cliffhanger, a western on water, dealing with an innocent Colorado rancher forced by a band of outlaws to help them make an escape by way of the raging Colorado River. The project would never be made. On October 15, the *Times* reported that Hackman was to be in producer Irwin Allen's next Fox film *The Walter Syndrome*. The thriller, adapted by Richard Neely from his own novel, would have him as a reporter who helps unmask a mass murderer of New Yorkers during the 1930s. This film was also never made.

The Francis Ford Coppola film *The Conversation* was in production in from November 26 to December 1972, with reshoots in March 1973. The drama was shot on location and at the American Zeotrope Studio in San Francisco. Hackman starred as 44-year-old Harry Caul, a surveillance and security technician assigned by The Director (an uncredited Robert Duvall) to record a conversation between Ann (Cindy Williams) and Mark (Frederic Forrest) in Union Square. Hackman wears a mustache and glasses and his short hair combed back to expose his receding hairline. His one costume is a dark green suit with matching tie worn with a white shirt under a gray plastic raincoat. He plays the saxophone though it was really played by an uncredited Justin Gordon. We see the actor semi-naked after a love scene with Meredith (Elizabeth MacRae). Hackman occasionally stammers but this has context for the repressed, controlled and haunted character. He expresses Harry's fear physically in the hotel room scene when he sees the murder of The Director on the adjoining balcony, but his best is perhaps when he speaks to Meredith about his girlfriend Amy (Teri Garr). The film gives the actor one scene with his old friend Duvall, and also features Richard Hackman uncredited as a security guard and as the priest in the church confessional.

It opened in Los Angeles on April 7, 1974, and then in New York on April 20 with the tagline "Harry Caul will go anywhere to bug a private conversation." The film received praise from Vincent Canby in *The New York Times* who wrote that Hackman was superb and fascinating and Roger Ebert who called the actor's performance a great one. Pauline Kael (*The New Yorker*) wrote that Hackman was a superlative actor but his limitation was his quality of anonymity which was right for this role. A box office success, the film was Oscar-nominated for Best Film, Sound and Original Screenplay. The January 10, 1995, *New York Times* reported that Coppola was to produce a CBS-TV drama series based on the film, but this apparently went nowhere.

The original cut was reportedly four and a half hours long. The dropped scenes: Harry dealing with his neighbors who complain about the building's plumbing problems, unaware that he owns the building; Harry consulting his lawyer (Abe Vigoda) about the apartment situation; and Harry convincing his teenaged niece (Mackenzie Phillips) not to run away from home.

Hackman based his character on an uncle and a man he had known in the Marines. He called Coppola a marvelous director who was very precise and knew exactly what he wanted. However making the film wasn't a pleasurable experience for Hackman because Harry was really a constipated character and difficult to play because it was so low-key. Later he said that the misery of making the film was partially due to Coppola letting it be known that he wanted Harry played by Marlon Brando, who had declined. On the March 21, 1974, *Tonight Show with Johnny Carson*, Hackman mentioned that an electronics expert on the film gave him a matchbox-size transmitter with an antenna which he kept. He didn't know if his telephone at home was bugged but he was paranoid enough being in the business to believe that people were listening to everything he said. Hackman did get a lot of strange calls, including hard breathers, since he had Wilt Chamberlain's old phone number.

Coppola felt Hackman was ideal because he was so ordinary, so unexceptional in appearance. He told him he wanted Harry to look like a "nudnik"—Yiddish for a boring person—so Hackman grew a pathetic mustache, wore ill-fitting glasses, and wore clothes that were at least ten years out of date. Coppola called him a very interesting actor to work with, but he so turned into the character

Hackman in *The Conversation* (1974).

that it really started to bug him and play with his head. Hackman would arrive to work wearing stylish casual clothes and looking handsome and youthful and then transform into this nerd. He was grumpy and impatient and Coppola felt this came from his being uncomfortable being in the skin of the character he was creating, though later he heard that Hackman enjoyed the film and felt it was good work on his part.

Sources claimed that Hackman had a growing drinking problem. He admitted to being depressed over the failure of *Scarecrow* and while he said he wasn't an alcoholic, but he did have two vodkas and tonics to start the night just to quench his thirst. And then he had a couple more later. In a 1972 interview, he said he kept telling himself that he would return to the theater but he supposed realistically he probably wouldn't. Plus Hackman said he now found it difficult to live in New York any more—it seemed to have gotten too big for him, or he had outgrown it. He would have liked playing some of the classic contemporary theater roles, the Eugene O'Neill or the Tennessee Williams roles that some of the better actors had performed, particularly as in the past he had always been involved in new plays and never got to do the classics.

The New York Times reported on January 4, 1973, that the actor was to begin shooting *Taylor's Bride*, a Warner Bros. film, from March 1 in Hollywood. Jan Troell, the Swedish film director, was to make his American directing debut and Hackman's co-star was to be Liv Ullmann.

At the 45th Annual Academy Awards (March 27, 1973), Hackman and Raquel Welch presented the Best Actress award, and before they announced the nominees he said something which appeared to be improvised: He said that the conventional wisdom was that one was born with talent, and maybe that was so, but talent was unusable and wasted without work, dedication and a deep feeling for others. The winner was Liza Minnelli for *Cabaret* (1972).

On April 22, 1973, *The New York Times* reported that director Costa-Gavras had thought about talking to him about playing the part of Mitrione aka Philip Michael Santore in the thriller *State of Siege* (1972) but decided on Yves Montand instead. On April 29, the *Times* said that he would star in the movie of Neil Simon's comic drama *The Prisoner of Second Avenue*. The play starred Peter Falk as Mel Edison, the role Hackman was presumably to play. However Jack Lemmon was cast in the 1975 film.

The western *Zandy's Bride* was shot on location in Big Sur, California, and at Warner Bros. in Burbank in the summer of 1973. The Marc Norman screenplay was based on the novel *The Stranger* by Lillian Bos Ross. The title character, 32-year-old Hannah Lund (Liv Ullmann), comes to Monterey from Minneapolis to marry 36-year-old cattle rancher Zandy Allan (Hackman). Hackman has wavy hair and a mustache, and his costumes by Pat Norris include a brown wide-brimmed hat and a brown jacket with a white fur collar and trim. He does a lot of horse riding, fights a bear and appears to do the stunt where he sits on a horse at it falls down a hill. Hackman delivers a controlled performance that is mostly free of mannerism, which matches Zandy being a man of few words. He manages to redeem the character after he rapes Hannah and treats her cruelly otherwise, even making some of his anger funny. Director Jan Troell let him do a lot of silent reacting, as when Zandy observes Hannah learning how to ride a horse. Hackman's best scene is perhaps in the finale: The actor expresses a range of emotions from anger to regret to humor to happiness in a long closeup, when Zandy tries to reconcile with Hannah and gets his first look at the twins she has borne him.

The film was released on May 19, 1974. Pauline Kael in *5001 Nights at the Movies* wrote that Hackman seemed defeated by the way the character was written. The film was not a box office success. When it was previewed, it ran nearly 20 minutes longer than the film that was eventually released. In deleted scene, Zandy knocks a man off a horse with a pitchfork.

Hackman described the film as a fresh, original love story—a left-handed romance. He said Zandy was a stubborn, egocentric mountain man and a real loner,

3. The Poseidon Adventure

who sends for a mail-order bride simply because he considered the women in his territory unworthy of him. He doesn't know how to relate to a woman, with no sense of tenderness, and thinks she has no mind of her own. To him, she is only a body to give him sons but he falls in love with her when he learns she is more than he had bargained for. Actually, Hackman felt Zandy was taken with her right from the beginning, but since he was such a cut-off guy he couldn't even admit that to himself. He thought that the relationship wasn't necessarily unique but it was something that was unique for him as an actor since he never played that kind.

An unpleasant exchange broke out between Hackman and Troell when the actor killed a snake and the director voiced his disapproval. The actor reported that difficulties arose because Troell had tunnel vision about what he wanted; and because he was working in a foreign country, it was sometimes hard to communicate it. However Hackman said that they finally got to a place where they respected each other. All in all, he thought Troell was very talented. Liv Ullmann commented that she loved working with the actor and found him very inventive. She said that though he played an unsympathetic character, he did wonderful things with him.

Eileen Heckart, who played Ma Allen, said that Hackman suffered personal problems and that as a way of releasing tension he threw his star weight around. In his memoir *Just Outside the Spotlight: Growing Up with Eileen Heckart*, Luke Yankee said his mother found him to be moody and temperamental.

Hackman's father died on July 9, 1973.

One proposed storyline for the *French Connection* sequel had Popeye in France searching for his elusive prey; Hackman was not happy. And since all sorts of interesting things were being offered to him, he began to dread going back to play that character again. Hackman didn't want to go to France and he knew enough about himself to realize that he wasn't going to be very docile about it. 20th Century–Fox gave the actor additional privileges, consulting him about storyline developments and director approval. This would lead him to choose John Frankenheimer, with whom he had enjoyed making T*he Gypsy Moths.* But the actor had the time to work elsewhere first.

On September 2, 1973, *The New York Times* reported that Hackman was to reteam with director Arthur Penn for Warners' *The Dark Tower*. Retitled *Night Moves*, the crime thriller had a screenplay by Alan Sharp. It was shot in late 1973, partly in Florida. Forty-year-old Los Angeles private investigator Harry Moseby (Hackman) is hired by former movie actress Arlene Iverson (Janet Ward) to find her runaway 16-year-old, Delly Grastner (Melanie Griffith). He wears a mustache and collar-length hair. The actor is scene semi-naked after Harry has unseen sex with his wife Ellen (Susan Clark), and bloody from fights with Tom Iverson (John Crawford) and when shot by Ziegler (Edward Binns). He has an awkward love scene with Paula (Jennifer Warren). His best scene is perhaps his reaction to Paula's request to run away with him rather than bring up artifacts from the bottom of the sea that she and John have been smuggling into the country. Hackman shows Harry's change from anger to consideration of her proposal and the conflict over the fact that the treasure has cost so many lives.

The film premiered in March 1975 and went into wide release on June 11 with the taglines "What private eye Harry Moseby doesn't know about the girl he's looking for... just might get him killed" and "Maybe he would find the girl... maybe he would find himself." Roger Ebert wrote that Hackman was subtle and riveting. The film was not a box office success.

In his book *Arthur Penn: American Director*, Nat Segaloff writes that the actor was sullen during shooting because of personal stress. Screenwriter Alan Sharp said that Hackman was an exceptionally professional and skillful actor, able to make very complex perceptions without having to verbalize or intellectualize them. He made the written word sound better than on the page and added a personal content which worked successfully. Sharp added that though it was hard to imagine who would have been better than him for the part, he was also one of the liabilities of the film. People didn't go to see him in films, though they might see a film he was in, because he was not a star. His name alone could not carry a film to box office success.

John Frankenheimer wanted to cast Hackman in the role of Hickey in the drama *The Iceman Cometh* (1973) but Lee Marvin was instead cast in the made-for-TV movie, broadcast on November 10, 1973.

Hackman next did a guest spot in the black-and-white comedy *Young Frankenstein* (1974), shot from February 26 to May 3, 1974. The film had a story and screenplay by Gene Wilder and Mel Brooks, and was directed by Brooks. Dr. Frankenstein (Gene Wilder), American grandson of the infamous scientist, is invited to Transylvania, where he discovers the process that reanimates a dead body. Hackman played the part of the blind hermit who says his name is Harold and whose house is visited by the Monster (Peter Boyle). It was a parody of the Blind Hermit played by O.P. Heggie in the Universal horror classic *Bride of Frankenstein* (1935). Hackman is not billed in the film's opening credits, and is billed 17th and last in the closing credits. He appears in two scenes that occupy four and a half minutes of screen time; in both, he wears the same white hair, mustache and a longer beard, and a black-colored smock like the one Heggie wore in *Bride*. Hackman is funny even when the scenes give him burlesque-style actions like pouring hot soup onto the Monster's lap, smashing his mug of wine in a toast, and lighting his thumb because he thinks it's a cigar. The film was released on December 15, 1974, with the tagline "The scariest comedy of all time!" Roger Ebert wrote that Hackman was very good. In *The New Yorker*, Pauline Kael said that Hackman provided a masterly bit. His performance was described as an inspired characterization by Les Keyser in *Hollywood in the Seventies*. The film was a box office success and earned Academy Award nominations for Best Writing Adapted Screenplay and Best Sound.

3. The Poseidon Adventure

One source claims that Hackman's scenes took two days, another says they took four. The blind hermit's last line, "I was gonna make espresso!" after the Monster leaves, was an ad lib. Brooks reported that very few people at the time realized that Hackman had played the part when they saw the film. Brooks found him to be a great comic actor who played the scene for all it was worth and was absolutely magnificent. Brooks said he never had to give Hackman direction and that the actor made suggestions to him. To play blind, he looked straight ahead, almost looking inside when he looked out, at the pictures he remembered or envisioned. Brooks cast him because of Gene Wilder, who had appeared with Hackman in *Bonnie and Clyde*. The pair were tennis buddies and when Wilder told him he was making *Young Frankenstein*, Hackman asked if there was a small part in it that he could play as he wanted to play comedy. According to one source, the actor was even prepared to audition for the part.

French movie card for *Night Moves* (1975).

Hackman returned to *The Tonight Show with Johnny Carson* on March 21, 1974, talking about *The Conversation* and the proposed *Poseidon Adventure* sequel. He was offered the part of Chief Brody in the adventure thriller *Jaws* (1975) by director Steven Spielberg but declined, and Roy Scheider was cast instead.

Hackman was invited to the Cannes Film Festival, which took place from May 9 through 24, 1974, in support of *The Conversation*. Hackman said on *Inside the Actors Studio* that he did not attend since he was "too busy being a serious actor."

By the end of the summer of 1974, Hackman had completed filming *Bite the Bullet* in New Mexico for writer-director Richard Brooks. The period western had location shooting in Arizona and Nevada. In the movie, a group of ex–Rough Riders, an ex-prostitute and a gunfighter enter a Western Press horse endurance 700-mile race in the desert. Hackman played the part of Rough Riders Sam Clayton, hired to deliver the horse Tripoli to J.B. Parker Enterprises for the race, and then decides to enter it himself. Hackman wears his mustache and collar-length hair. He speaks Spanish and is funny when he suffers the agony of alcohol poisoning. The actor's best scene is when Sam tells fellow racer Miss Jones (Candice Bergen) about his deceased wife Paula, a Cuban insurrectionist in the Spanish-American War. The scene shows Sam's change from glorifying the San Juan Hill battle to confessing what really happened and how Paula was killed. On *Inside the Actors Studio*, he commented that this scene was a wonderful one for him as an actor.

Hackman said that it was the toughest film he ever worked on. It was released on June 25, 1975, with the taglines "In the tradition of *Shane* and *High Noon*, a new Western Classic is born!" and "A Western Classic in the tradition of *Shane* and *High Noon*." The film received Oscar nominations for Best Sound and Best Dramatic Score.

Brooks said Hackman was a really good actor with insight and intuition. The actor reminded Brooks a lot of Lee Marvin, but without the hellraising. Bergen wrote in her memoir *Knock Wood* about an argument with Hackman. She verbalized her disapproval of the screenplay's dialogue, feeling that it was an anthology of cowboy clichés. He had been sitting silently beside the driver in the front seat of the station wagon which carried the actors to location and swiveled sharply, turning his fury on her full force. "Shut up about the dialogue!" he said. "I don't need to hear any more of your wisecracks about how it can't be done. My job is to do it." Bergen admitted that Hackman was right. He didn't give a damn about what anyone thought of him and never wasted his time buddying up to crew members or getting chummy on the set. He funneled his energy fiercely into his work, and made bad material good, mediocre writing great. Bergen said he gave her a sense of respect for acting and the complexity and infinite challenge of the profession.

Interviewed in *The Guardian* (October 21, 1974), Hackman said that he had been doing too many films and needed six months rest because he felt dried up. The actor couldn't bring something new to each character and found himself being lulled into a false sense of security which took a lot of discipline to overcome. Director Stanley Donen offered him the part of The Pilot in the family fantasy musical *The Little Prince* (1974), but he declined and Richard Kiley was cast.

The actor came to the aid of old friend Dustin Hoffman, who had decided to make his Broadway stage debut as a director. The piece was a revue entitled *All Over Town*, written by Murray Schisgal. When Hoffman faced difficulty in finding a backer for the production, he enlisted Hackman and together they raised $300,000. The show ran at the Booth Theatre from December 29, 1974, to July 20, 1975. It was praised by Clive Barnes in *The New York Times*.

4

The French Connection II

The crime drama *French Connection II* had a screenplay by Alexander Jacobs and Robert and Laurie Dillon, with uncredited work by Pete Hamill, based on a story by the Dillons. Directed by John Frankenheimer, it was shot on location in France and at the Paris Bois de Boulogne Studios. Forty-two-year-old "Popeye" Doyle (Hackman) has traveled to Marseilles to find Alain Charnier (Fernando Rey), who had eluded him in New York. The actor is clean-shaven and his hair is short. The costumer is credited as Pierre Nourry but producer Robert L. Rosen reported that Hackman's wardrobe was actually supplied by an American who spent $500 at thrift shops to find mismatched and uncoordinated choices. Frankenheimer said the budget was $200 for off-the-rack clothes in California. The role gives him the chance to be drunk twice, sing "Mademoiselle from Armentières" and swim in the ocean-flooded freighter. Frankenheimer gives him a closeup when Popeye yells at Charnier in anger, showing his fiery eyes. One of the actor's drunk scenes has a long monologue about baseball which climaxes in his crying. Hackman is perhaps better in the physicality he brings to his drug withdrawal and the mix of vulnerability and anger he provides.

The film was released on May 18, 1975, with the taglines "Don't miss the final showdown!," "Gene Hackman continues his Academy Award winning role" and "*The French Connection* was only the beginning. This is the climax." According to *Variety*, Hackman's performance was another career highlight, ranging from cocky narc, Ugly American, helpless addict, humbled ego and relentless avenger. Roger Ebert wrote that Hackman supplied a lot of good acting, leaving no emotion unchurned. The film was a box office success.

For the first few showings of the film, it was approximately eight minutes longer. Fox took out a couple of scenes, including one with Popeye and the Young Girl on the Beach (Reine Prat) in his hotel room. A ten-minute scene where Popeye asks a traffic policeman for directions to the police station could not be used since the policeman was the son of the mayor of Marseilles, who felt it made his son look bad. The original end had Narcotics Detective Barthelemy (Bernard Fresson) talking to Popeye after he had shot Charnier, but Frankenheimer decided it was better to end the film on the shock of the shooting.

Hackman brought his wife and children with him and they stayed at the hotel Le Petite Nice. He said it was a nightmare trying to keep them happy, particularly his children who were on school vacation, while he worked although they did have all-day room service. Hackman had only been to Europe once before and he didn't speak French, and the crew didn't speak English. The actor used his inability to speak French to play this fish-out-of-water Ugly American. He felt that making Popeye a drug addict was inspired since you saw this tough guy melted down into a limp washcloth. To research, he watched documentaries about drug addicts in withdrawal and the great pain they went through. Hackman said that the drug withdrawal scene was one of the most important ones he ever did as an actor, and something any actor would kill to do. The drunk monologue was based on facts from the life of Eddie Egan, who had played baseball before he was a policeman. The speech was originally about Popeye's patriotism, and the actor used effective memory of a past trauma and his knowledge of drinking. He also liked Frankenheimer, and although they had their differences making the film, said he would always be grateful to him.

Hackman found Fernando Rey to be a gentleman—sophisticated and erudite. He also thought Bernard Fresson was wonderful and they had a good rapport. The actor liked having Cathleen Nesbitt play The Old Lady because she was truly a lady of the theater in the grandest way. In the scene where the dry dock was flooded, the scariest part was the amount of water that was used since too much would have made the docked ship float and the technicians would have lost all control of the situation. For the climactic chase scene, Hackman reported that his bad knees bothered him when he had to run, so his limping pain was not acting.

The actor commented that what was endearing about the film was that Popeye wanted to do things his way. He didn't respect the fact that the French might have a point of view. He just wanted to get things done, which frustrated Barthelemy. Hackman felt that a sequel relying upon the success of the original film was a mistake, and he wasn't sure that the studios knew how to market sequels anyway. Although he was unhappy being in France and he found the experience of making the film appalling, he said he ended up liking the film a lot. In some ways he felt it was more his film than the first because he put more of himself into it.

Frankenheimer said he found Hackman's portrayal of a drug addict extraordinary and perhaps the best he had ever seen. When he planned the running climax of the film, he was unaware that the actor had bad knees which became inflamed in the process. Despite this, Frankenheimer claimed that no double was used for him.

Producer Robert L. Rosen reported that Hackman improvised scenes, like the one at Le Florida Café-Bar, where Frankenheimer had him miked and used multiple hidden cameras. The actor came to work pretending he did not know what scenes

4. The French Connection II

were to be done that day, when in actuality it was obvious that he had done a lot of preparation and he was always letter-perfect in dialogue scenes. Rosen said that watching the beach volleyball players, he and Hackman thought they could easily be beaten by American players. They challenged the French to a match but on the first ball, he and Rosen collided and Hackman kneed and broke the producer's ribs.

Poster for *Lucky Lady* (1975).

Hackman now took on what he called real establishment thinking. He would play safe and only do movies that he thought would definitely make money, so that he would have plenty of it. Hackman referred to this period in his career as his felony period. Later he would feel he did these films for the wrong reason, but he believed at the time that he could do no wrong and he would always be good no matter the role.

His next film, the comedy *Lucky Lady* (1975), was shot in Nevada, Mexico and California from February 23 to July 1975. The cast was later called back for one day in November 1975 for a reshoot of the ending. The screenplay was by Willard Huyck and Gloria Katz and the director was Stanley Donen. Kibby (Hackman), Claire (Liza Minnelli) and Walker (Burt Reynolds), a trio of Prohibition Era rum-runners, travel from Tijuana to San Diego on the yacht with the film's title. Hackman is top-billed but he appears in less scenes than Reynolds, who is third-billed. He is clean-shaven and wears his hair in a collar-length style, and his wardrobe by Lilly Feniche has a distinctive white turtleneck sweater with white pancake beret and gray pants and suspenders. He makes Kibby's anger funny. Hackman's best scene is perhaps when he swears in period slang at a Coast Guard captain (Geoffrey Lewis) as he sinks into the ocean in a boat.

The film was released on December 25, 1975. It was lambasted by *The New Yorker*'s Pauline Kael, who wrote that Hackman kept a low profile and came off better than the others. *The New York Times*' Vincent Canby said his comedy touch would punch a hole in the side of a battleship. The film was a box office success.

The original ending had Kibby and Walker gunned down by government agents with Claire watching, and was followed by scenes ten years later of Claire, now married to her wealthy but dull boyfriend and with a son, reminiscing about her romantic youth. Donen felt the finished film was too comedic in tone for such a downbeat ending so Donen, Hackman and Reynolds went to Rome where Minnelli was shooting *A Matter of Time* (1976) to film the new ending. According to the December 14, 1975, *New York Times*, the actors agreed to the reshoot without requiring that theybe paid. This ending had the trio shown (with old age makeup) together in bed at age 70. Another source claims that a new ending was shot after test audiences didn't like the unhappy ending. Stephen Farber in the *Times* wrote that he attended two previews, one with the original unhappy ending and one with the happy ending, and in both cases the audience reaction was enthusiastic. The screenwriters said it was a minority that objected to the unhappy ending but since the studio also wanted a happy ending, Donen decided to use footage shot earlier of the threesome young and happy continuing their rum-running ways instead. The original unhappy ending was featured in the July 13, 1978, episode of the documentary series *That's Hollywood*.

Donen had wanted Paul Newman and Warren Beatty for the lead roles.

4. The French Connection II

Reynolds was later signed along with George Segal, who dropped out after suffering a leg injury. Donen reportedly approached agent Sue Mengers about Steve McQueen, but he declined as he was in semi-retirement. He then asked about Beatty, who also declined. Producer Michael Gruskoff, who had done *Young Frankenstein*, suggested Hackman.

Hackman in the meantime had been approached about two high-profile roles. Producers Michael Douglas and Saul Zaentz were making the drama *One Flew Over the Cuckoo's Nest* (1975) and Douglas offered Hackman the leading role of recidivist criminal Randle McMurphy, who in 1963 conned his way into 90 days of psychiatric observation in an Oregon mental hospital. It was based on the novel by Ken Kesey, who had said that Hackman was his choice to play his protagonist. The novel had been adapted by Dale Wasserman into a 1963–64 Broadway play that had starred Kirk Douglas. Hackman declined the offer, perhaps because the fee was not enough or perhaps because he didn't think it would be a box officer winner. Jack Nicholson took it and won the Best Actor Academy Award for his performance.

Hackman also turned down the role of Howard Beale, the suicidal veteran news television anchor who becomes the mad prophet of the airways, in the drama *Network* (1976). Its director Sidney Lumet said that Peter Finch was his first choice for the part (Finch won the Best Actor Academy Award posthumously). Screenwriter Paddy Chayefsky was said to have wanted Hackman for the part of Max Schumacher, the news division president. In the movie, Max was played by William Holden, who was nominated for the Best Actor Academy Award for his performance.

Hackman initially did not want to do *Lucky Lady* but 20th Century–Fox kept offering him more and more money so that Mengers said that it was almost obscene for him *not* to do it. He said he was seduced and Fox agreed to his terms of chartering him his own King Air twin-engine plane for ferrying supplies to and from the set. Hackman was cast only a week before principal photography started in Mexico.

The work wasn't satisfying. Hackman didn't call it acting, he called it trying to remember what went on before, and the major effort of each day was just getting to the location. He also got weary of waiting to be called and asked himself why as an adult was he sitting his life out on the sidelines? Hackman's observation of Donen setting up scenes, checking the cameras and interpreting the script while he sat idle made him more determined to become a director.

In a *New York Times* article (June 29, 1975), it was reported that he was looked upon with contempt because he insisted upon absolute privacy when he wasn't working. The driver who delivered Hackman to the set was the only person who knew where he lived, and he had his private plane standing by to whisk him away whenever shooting halted for more than a day at a time. Regarding the boat, Hackman said he didn't go below because it smelled bad because of the diesel fumes. He had to find a good spot on the deck and stand up the whole time. On the general working conditions on the film, he said he had a limit but he wasn't there yet. The water didn't bother Hackman but being out all day in the sun and the wind wiped him out. In terms of physical pressures and mental strain, it was the hardest film he had ever had to do. He was also critical of Donen's directing, editing and general misunderstanding of the film, with its odd mix of comedy and violence.

Burt Reynolds wrote in his memoir *But Enough About Me* that Hackman was tough and that every once in a while he would tell Liza Minnelli to "Shut the fuck up!" and everyone would walk off the set until the actor cooled down. Hackman was also critical of Minnelli's acting. After one rehearsal, he told her "You're not gonna do it that way, are you?," and she fell apart. Between takes, Hackman played basketball with Robby Benson, who played Billy in the film. According to Reynolds, Hackman got pissed when Benson ran circles around him and he tried to rough the boy up.

Producer Julia Phillips wrote in her memoir *You'll Never Eat Lunch in This Town Again* that he was visited in Mexico by his entertainment lawyer and close friend Norman Garey, who gave him the script for the science fiction film *Close Encounters of the Third Kind*. Director Steven Spielberg was interested in Hackman playing the lead role of Indiana electric lineman Roy Neary, who has a close encounter with a UFO. Phillips says he wouldn't read the script since the film was to be shot away from Hollywood for 16 weeks. Hackman was trying to keep his marriage from failing and thought he should stay in town. Some sources claim that Jack Nicholson was the director's first choice and Spielberg says it was Steve McQueen. Richard Dreyfuss eventually played the part.

The actor's desire to direct remained, though he confessed that he had no idea if he had the credentials. In partnership with Irwin Allen, Hackman purchased the rights to a mystery book by Richard Neely entitled *Walter*, but the film was never made. Taking a break from work, he relaxed by painting and flying his plane. Hackman bought property in the U.S. and Europe. One of his favorite spots was in the south of France where he purchased a luxury home which had three floors, 20 rooms, an elevator, a 30-foot playroom, a pantry complete with soda fountain, nine bathrooms and a croquet court.

Hackman was mentioned in a *New York Times* article (October 12, 1975) about stars who could do nothing to save a movie if the word of mouth was bad. Writer Charles Higham said that the actor failed to draw crowds in five recent pictures in a row: *Zandy's Bride, The Conversation, French Connection II, Night Moves* and *Bite the Bullet*. In a December 14, 1975, *New York Times* article, Vincent Canby wrote that Hackman was a fine actor but appeared to lack pliancy—the way he looked and his physical shape. Canby felt that Hackman also had an exposure problem

4. The French Connection II

since he seemed to have been on screens non-stop all year and, though the movies were different, he wasn't.

Hackman was offered the title role in the sports drama *Rocky* (1976) but declined. Screenwriter Sylvester Stallone was cast and his performance earned him a Best Actor Academy Award nomination. Another offer that the actor rejected was from director Francis Ford Coppola to star as a helicopter pilot in the version of the war drama *Apocalypse Now* (1979) that was then known as *Apocalypse Three*. One source reports that the part offered was Lieutenant-Colonel Bill Killgore. It was said that the upfront fee was paltry by Hackman's standards but Coppola offered him a percentage of the profits. Hackman declined, saying that the director had a way of asking you to work on deferment, which he didn't think he should do. Another factor may have been that filming was to take place in the Philippines. Robert Duvall was cast instead. Other sources suggest that Hackman was considered for the leading role of Captain Willard. Harvey Keitel accepted that part but was then fired after a week of shooting and replaced by Martin Sheen.

Hackman next made the drama *The Domino Principle* (1976), scripted by Adam Kennedy and based on his novel. Director Stanley Kramer shot the film at the San Quentin prison and in San Francisco and Mexico from April 12, 1976. Roy Tucker (Hackman), a convicted murderer, is freed from San Quentin so that the Vietnam War marksman can assassinate a Costa Rican diplomat for businessman Marvin Tagge (Richard Widmark). The actor has a graying mustache, graying sideburns and collar-length hair. Hackman underplays Roy's climactic confession that he did not kill the man he was prosecuted for murdering, but his best scene is perhaps when he talks about hating to be alone.

The film was released on March 23, 1976, with the tagline "Trust no one. No one." It was not a box office success. Re-edited, it was released in Britain as *The Domino Killings*. Hackman called it an interesting little film and said that Roy Tucker was an interesting and exciting character to play. He had great fun working with Widmark and Eli Wallach (who played General Reser), whom he described as old professionals. He had known their work for years and they had a backlog of wonderful material they had done. Mickey Rooney, who played Spiventa, had more energy than anyone Hackman had ever worked with.

Kramer found him surprisingly and unreasonably argumentative, and wondered if the actor was affected by the heat of the location shooting. Hackman said the arguments came about because he didn't understand what he was doing in the film. After a magazine published the daily journal that Kramer kept, Hackman confessed that the tales of his problematic behavior were embarrassing to read, but accurate. The truth was that they were in trouble on the film and Hackman got scared.

In her memoir *Cloris*, Cloris Leachman wrote that in San Francisco she had

French lobby card for *The Domino Principle* (1976).

4. The French Connection II

dinner and then made love with him in her hotel room, and the next day they both returned to the films they were making in the city. Hackman admitted that due to his deteriorating marriage, he found his personality changing. He was becoming mean and arrogant. His wife or children noticed the difference in him.

He was offered the role of Jackie Scanlon in William Friedkin's adventure thriller *Sorcerer* (1977), but declined as the film was too violent, and Roy Scheider was cast.

Hackman was part of the all-star cast of *A Bridge Too Far*, a World War II movie adapted from Cornelius Ryan's best-seller about an Allied attempt to capture five bridges in the Netherlands. The director Sir Richard Attenborough worked from a screenplay by William Goldman. The war drama was in production until October 1976 in the Netherlands and at the Twickenham Film Studios in Middlesex, England. Hackman's Major General Stanislaw Sosabowski has a mustache and short hair, speaks with an accent with odd intonation, and also speaks Polish. He appears in one battle scene, but otherwise has little to do. In his best scene, the major general hears that the Allies have decided to withdraw from the operation and Sosabowski comments, "When one man says to another, 'I know what let's do today. Let's play the war game,' everybody dies."

The film was released on June 15, 1977, with the tagline "Out of the sky comes the screen's most incredible spectacle of men and war!" Vincent Canby in *The New York Times* wrote that Hackman scowled a good deal. Roger Ebert said that the actor turned in a performance that looked as if it was trying to hide underneath itself. The film was a box office disappointment in North America but performed well in Europe. He received $1 million for his participation, which took ten days. Hackman admitted he did it for the money but it was all good company and it was a worthwhile role on a worthwhile film. He chose to play the part because Sosabowski was a strong individual with a questioning mind, and his kind of hero despite his outspoken criticism which made him unpopular with his fellow officers. Hackman agreed that many actors could have played the part as well if not better than he did, but what the company was going for was using his name for whatever that was worth. Hackman said that it was attractive to be able to go off to Holland for a few weeks and work with people you enjoyed working with.

After *The Domino Principle*, Sir Lew Grade wanted to work with Hackman again and sent him a variety of scripts and books from which to choose. The actor went with a project that he had once rejected; now more money and the persuasion of Grade secured his commitment. The war adventure *March or Die* was shot from August 23, 1976, in Morocco, Spain, Arizona and California. The screenplay by David Zelag Goodman was based on a story by Goodman and Dick Richards, and the film was directed by Richards. In 1918 Morocco, French Foreign Legionnaires are sent to an archaeological excavation in Erfoud and the tomb of Joan of Arc, known as the Angel of the Desert. Hackman, second-billed behind Terence Hill, played Major William Sherman Foster, the American in charge of the Legion. He wears his mustache and short hair and speaks French, sings and gets a death scene. He is surprisingly unconvincing in a mad scene. In his best scene, Simone Picard (Catherine Denevue) attempts to seduce him and he rebuffs her.

The film was released on August 5, 1977, with the taglines "The Foreign Legion—they were the greatest fighting force of all time and they obeyed but one command–March or Die," "The Foreign Legion! Only the desperate joined. Only the lucky ones survived" and "The magnificent story of every courageous man who has ever gone out to face death and every brave woman who has ever waited for him to return." The film was not a box office success. A different ending and additional footage (none featuring Hackman) were included in its television broadcast.

Hackman described the major as a born leader but a complex character, either a neurotic or psychotic. For research, Hackman read a couple of technical pieces on the Foreign Legion—where they operated and what they did—and there were some real-life Legionnaires on the set as advisers. During Morocco filming, the actor was thrown from a horse that had been frightened by a camel. The sciatic nerve in his hip was injured and he had back pain. Fearing that it would be permanent and cost them money, the film's insurance company had sand from the Agadir dunes sent to Nevada, since the color of the sand there wasn't the same, so that shooting could be completed in the U.S.

Hackman appeared in the documentary *America at the Movies* (1976) which was directed by an uncredited George Stevens, Jr. It was a compilation of scenes from 83 films, divided into five segments: The Land, The Cities, The Families, The Wars, The Spirit. It was released on September 22, 1976, with the tagline "You want superstars? We got 'em."

The actor commented that he was doing far too many films for just the money—and it showed. People were saying he was getting difficult to work with, which he confessed was possibly true. In 1976, John Sturges wanted him to play the U–Boat Captain Kapitänleutnant in a film of *Das Boot*, based on the novel by Lothar-Günther Buchheim, to be shot at the Bavaria Film Studios. But neither Sturges nor he would make the eventual film, which was produced in West Germany by director Wolfgang Petersen and released in 1982.

The action adventure *Superman* aka *Superman: The Movie* (1978) and its sequel *Superman II* were shot simultaneously in 1977 and 1978; the first film was released when the second was only 75 percent completed. Shooting took place in Canada, New Mexico and New York and at England's Pinewood and Shepperton Studios. The first film's screenplay was by Mario Puzo, David Newman, Leslie Newman, Robert Benton and an uncredited Tom Mankiewicz, based on a story by Puzo, with additional script material by Norman Enfield, and based on the DC Comics char-

4. The French Connection II

acter by Jerry Siegel and Joe Shuster. Superman (Christopher Reeve) aka Kal-El was the sole survivor of the planet Krypton, sent to Earth where he's become a superhero disguised as Metropolis *Daily Planet* reporter Clark Kent. Hackman, second-billed behind Marlon Brando, played Lex Luthor, who attempts to destroy California's San Andreas Fault by hijacking two missiles. He is clean-shaven and wears spectacles in one scene, and his hair is worn in a variety of styles to suggest wigs, since Lex is bald. (Hackman refused to have his hair shaven so he wears a bald cap.) His clothes by Yvonne Blake include a memorable blue-checked suit worn with a yellow shirt with yellow boutonniere and a black-and-white patterned scarf, and green swimming trunks. His anger is funny and he gets to perform some slapstick. His best scene is perhaps when Lex explains his ownership of Californian land to Superman.

The film premiered in Washington on December 10, 1978. Adrian Havill in his book *Man of Steel: The Career and Courage of Christopher Reeve* wrote about Hackman's appearance at the premiere with his children. He had staked out a corner at the Kennedy Center atrium and defended his million-dollar salary, saying that he hadn't asked for it, the amount was volunteered. Hackman became flustered when asked why the film didn't deal with the black question, shouting, "That's the most idiotic question I've ever heard and you are an ass," before storming away. *Superman* opened on December 11 with the taglines "You'll believe a man can fly" and "The movie that makes a legend come to life." James Harwood in Variety wrote that Hackman was a charming jackanapes. Pauline Kael of *The New Yorker* wrote that Hackman was strenuously frivolous like a guest villain on a *Batman* TV episode. The film was a box office success and received Academy Award nominations for Best Film Editing, Original Score and Sound Mixing, and it got a Special Achievement Academy Award for Visual Effects.

Hackman also appeared in four deleted scenes. Lex is seen ordering Otis to feed his "babies," which are unseen but sound like lions; he plays the piano as Eve Teschmacher (Valerie Perrine) asks why she loves him; he plays the piano and sings "You Must Have Been a Beautiful Baby" as she is fed to the babies after freeing Superman from his Kryptonite chain; and he sees Superman save her and bring her back up to his lair.

Paul Newman was offered the part of Lex first and declined; Dustin Hoffman may also have been considered. Ilya Salkind and Pierre Spengler reported that Sue Mengers approached them to tell them of Hackman's interest after Brando was signed. Hackman wanted to work with Brando, although the two would have no scenes together and their shooting schedules did not coincide. Hackman said he had been a comic book fan as a child but probably wouldn't have done the film had Brando not been in it. He couldn't deny that the money was a big inducement. Hackman said the producers originally wanted him to sign to do *four* films for what was anticipated to be a franchise series, but he declined this part of the offer. He liked that Lex was a departure from anything he had ever done before: He wasn't normally one for makeup and hair and that's what Lex was all about.

Hackman was cast when Guy Hamilton was attached as director. Hamilton dropped out after Brando was unable to film in Rome. Hackman then met with new director Richard Donner at the Beverly Hills Hotel. He really loved Donner, thinking him a fascinating man full of life and enthusiasm. Hackman told him he was afraid that his image as a serious actor would be tarnished since he thought of Lex as only a cartoon character but Donner helped him recognize that he could make it something to be proud of. He refused to cut off his mustache and the director told him they would discuss it when the actor came onto the set. When Hackman reported on the first day, he told Donner he still wanted to keep the mustache. Donner proposed that he would shave his own mustache if the actor shaved his. Hackman agreed. After he did so, Donner peeled off his mustache—a fake one. Hackman said he loved the director because of that. Hackman found that Donner had that rare quality of being able to instill in him a sense of fun and a sense of "This is yours. Let's see what you can do." Because of Hackman's refusal to shave his head, special makeup effects artist Stuart Freeborn made him a pure white bald cap to which he added makeup. Hackman reacted to the white cap with concern by exclaiming, "What are you doing? Trying to turn me into a ping pong ball?!"

Hackman in *Superman* (1978).

Hackman was also impressed with the talent of Christopher Reeve, saying that the young actor really came into his own when he played Clark Kent. He described him as like Cary Grant in his younger days, and you could also see that under the tights and cape there was really a fine character actor waiting to burst out.

But Hackman was unhappy

making the film. He thought it would be a lark but it turned out to be boring because it was a big production and a long schedule. Hackman said that the more technical a film became, the more inhibited he was, so the harder he had to work. Sometimes it took an hour or two to get a character to fly from one wall to another in the proper way, so when it was time to do his section, Hackman became a little soft and he was disappointed with his performance.

Bruce Scivally in his book *Superman on Film, Television, Radio and Broadway* wrote that the actor pulled a prank on Reeve for the scene where Superman threw back the lid of a lead box to find Kryptonite: Hackman had the lid nailed shut. Reeve commented that Hackman helped him a lot, and he had told him that he knew what he was going through (Reeve was new to films). To see what Hackman had attained was an inspiration but Reeve saw him often morose. When he asked him why he agreed to do the film, the actor replied, "You mean besides the $2 million?"

Donner considered Hackman an extraordinary actor and felt that he and Ned Beatty were magic together. They were both something very difficult to find—giving actors—and they would give a line written for them to the other if they felt he could more with it, and if it was an action this would then make their reaction stronger. Donner said the love between Hackman and Beatty was obvious on-screen, and they would become real-life friends.

Creative consultant Tom Mankiewicz called Hackman a natural for comedy though he could play anything. He reported that about two years after making the film, he was at the Kahala Hilton Hotel in Hawaii and ran into Hackman. The actor spoke a variation on a line from the film that Lex had said to Otis as he saw him sign in at the reception, "It's amazing how that brain can generate enough power to keep that pen moving."

The sequel *Superman II* (1980) was shot at Pinewood Studios and on locations in Canada, France, England, Norway and St. Lucia. Hackman refused to come back for his final scenes so a body double and a voice impersonator were used, best exemplified in a *Daily Planet* scene where Lex arrives after the three Kryptonian criminals. There is a moment in a hallway which is not in the Richard Donner cut of the film where Hackman speaks but is dubbed when he says, "Even with all this accumulated knowledge, when will these dummies learn to use a doorknob?"

Producers Pierre Spengler and Ilya Salkind reported that the actor's decision was not made from spite. They said Hackman was too busy, though at the time he had retired. In order to receive full director's credit, Richard Lester had to shoot up to 51 percent of the film, which included refilming several sequences originally filmed by Donner. According to Donner, roughly 25 percent of the theatrical cut contains footage he shot, including all of Hackman's scenes. In 2006, a re-cut of the film was released: *Superman II: The Richard Donner Cut* restored as much of

Donner's original conception as possible, including deleted footage of Marlon Brando as Jor-El.

The story had Superman sacrificing his powers to start a relationship with Lois Lane (Margot Kidder), unaware that three Kryptonian criminals are conquering Earth. Hackman returns as Lex Luthor who escapes from prison and joins up with the criminals determined to destroy Superman. The actor is top-billed before the film's title though again he plays a supporting role to Reeve. Hackman wears the bald cap for Lex's scenes in prison and his own hair in other scenes and he has two memorable costumes: a comic-book style horizontal striped prison uniform and a brown fur coat with a yellow turtleneck sweater. He has a nice underplayed reflective moment in prison, and a funny moment when Lex is frightened by the shadow of rabbit ears Otis (Ned Beatty) makes during their escape. Hackman's best scene is perhaps when he is grovelling to General Zod (Terence Stamp) in order to align himself with the criminals who have taken control of the planet.

The film was released on December 4, 1980, in Australia. In the U.S., there was a screening on June 1, 1981, in New York to benefit the Special Olympics. It opened on June 19 and Hackman attended the New York premiere and opening night party. He was photographed with Richard Lester and the producers, which supposedly confirmed that there was no ill feeling towards them from him. The film's taglines were "The adventure continues," "The Man of Steel meets his match!" and "The Man of Steel is back, and better than ever!" Pauline Kael (*The New Yorker*) wrote that Hackman grew in vitality when he did comedy and Janet Maslin (*The New York Times*) said that the actor very nearly stole the movie as a hilariously conniving bad guy. The film was a box office success. After *Superman III* (1983), Hackman returned in *Superman IV: The Quest for Peace* (1987).

The television versions of the film include previously deleted

Hackman in *Superman II* (1980).

4. The French Connection II

scenes which feature Hackman. These include the Phantom Zone villains landing outside the Fortress of Solitude with Lex and Lois Lane, trying to figure out how to get in; Lex taking the coffee of Perry White (Jackie Cooper) during the Times Square battle; Lex and Miss Teschmacher admiring the Fortress of Solitude; and a longer scene of Lex negotiating with Superman after they leave the Fortress. These scenes also appear on the *Superman II: The Richard Donner Cut* DVD. The Donner cut features a reprise of the *Superman I* scene where Lex puts the Kryptonite chain on Superman in a pre-credit sequence and some scenes with Hackman that were deleted from *Superman II*. These include Lex with Miss Teschmacher in the hot air balloon where he uses a machine to track Kryptonite alpha waves to find the Fortress of Solitude; the couple on a jet-ski traveling in the snow (Hackman's voice sounds like the impersonator); climbing through the Fortress; and listening to a crystal education recording of Jor-El. Donner also still had scenes with Hackman that are not in *Superman II* and that he also deleted from his own cut of the film. These include Lex and Miss Teschmacher heading south with the tracking machine, the couple arriving at the Fortress (Hackman's voice sounds like the impersonator), the Kryptonian criminals entering the Fortress with Lex, Superman handing over Lex to the U.S. Arctic Patrol outside the Fortress, and Lex escaping from prison with Miss Teschmaker (perhaps again with the impersonator).

Hackman said he liked to see Lex as playful even though he was written as a villain. The actor didn't know how to play a villain and could only play what was in him. He wasn't going to sneer and have people hiss at him. Pierre Spengler and Ilya Salkind called Hackman a fantastic actor who could go from comedy to drama believably, negotiating the fine line between humor and danger. He gave Lex dark moments that made him frightening, like the killing of the policeman in the train tunnel in *Superman I*, and also in a filmed but deleted scene in *Superman II* where he dumped Miss Teschmacher in the Fortress of Solitude.

Sarah Douglas, who played Ursa, said that it was so much fun to work with Hackman—she knew she was working with a seriously great actor and a gentleman. She recalled one day when they were going to a restaurant for lunch, they passed a big photograph showing her in the film *The People That Time Forgot*. Hackman didn't recognize her, and said the girl in the photograph was pretty, "but not in your class though." Douglas didn't have the heart to tell him that it was she.

In the September 2, 1977, *New York Times*, Elliott Gould said he hoped to star with Hackman in *A New Life*, based on the Bernard Malamud novel. This film was never made.

5

Semi-Retirement

Hackman said he had grown to hate himself on screen. He saw an old man, an uncle figure of around 50 when he still believed he was a guy in his 20s. He also regretted his choices, having made four bad films in a row: *Lucky Lady, The Domino Principle, A Bridge Too Far* and *March or Die,* and he should have stopped after *Lucky Lady.* Things suddenly seemed very simple to him. Hackman decided to stop acting before he was forced to stop. His life after winning the Oscar had become a long, nightmarish blank and all he knew was there was a lot of money to be made. For ten years, he had done nothing but work because he never could believe that an ugly schmuck like himself could stay so lucky.

The actor's professional reputation had also taken a hit. In the June 12, 1977, *New York Times,* director Joan Micklin Silver criticized his choice of "junky biggies" as opposed to someone like Al Pacino who she said allocated his time to theater and independent filmmakers. She could think of ten small movies that Hackman could illuminate if only he was willing to do them. Even if the studios weren't interested, his very presence in one of her films or a Barbara Kopple film would guarantee backers and distributors.

In a March 1989 *New York Times* interview, Hackman commented on his retirement. He had decided to quit when he walked on the set of *Superman* in London the first day of filming and there was Christopher Reeve in a skin-tight blue suit and red cape. Hackman looked at him and thought he had committed suicide. He was tired and he couldn't get himself motivated to work. He had become very selfish as an actor, spending so many years wanting desperately to be recognized as having talent; and then when he was starting to be offered parts, it was very tough to turn anything down. Even though he had a family, Hackman took jobs that separated them for three of four months at a time. The temptation of money and recognition was too much for the poor boy in him and he wasn't able to handle that.

Hackman feared that he would lose his wife forever if things didn't change so he had to retire. He wasn't easy to live with and his home and his life were in turmoil as a result. He believed that if he kept acting, it would have been a disaster. His wife was not an actress so she could see what was happening to him and she didn't want the effects to rub off on her.

He moved his family to a little Spanish-style house in Monterey that was chosen in contrast to the big mansion and the Hollywood lifestyle. Hackman wanted a pick-up truck, yearning for the simple life, despite the massive wealth he had accumulated. His hobby of oil painting soothed the stress because it was a private activity. He would never put himself in a position where his paintings would be judged, since they immediately became "The Paintings of Gene Hackman, the Actor" and he wouldn't get an honest reaction. He watched his sons race motorcycles, he read, he took up tennis, he learned to sculpt, and he flew his Pitt biplane solo above the clouds where there was perfect peace and relaxation. Hackman also took a five-day course at the Bob Bondurant School of High Performance Driving in Northern California. He was soon competing in car races at Sebring and Riverside which perhaps explained his appearance in the Italian documentary *Formula 1—Febbre della velocità* aka *Speed Fever* (1978). Written by Mario Morra and Oscar Orefici and directed by Morra, Orefici and Ottavio Fabbri, it focussed on the world's most important car racing, was shot on worldwide slopes, and was interspersed with interviews with famous drivers.

There was no official announcement of Hackman's retirement. He just let Sue Mengers know that he was no longer available for work. She would occasionally contact him with new film offers but Hackman told her he was not interested. One of these was the part of dancer-choreographer Joe Gideon in the Bob Fosse–directed musical comedy *All That Jazz* (1979); he had been recommended by Sidney Lumet. Roy Scheider was cast instead. A part opposite Diana Ross in *Tough Customers* was offered but the film was never made. Hackman wouldn't read any new scripts and he didn't want producers to approach him directly. The actor was a guest on the December 22, 1978, episode of the West German–Austrian documentary television series *V.I.P.—Schaukel.*

Growing restless, he tinkered with the idea of starting his own theater group in Monterey, still feeling the desire to act. But when the rumor leaked out, he quickly quashed it, stating that he had lost enthusiasm for show business, which he described as ugly and corrupt.

But in retirement, he felt he couldn't accomplish anything and that he was a mess. He gave up playing tennis, the solo flying jaunts, and the other hobbies that used to occupy his free time. Now he just loafed around and came to believe that retirement was a kind of death. He finally had to admit that the thing he did best was acting, though he didn't mean that in any egotistical sense. He thought that after 20 years of acting, he would have been glad of the rest, but sailing off to Tahiti was not the answer. Perhaps there was no answer, but he had come to accept that the rest of his working life had to be devoted to acting. It is what he looked forward to most of all when he woke up in the morning. The good thing about his time away was that it had gotten him off the take-the-money-and-run bandwagon. He certainly was going to stop making three films a year, because there weren't three *good* films a year to be made. He had done a lot of things he wasn't proud of in his time and now he would make fewer but better films.

He was a guest in the biographical documentary *A Look at Liv* (1979), a celebration of Liv Ullmann written by Richard Kaplan and Jerry Winters and directed by Kaplan. *The New York Times* reported on October 5, 1979, that Hackman had placed first in the pro-celebrity race and third overall in the prelude to the United States Grand Prix, held in Watkins Glen, New York.

Robert Redford wanted Hackman for the drama *Ordinary People* (1980), which he was directing. One source claims he was sought for the part of Calvin Jarrett, another says it was for the psychiatrist Dr. Berger. The actor was uncertain which part he had been offered and said they just couldn't make a deal. Though he would have loved to have made the film, Hackman wanted some points and they were not willing to give him enough. He also had some concerns about the script and the characterization but Redford was unwilling to compromise. Donald Sutherland was cast as Calvin and Judd Hirsch as Berger, the latter's performance earning him a Supporting Actor Oscar nomination.

One offer Hackman did accept was from Warren Beatty. He was in England producing, directing and starring in the historical biography *The John Reed and Louise Bryant Story* (released as *Reds*) and he had a part for him. Hackman was hesitant but agreed after Beatty reminded him of how his casting in *Bonnie and Clyde* benefited his career. He conceded that he owed Beatty and flew to England. Scripted by Beatty and Trevor Griffiths, it told the story of Reed (Beatty), a radical American journalist who becomes involved with the Communist revolution in Russia and hopes to bring its spirit and idealism to the U.S. The film was shot in the U.S., Norway, Finland, England, Spain and Sweden and at England's Twickenham Film Studios. Shooting took place from August 1979 to December 1980. Hackman is Pete Van Wherry, a Greenwich Village magazine editor. He is not in the film's opening credits and is listed 26th in the end credits. In one of his two scenes, he is clean-shaven and in the other he has a mustache. The performance includes a drunk scene, which is perhaps his best since he gets to overplay opposed to his underplaying in the other. He shows sensitivity when telling Reed that his journalist wife Louise (Diane Keaton) has been fired by John K. Wheeler's Wheeler Bell Syndication.

The film premiered on December 3, 1981, and was given a wide release on December 25 with the tagline "Not since *Gone with the Wind* has there been a great romantic epic like it!" Pauline Kael in *The New Yorker* wrote that Hackman was too good for his role and that he had such audience rapport that he jumped out from the screen. The film was a box office success and received Oscars for Best Director,

Cinematography and Supporting Actress (Maureen Stapleton). It also received nominations for Best Picture, Actor (Beatty), Actress (Keaton), Supporting Actor (Jack Nicholson), Art Direction–Set Decoration, Costume Design, Film Editing, Sound and Original Screenplay.

According to Suzanne Finstad's *Warren Beatty: A Private Man*, Hackman accepted the offer without having seen the script, and also refused to take a salary. The actor said that it was a pleasure to work for Beatty, even though he did about 50 takes. The director didn't say a lot but Hackman hung in there because but there was something about somebody who was that tough and persevered that way that was attractive to an actor who wanted to do good work.

Screenwriter-producer Steve Shagan wanted Hackman for the part of Los Angeles detective Barney Caine in the crime thriller *The Formula*. The part was taken by George C. Scott. Hackman's next film role was in the romantic comedy *All Night Long* (1981), which had the working title *Night People*. Written by W.D. Richter and directed by Jean-Claude Tramont (the husband of Hackman's agent Sue Mengers), it began production in April 1980. Soon afterwards, leading lady Lisa Eichhorn was fired and Barbra Streisand took over the role of Cheryl Gibbons. In July, the last week of filming was disrupted by a strike by the Screen Actors Guild and the American Federation of Television and Radio Artists; the film was finally completed in October.

Hackman stars as George Dupler (Hackman), an Ultra Save Corporate Office executive who is demoted to become the night manager of one of the company's 24-hour drug stores. A married man, he has an affair with the married Cheryl. Hackman is clean-shaven and his hair is in a short, wavy style. Hackman gives a funny and understated performance and is particularly sweet playing off Streisand. In one scene he sings the "Anvil Chorus" from the opera *Il Trovatore*. In perhaps his best scene, he leaves his marriage home and says that he "assumes responsibility for everything" as he packs.

The film was released on March 6, 1981; Hackman, Tramont and Streisand attended the New York premiere. The tagline was "She's got a way with men. And she's getting away with it…" It was praised by Pauline Kael in *The New Yorker*, who wrote that Hackman gave one of his most likeable performances, doing the kind of comic acting that rang true. It was not a box office success.

Some deleted scenes featured Hackman. They included a longer scene of George signing into the hotel where he lived after moving out of his home, being treated by Cheryl with something from the drug store pharmacy after the battle with the Holdup Woman (Faith Minton), arriving at the office of Richard H. Copleston (William Daniels) to talk with Helen (Diane Ladd), on a street pay phone talking to Cheryl, driving to the house of Bobby (Kevin Dobson) after finding the tape from Cheryl, and two scenes inside Bobby's house looking for Cheryl.

William Goldman wrote in his book *Adventures in the Screen Trade: A Personal View of Hollywood and Screenwriting* that Hackman was so keen to play the role that he was willing to forfeit at least part of his up-front salary in exchange for a larger percentage of the box office. Universal insisted on paying his regular salary. Hackman considered the project his comeback film and said it gave him a chance to play a light role for the first time, since almost all of his previous ones were packed with action and heavy drama. The experience reignited the actor's desire to direct and he was described as a prowling lion on the set, observing every minute detail.

About Eichhorn's firing he said, "She's got enough problems, and I've been fired myself. I know how it hurts." He also commented on Streisand's casting, saying the way the part was written it wasn't that big and would have been a waste of her time and talents. Hackman still insisted that, while the actress had five or six good scenes, it was unfair to audiences to suggest that it was her movie. It was reported that when Hackman heard that she would be getting paid $4 million for her participation, he refused to go to the set until his salary for this picture was adjusted accordingly. The actor said they had a good time and a real rapport and the chemistry worked for them.

Hackman in *All Night Long* (1981).

Jean-Claude Tramont commented on the casting of the actor, saying he had doing these harsh roles but he was so funny in *Young Frankenstein* (1974) that he always wondered why nobody used him in comedy. Brian Kellow in his book *Can I Go Now? The Life of Sue Mengers, Hollywood's First Superagent* wrote that in the evenings during the two weeks of rehearsal, Eichhorn would go to Hackman's house for a swim and further discussions about the film. She said she was in awe of him and that their time alone got perilous. Eichhorn knew he was a married man and was intrigued by him but went home before anything happened. However, once shooting began, things began to change and there was trouble between the pair. Screenwriter

Richter reported that the actor was withholding something vital in their scenes together and he believed that Hackman didn't want Eichhorn as his co-star and subverted the process. Richter said he was a pain in the ass to her, doing weird little actor-ish things to her in closeups, making it harder for her to be her best. Hackman was being cold to Eichhorn in a weird subtle way and none of his charm came through. She was thrilled to be working with him, and recalled that he commented that she was so beautiful and looked luminescent on screen. Producer Leonard Goldberg said there was nothing wrong with the Hackman-Eichhorn rushes.

In Peter Biskind's book *Gods and Monsters: Thirty Years of Writing on Film and Culture*, he wrote that Richter said Hackman wanted Streisand from the start, and felt it was a way for him to realign himself in the Hollywood superstar structure by being in a romantic comedy with her. But she turned down the part. So did Tuesday Weld and Loni Anderson, before Eichhorn was signed. Richter claims that Hackman was inconsolable about the loss of Streisand and made Eichhorn, Tramont and everybody else miserable. Sources differ as to why Streisand changed her mind about doing the part.

Streisand said that she loved Hackman and that was one of the reasons she agreed to do the film. She also reported that he was very hard on Tramont and she tried to protect the director because she felt bad for him. Streisand said Tramont couldn't handle someone like Hackman.

The actor was sought by director Steven Spielberg for the part of archaeologist Indiana Jones in the action adventure *Raiders of the Lost Ark* (1981), but Harrison Ford was cast instead. Hackman was considered by director Ridley Scott for the title role in the science fiction thriller *Blade Runner* (1982) but again Harrison Ford got the part. He turned down the role of Sheriff William Teasle in the action adventure *First Blood* (1982), and Brian Dennehy was cast.

In the biography of Oliver Reed by Robert Sellars, *What Fresh Lunacy Is This?*, Steve Neill recalls a reunion between Reed and Hackman after they had made *The Hunting Party*. It occurred while Reed was making the comic horror film *Dr. Heckyl and Mr. Hype* (1980): He was staying at the Montage Hotel in Beverly Hills and one night in the hotel's restaurant the actor spotted Hackman. Reed could see that he recognized him but he also saw a horror in Hackman's eyes, as if he didn't want to be seen. He went over and grabbed Hackman and brought him back to his table. Neill doesn't report what happened after that though presumably, as the actor is not mentioned again, he did not stick around for the night of drinking.

Hackman was a driver in the Toyota Pro/Celebrity Auto Race held on March 24, 1981, at the Long Beach Racetrack in California. He attended the American Film Institute Salute to Fred Astaire, held at the Beverly Hilton Hotel on April 10, 1981, and screened on CBS on April 18. It featured highlights from his films and reminiscences from his co-workers. Hackman presented the National Board of

Review's Best Director award to Warren Beatty for *Reds* on December 15, 1981, in New York. The actor recalled one scene in the film where he made a comment after the 51st take, and the room erupted in laughter.

The murder mystery *Eureka* (1983) was shot on location in Canada, Jamaica and Florida, and at the EMI Elstree Studios and Twickenham Film Studios in England. Filming took five months to take advantage of the British Columbia winter and Jamaica spring. The director was Nicolas Roeg and the writer was Paul Mayersberg, basing his script on the book by Marshall Houts. Hackman stars as Arctic prospector Jack McCann, who becomes the richest man in the world when he strikes gold and buys the island of Luna Bay off the coast of Miami, to live on a property called Eureka, in the 1940s. The actor has a beard in the early scenes and then collar-length white hair and clean-shaven for the later scenes. He is funny when talking to a parrot, and has a grisly death scene. His best scene is perhaps when Jack is in bed with his wife Helen (Jane Lapotaire) and talks about being "under siege."

The film was released in the United Kingdom on May 20, 1983, and in the U.S. on October 5, 1984, with the tagline "Richer than Getty, stranger than Hughes, the bizarre tale of Jack McCann." Roger Ebert wrote that Hackman was wonderful with the intensity of his obsessions, *Variety* said that Hackman performed with predictable credit and Walter Goodman of *The New York Times* wrote that he was plainly adrift. The film was not a box office success.

Hackman said he had wanted to make a film about ecstasy and what happened after one had achieved one's greatest ambition. It was the story of the obsession of a man, a maypole figure around which the other characters danced. He found the script to be one of the most unusual he had read in quite some time. It was not a normal adventure story, not a mystery, and not a drama of a family, though it had elements of each. It also had a variety of really exciting locations—everything it took to make a really interesting movie. Hackman said what really attracted him to the role was the change in character in 20 years, from adventurer to great patriarch and one of the richest men in the world.

He also admired Roeg as a filmmaker. After seeing his *Don't Look Now* (1973) and *Bad Timing* (1979) Hackman felt that Roeg had a complete knowledge of what the camera could do, and could exploit an actor to the best advantage of the script. He thought Roeg was somebody he was on the same wavelength with, but when filming began, the actor's patience was tested. He had begun to be more interested in aspects like art direction and cinematography, and less concerned about his performance, and Roeg's working methods were not what Hackman was used to. He only used one camera and enjoyed taking the time to light each set-up individually, following his experience as a cinematographer, and shot numerous takes from different camera angles. Hackman preferred multiple cameras and rarely doing more

5. Semi-Retirement

than two takes, so Roeg's method resulted in a lot of waiting around. This set off the actor's temper and the pair argued after the director rejected take after take. Hackman's reputation for being difficult seemed to be confirmed by observers.

Chris Hackman, the actor's 22-year-old son, accompanied his father on location and was hired by Roeg to work with the crew. This helped Hackman, who didn't like to socialize with his fellow actors, since they would often want to talk about their roles and he preferred not to. However the actor relented by joining in a cast vs. crew darts match and a beach volleyball match.

After making *Eureka*, Hackman said he felt fortunate to have been given a chance to start the process as an actor again. Now he had a better view of what he wanted: personal satisfaction from being proud of the work, and the realization that if he did something not up to his standards, it would come back and haunt him. He tried to hold out for a really good story and script, and he said if he couldn't have that, he had to have a lot of money and good locations. The actor also had the feeling that he didn't want to be ugly any more. Perhaps, as a man in his fifties, he hoped that he could be cast in more refined and polished roles to avoid the brutal and violent ones that seemed to define his prior screen image.

Interviewed in the March 28, 1982, *New York Times* about winning an Oscar, he said that winning had caused a lot of actors to price themselves out of the market or they expected too much. Hackman seemed to have been lucky, saying he had been working pretty steadily, although not as much as he would have liked. The actor added that there was a loss of privacy but that kind of thing was crying poor mouth. He said acting was exciting—you paid for it in many ways and in many ways it paid you.

The August 18, 1982, suicide of 46-year-old Norman Garey made on impact on Hackman since he was his lawyer and close friend.

Shot in Oaxaca, Mexico, *Under Fire* was about the 1979 Nicaraguan revolution. Directed by Roger Spottiswoode, it told the story of a tough "seen-it-all-before" photojournalist (Nick Nolte) who is gradually convinced by the Sandinista cause and eventually risks his own career to promote the revolution. The war drama had a screenplay by Ron Shelton and Clayton Frohman based on Frohman's story. Second-billed as senior correspondent Alex Grazier, Hackman looks thinner and wears his mustache. He gets to play a mouth organ and a piano and sing "Spring Can Really Hang You Up the Most." He has a funny line when Alex tells Russel (Nolte) and Claire (Joanna Cassidy), "The cutest couple in town's got me looking up a horse's ass on a midnight tour of Managua." Perhaps his best scene is when he looks in the mirror and talks to Claire about how he has a face for television.

The film was released on October 21, 1983, with the taglines "This wasn't their war but it was their story ... and they wouldn't let it go!," "Dateline: Central America. The First Casualty of War is the Truth" and "Nick Nolte and Gene Hackman in a

Riveting, High-Tension Thriller." Pauline Kael in *The New Yorker* wrote that Hackman was totally believable, and Roger Ebert said he was convincing. The film was not a box office success. It received an Academy Award nomination for Best Original Score.

Spottiswoode reported that he got Hackman for less than his usual price, bypassing sending the script to his agent and getting a quicker response. He said what most appealed to him was the idea of the interplay between the three main characters, and since they covered the Central American war it was a fascinating attempt to make a triangle work within that context. Spottiswoode said Hackman was a writer-director's delight, an actor who found all the options, explored all the possibilities and then came up with surprises on every take. He prepared for his singing scene by renting a piano, choosing a music teacher and diligently practicing.

Joanna Cassidy commented that in one scene with her, Hackman said it was one of the rare times that he felt he disappeared into his acting. He was able to remove the room and go into a zone with her and that was really quite wonderful. Cassidy took it as a compliment to her.

After finishing the film, Hackman contemplated directing a film called *Open and Shut*, about a rape case. He had promised himself that he would not go on the set on the first morning without having some experience, and intended to do some second unit work before starting principal photography. He preferred not to act in the film. The film was not made.

In 1982 the Hackman house was put on the market for $8 million because it was too big for his family. But that year he also separated from his wife again, citing irreconcilable differences. Being on location for *Eureka* had added more strain to the relationship, since Faye seemed to be happiest when her husband wasn't working. He admitted that it was very difficult to have a personal life in show business, particularly when he was away from home so much. Though his daughters were now teenagers, Hackman still felt that a celebrity's children had a tough life. They remained living with their mother in a smaller house he provided while he stayed in hotels. He retained some of his property in Europe and kept their locations secret.

Hackman admitted to not feeling content, believing his career was slipping away from him because he didn't really care enough about it to give it 100 percent. It meant a great deal to him to be well thought of as an actor, but it didn't mean enough to do a hell of a lot about it.

Warner Bros. considered him for a role in the biographical drama *The Killing Fields* (1984), but producer David Puttnam preferred an actor who didn't bring the baggage of other roles. The role was presumably that of Sydney Schanberg, the *New York Times* journalist trapped in Cambodia during tyrant Pol Pot's bloody "Year Zero" cleansing campaign. Hackman drove in the Grand Prix of Long Beach on March 27, 1983.

5. Semi-Retirement

Hackman was uncredited as the voice of God in the fantasy romantic comedy *Two of a Kind* (1983). Written and directed by John Herzfeld, it told the story of struggling inventor Zack (John Travolta) and bank clerk and aspiring actress Debbie (Olivia Newton-John), who must demonstrate a willingness to sacrifice each other or God will flood the world. Hackman is heard in five scenes and his God is represented by the optical effects of the sun and rolling clouds. The film was released in Canada on December 13, 1983, and then the U.S. on December 16 with the taglines "It took a twist of fate to make them two of a kind" and "A match re-made in Heaven." The film was not a box office success and scored Razzie Award nominations for Worst Picture, Screenplay, Director, Actor and Actress. Its producer Joe Wizan had produced *Prime Cut*.

The drama *Misunderstood* was shot in Tunisia and directed by Jerry Schatzberg, who had worked with Hackman on *Scarecrow*. Scripted by Barra Grant (based on a novel by Florence Montgomery), it was a remake of the Italian Luigi Comencini–directed *Misunderstood* aka *Incompresso* (*Vita col figlio*) (1967). The new film told the story of Ned Rawley (top-billed Hackman), a shipping magnate in Tunisia, North Africa, who must take care of his boys Andrew (Henry Thomas) and Miles (Huckleberry Fox) after the death of his wife (Susan Anspach). The actor wears his mustache and spectacles. He is given the difficult task of acting mostly with two children; his real-life experience as a father no doubt explains his physical comfort with them. His best scene is perhaps the final one where he expresses controlled emotion when he is faced with the injured Andrew.

Hackman in *Misunderstood* (1984).

The film was released on March 30, 1984, with the tagline "For every kid who wants to be hugged. For every parent who wants to love and understand." The film was a box office success. The story would be remade again as the Taiwanese *Zu sun qing* aka *Grandpa's Love* (1994), the Canadian made-for-TV movie *L'incom-*

pris aka *The Misunderstood* (1997) and the Italian made-for-TV movie *Incompreso* (2002).

Hackman was interviewed in San Francisco by Bobbie Wygant on television about the film, and though he admitted that promoting was a painful process, he was now prepared to do so as he wanted his films to be successful. The actor didn't believe he took any chances making the film though the subject made him consider his own relationship with his father, which was not as good as he would have liked. Hackman felt a film like this had its place and touched some people, though he knew others wouldn't like it. He said his youngest daughter was very affected by it, and she recommended it to her girlfriends. Hackman hoped his older children were equally taken with it.

He said working with Henry Thomas was quite remarkable. Hackman found him very professional, completely concentrated and very much aware of what was going on and what was needed. Thomas was like a lot of child actors who suddenly reverted to being a 12-year-old boy as soon as the scene was over (he and Huckleberry Fox would then play Dungeons and Dragons). It was the first time Hackman had worked with children and he loved doing it because he had to take a whole different attitude with them. The actor knew that W.C. Fields said that the worst things to work with were animals and children because they stole the scenes, but he didn't feel that way. Schatzberg reported that he had thought of a number of people to play Ned, Hackman among them, and the more he thought about it, the more he realized that Hackman was right.

Hackman's next film was the action thriller *Uncommon Valor* (1983), originally known as *The Last River to Cross*. It was shot from June 6 to August 1983 on location in Thailand, Hawaii and California. In preparation, cast members spent a week in intensive military training. The screenplay was by Joe Gayton, based on a story by an uncredited Wings Hauser, and the director was Ted Kotcheff. U.S. Marine Colonel Jason Rhodes (Hackman) assembles a private rescue team to find Americans, including his son, held in a Laos P.O.W. camp. Top-billed Hackman wears his mustache and is seen with a military haircut in a 1973 scene and with his hair in a short but less military cut in scenes from 1977, 1982 and 1983. He gets to fire a rifle and machine gun, use a machete and fly a helicopter. His best scene is perhaps when Jason recites a speech from *Julius Caesar* to his rescue team.

The film was released on December 16, 1983, with the taglines "C'mon... we're going home" and "Seven men with one thing in common..." Pauline Kael in *The New Yorker* wrote that Hackman offered a range of held-in, adult emotions that you didn't expect to see in an action movie. The film was a box office success.

Hackman asked his *Cisco Pike* co-star Kris Kristofferson, a former Airborne Ranger, if he wanted to do a cameo in this film but he declined because he was on a concert tour. According to Hackman, the film had something to say about the

Vietnam War and about the unresponsiveness of the U.S. government towards people affected by the war years down the line. He spent his Sundays off on location painting and sculpting.

Ted Kotcheff said he cast Hackman because he had a credible quality, not gung-ho but the way anyone would have behaved in such a situation. In his book *Director's Cut: My Life in Film*, he wrote that the actor said he only wanted three directions from him: "More, less—faster, slower—louder, softer." Anything else screwed up his brain. Kotcheff had no intention of restricting himself like that but had to find a way to communicate to Hackman the shadings he wanted without upsetting his artistic equilibrium. Presumably he found the way since he said that what Hackman did in the film was not acting, it was being. The director reported that the actor prepared for two months beforehand and that becoming the character took total possession of him so Hackman would do anything he was asked of him without objection because this is what the colonel would do. Kotcheff found his ability to switch in and out of character mesmerizing. They often dined together after work at restaurants, like the rooftop restaurant at Bangkok's Oriental Hotel. One day the pair stood next to the camera waiting for the cinematographer to finish setting up a shot and bantering about food and wine. Then Hackman turned away and in a second he became the colonel, having so digested the character that he was able to call upon this at a moment's notice.

Kotcheff reported that the actor was also very intuitive about the filmmaking process and what made a scene work. The director was staging a scene where the colonel tells his rescue team what they would be doing on the mission. Hackman didn't want to be standing making a speech and wanted some business because then he wouldn't have to think about the words. Kotcheff suggested Hackman put camouflage makeup on as he spoke and the result was brilliant. According to Kotcheff, Hackman was the finest actor he had the good fortune to work with.

In his memoir *The Time of My Life*, Patrick Swayze wrote that Hackman took him under his wing on the set, being unfailingly professional and very generous with his time and insight. He also taught Swayze a very big lesson about acting, telling him that he was not there for himself but to only to serve. Hackman devoted himself to his movies and if it took 20 takes for the other actor to get it right, he would be right there, delivering his lines every single time with the same energy and dedication.

6

Twice in a Lifetime

Hackman was referenced in the Arthur Hiller–directed comedy *The Lonely Guy* (1984), based on Neil Simon's adaptation of the Bruce Jay Friedman book *The Lonely Guy's Book of Life*. In one scene, greeting card writer Larry (Steve Martin) attends a party held by his Lonely Guy friend Warren (Charles Grodin), which is populated with life-size celebrity cut-outs. Lonely Cop (Madison Arnold) asks if there is one of Hackman, and Warren replies that there is but you had to reserve it a week ahead.

The actor attended the 41st Annual Golden Globe Awards, held on January 28, 1984, at the Beverly Hilton Hotel in Los Angeles. A nominee for Best Actor in a Supporting Role in a Motion Picture for *Under Fire*, Hackman lost to Jack Nicholson for the comic drama *Terms of Endearment*. He was also the presenter of the Best Actress in a Motion Picture Drama to Shirley MacLaine for *Terms of Endearment*.

Hackman had been sought by Paul Newman for the part of demolition crane operator Harry Keach in the drama *Harry & Son* (1984), which Newman was going to direct. But no studio would bankroll the project unless Newman also starred, so that is what he did.

At the 56th Annual Academy Awards, held on April 9, 1984, at the Dorothy Chandler Pavilion in Los Angeles, Hackman was co-presenter (with Dyan Cannon) of the Best Actress in a Supporting Role award to Linda Hunt for *The Year of Living Dangerously* (1982).

Hackman and his wife began their divorce proceedings. He had reportedly been linked with the Hawaiian pianist Betsy Arakawa, who was only a year older than his own son Christopher. Arakawa would later become Hackman's second wife. The actor's choice to make the romance *Twice in a Lifetime* (1985), with its story of a man who leaves his family for another woman, paralleled his personal situation. Originally known as *Kisses at 50*, it was shot in Seattle and other areas of Washington from July to September 1984, after two weeks of rehearsals in Los Angeles and on location. Hackman said that he didn't think the film would have worked on any level without the rehearsals because there was too much to find and it was too difficult an acting piece.

6. Twice in a Lifetime

Scripted by Colin Welland, it starred Hackman as Harry MacKenzie, a 50-year-old who leaves his wife of 30 years, beauty parlor worker Kate (Ellen Burstyn), for widowed barmaid Audrey Minelli (Ann-Margret). The actor gets to sing and dance and makes his character likable and funny. He differentiates Harry's boredom with Kate and the excitement of being with Audrey. Hackman's best scene is perhaps in reaction to Audrey's demand for "Nothing but us," where he shows Harry's mix of guilt and fear about making a new commitment.

The film premiered at the Toronto Film Festival on September 9, 1985, had a New York premiere on October 21 (Hackman attended), and was given a wide U.S. release on November 8. The film was not a box office success but earned Amy Madigan a Best Supporting Actress Oscar nomination. Hackman received a Golden Globe nomination for Best Performance by an Actor in a Motion Picture—Drama (but lost to Jon Voight of *Runaway Train* [1986]).

Hackman commented that, while the film was not that different from other films about divorce, it had terrific actors and it was quite a thrill to make. He went through a divorce, and his parents were also divorced, so he knew something about the subject. It was a painful experience, probably more so for the children of the family then the parents. If one could make it through still being friends with your former mate and having some kind of relationship with your children, you had done a marvellous job. That is what they tried to do in the film, and making it allowed the actor to get a lot of his own emotion into it. Hackman said the film offered a different kind of challenge. The character wasn't particularly sympathetic in his actions but you had to keep an audience interested and caring about him. The story moved him more than a lot of other things he had done. He was at an age where he got offered fatherly parts but this one interested him: Harry had a hard edge to him but also a soft side. The longer he was an actor, the more he became attracted to doing things he had never done before and he liked films that came out of relationships rather than stories of men against the system. Hackman thought he could use some of what he went through, but it didn't really work out that way. He found the scene where Harry's daughter Sunny (Amy Madigan) confronted him an uncomfortable one, and being uncomfortable and self-conscious was something he dreaded. When it came time to shoot, just about all the actors in it wanted their lines reduced and some just didn't want to do it. But they did.

Director Bud Yorkin reported that after he sent the script to Hackman, he heard back from him the next day to say that he had to play the role. Yorkin felt that his interest came from the fact that he was going through a divorce at the time.

After *Twice in a Lifetime*, the actor unwound by taking lessons from a Russian painter. Then he received another film offer from one of his favorite directors, Arthur Penn. Penn's action adventure *Target* (1985), originally known as *On Target*, was shot from October 1984 to January 1985 with an 11-day break for Christmas.

It was made in Texas, West Germany and France with interiors shot at the Studios De Boulogne in Paris. The screenplay was by Howard Berk and Don Peterson, based on a story by Leonard Stern. The story involved the relationship between Dallas lumberyard businessman Walter Lloyd (Hackman) and his racing car mechanic son, Chris (Matt Dillon), who come together to look for Walter's wife Donna (Gayle Hunnicutt) who was kidnapped in Paris. Hackman's costumes by Marie-Francoise Perochon include a dark blue shirt that sets off his blue eyes. The role has the actor speak French and German, sing, fish, smoke and shoot a gun. The actor is simple and earnest when Walter tells Chris that he "needs his strength"; his best scene is perhaps when Walter meets with the German agent Schroeder (Herbert Berghof) in a hothouse. Here Hackman remains still and just listens and observes.

The film was released on November 8, 1985, with the tagline "It's Harder to Win When You Play by the Rules!" Vincent Canby (*The New York Times*) wrote that Hackman acted with stylish conviction. Pauline Kael in *The New Yorker* said that the actor worked like a saint to give the film a rootedness. The film was not a box office success.

Interviewed on the set, Hackman reported that he didn't think he would have done the film if it had been any other director. When he first read the script, it wasn't anywhere near in the shape it later took. He felt it was an interesting role for him, after having been offered so many recent father-son relationship films. This one was totally different because his character changed so radically as he came out of his shell. It was fascinating having two sides to the man—soft and hard— and seeing how the son seems to have those same qualities. One of the things about this genre was that if you could convince the audience that you were respectable, attractive and sympathetic, they believed that and went with you.

Talking to interviewer Bobby Wygant, Hackman reported he did his own dive into the river because he was bored that day. The water was very cold even though he had an exposure suit on under his costume, and it was fun to know that he did his own stunt although the production didn't want him to for safety and health reasons. Hackman was only required to do it two or three times, and he felt it was part of the actor's job to do as much as he could. But narratively, it was also important because he had to signal his son from the water to run so it had to be him, so he thought "Why not get it done and get it over with?"

He also commented that the film had one of the best crews he had ever worked with, and also praised Arthur Penn, saying he asked a lot of everyone but then he asked a lot of himself. At three or four in the morning you really wanted to quit— one night in Hamburg was really miserable—but they went on till 5.15 a.m. and Penn was still there, punching away.

Co-producer David Brown said that he had never known an actor who spent so little time relaxing in his trailer between takes. Hackman wanted to know everything that was going on. Penn added that he was a consummate actor and a perfectionist. Every move, he knew exactly what he was doing, but he agonized over it for hours, even days, before he got to the camera.

In his book *Arthur Penn: American Director*, Nat Segaloff wrote that the father-son tension between the characters was paralleled offscreen between the actors one day. Hackman blew up at the 21-year-old Dillon, when he made a suggestion for a scene. He told him, "That's not what you do," and gave him a five-minute lecture on what it was to be a serious actor and an artist. Dillon reported that this changed his life, giving him a new respect for the art.

The New York Times of October 15, 1984, reported that Hackman had considered playing the part of New York security guard John Mack in the thriller *The Guardian*, a 1984 made-for-TV movie. Louis Gossett, Jr., was cast as Mack. In a November 28, 1984, *Times* article, it was reported that Hackman's asking price for a film was now $1 million, and the price of Robert Redford and Dustin Hoffman was $5 million.

He appeared in ABC's *Night of 100 Stars II* (1985), shot at New York's Radio City Music Hall on February 17, 1985, and broadcast on March 10. A celebrity benefit for the Actors Fund of America, it featured music, songs, dances and comedy. Three hundred eight stars participated in a seven-hour marathon that was edited to three hours for television. It was nominated for Emmy Awards for Outstanding Directing in a Variety or Music Program, Outstanding Achievement in Music Direction and Outstanding Achievement in Choreography.

Hackman next signed on for director Sidney Lumet's film *Special Action*, a title later changed to *Power*. It was shot from April 1 to June 1, 1985, in California, Seattle, Washington, New Mexico, New York and Mexico with interiors at the Kaufman Astoria Studios and Telecommunications in New York. Scripted by David Himmelstein, it featured Richard Gere as Pete St. John, a political consultant hired to help with the campaigns of New Mexico gubernatorial candidate Wallace Furman (Fritz Weaver) and Ohio Senatorial candidate Jerome Cade (J.T. Walsh). Hackman played Wilfred Buckley, Pete's former employer and another consultant who runs the campaign for New Mexico candidate Frank McKusker (Glenn Kezer) and Ohio Senatorial candidate Phillip Aarons (Matt Salinger). Third-billed Hackman sports a mustache and his hair is a little longer at the back. Wilfred is a drunk, Southern and presumably gay. He speaks with a Southern accent and shows his range from overplaying good humor and drunkenness in a comic style and then showing Wilfred's real fear and hurt when Pete speaks to Phillip about his campaign strategy. In Hackman's best scene, he drunkenly ridicules Pete at an airport and falls down unconscious.

The film was released on January 31, 1986, with the taglines "Nothing else comes close" and "You have the ballot. But who has the power?" The film was not a box office success and it earned Beatrice Straight a Razzie nomination for Worst Supporting Actress.

Hackman commented that Lumet was such an energetic guy that he really overwhelmed him with his positive attitude about what he was doing and what he wanted from his movies and his people. The director shot like nobody he had ever seen, with the New York crew moving sometimes two or three times a day on locations, whereas other films would never move once because that would have meant losing the rest of the day. Doing the film was a bit like doing a play, especially for the first five days when the creative process was taking place, where Lumet allowed ideas and the freedom and the looseness that Hackman enjoyed most. Then the following week he had to know his lines and it started to get serious because then it was all in cement. It was an interesting, involved and calculated process and by the second Friday it was like they were ready to open on Broadway if they could.

He was very pleased with the film and the other performers, especially Richard Gere. Lumet liked theatrical performances which Hackman found refreshing as opposed to a lot of naturalness that you saw in a lot of films. Here everybody was very much intent and knew exactly what they were doing. He also thought Denzel Washington as Arnold Billing was a very strong actor.

Hackman was back before the cameras for the sports drama *Hoosiers* (1986), shot in Indiana. The screenplay was by Angelo Pizzo and the director was David Anspaugh. Fifty-year-old Coach Norman Dale (Hackman), a former Marine, is hired in 1951 as the history and civics teacher and basketball coach for the Indiana Hickory High School Huskers. Dennis Hopper as Shooter has the showier role but Hackman has some good quiet moments, like Norman reacting to the town meeting held to decide if he can stay on as coach. His best scene is perhaps when he listens

Hackman in *Hoosiers* (1986).

6. Twice in a Lifetime

to the information that fellow teacher Myra Fleener (Barbara Hershey) has found out about his past.

The film went into limited release on November 14, 1986, and then a wide release on December 11 with the taglines "It'll go straight to your heart" and "They needed a second chance to finish first." It was praised by Janet Maslin in *The New York Times*, who wrote that Hackman brought shrewdness and a varied temperament to a man who might otherwise have seemed bland. Roger Ebert said that the actor gave a great performance, combining likability with complexity. The film was a box office success and received Academy Award nominations for Dennis Hopper as Best Supporting Actor and for Best Score.

The film's rough cut ran 168 minutes; it was reduced to 138 for the first audience screening, and the final running time was 114 minutes. Deleted scenes showed more of the romance between Norman and Myra, including his writing on a class chalkboard and asking her on a date, having dinner with her and her mother Opal (Fern Persons) and thanking Myra for what she said at the town meeting. Other deleted scenes featuring Norman had him in a motel room looking through a scrapbook of his past and removing stripes from an old military jacket with a razorblade, stopping for gas on the way to Hickory and talking to the attendant, walking with Cletus (Sheb Wooley) through the school, having dinner at Cletus' house, helping with the town harvest, eating a meal at the harvest, sitting on a haystack, drinking water from a pail, losing his temper in Cletus' office, talking to Everett (David Neidorf) about his father, asking Preacher Purl (Michael Sassone) to pray for the team, and getting a hair trim from Opal.

Jack Nicholson wanted to play Norman but he was unable to because he was serving as a witness in a lawsuit, which sidelined him for six months. He told the producers he knew they were on a tight schedule to shoot, and if they found another actor, to go ahead. If not, he could do it the next year. After seeing the film, Nicholson told director Anspaugh that Hackman was great in the part. Burt Reynolds was also considered, as was Robert Duvall. Hackman's salary was $400,000, lower than his normal rate, in exchange for also receiving ten percent of the film's gross profits including videocassette sales.

Hackman said that sometimes it was more satisfying as an actor to be in a small film since you had more to do and they were really more interesting. The film told an interesting story and he chose films based on story rather than character because he felt he could find something to make a character interesting if the story was strong enough. The role also appealed to him because he went through a lot of changes in the course of events and through people he met. If it was just about basketball it wouldn't have worked because it had to be about the people. Hackman viewed his character as a very competitive man, who did what he felt was the right thing to do rather than play the political game.

Hackman praised screenwriter Pizzo, saying he was good for Anspaugh because he was always on the set and knew exactly what he wanted from the film. In a montage of Hickory winning a string of games, Norman is shown saying something to Shooter on the bench that makes him laugh. Hackman had reportedly told Hopper that he hoped he had invested well because they were never going to work after the movie, since he considered it a career-ending experience.

He said he felt that there was something special about the film because he had grown up just 75 miles from where they shot it so he knew the area and that era, having played basketball himself during that time. Hackman had never worked as an actor in the Midwest and he was looking forward to it, but when he got there it was difficult. Everything was in disarray because there were so many non-professionals in the cast and so many unpaid extras. But the people in the small towns were nice and the experience was pleasant. Hackman reported on *Late Night with David Letterman* (February 10, 1986), that men came over from Danville where he had grown up to see him, men he had gone to grade school with, and they had a great time together.

Anspaugh said that because of Hackman's age and weight, the actor fit the character to a T. He and the screenwriter spent a great deal of time with Hackman starting at page one and going through every scene, even scenes he wasn't in, wanting his opinion and feedback. They found he was smart and his instincts were so good, since with certain scenes, Hackman would say he didn't need so many lines. He could act their intention instead. When they had a read-through of the script, Anspaugh knew they had stumbled into the best choice they could have made. Hackman was also helpful in doing daily acting workshops between basketball practice for the boys in the film because none of them had acted before. Brad Long advised that the acting instructions they received included monologues where they would make up a story. To produce emotions they did forced-emotion exercises that would make you think of something that would make you very sad, and you'd try to cry. Long said that was hard to do but Hackman was easygoing about it. They also had to sing a song of their choice. In return, the boys schooled Hackman in basketball lingo, which helped make it natural for him to yell "Cover the weak side" and "Get back on defense." Hackman also offered the boys advice, saying they had to give it the best since what they did would be on film forever. When they asked him if they should pursue acting careers, he told them about going to restaurants in Los Angeles and having starving actors wait on him, and asked if that was really their goal in life. He advised if acting wasn't something you wanted to do your whole life more than anything, then it wasn't worth doing.

Hackman participated in publicity by autographing t-shirts that were sold in town. He also interacted with the locals. The grocery store owner called him congenial and nice and someone else commented that if you didn't know who the actor was, you would have thought he lived there. Local Fannie Stevens introduced herself

6. Twice in a Lifetime

to Hackman, telling him that she and his mother were his neighbors and best friends in Danville. She gave him two pictures of his mother and Hackman reminisced with Stephens and her husband. What really got to him was how they kept calling him Gene Allen, using his middle name, since no one had called him that for years. Ralph "Whitey" Shively proclaimed that Hackman was probably one of the nicest people he had ever met, and gave him a Shively Auction hat which he wore that day. Shively described the actor as common as an old shoe. One woman baked him a pie and another gave him a plaque.

After these encounters, Anspaugh thought making the film would be a magnificent experience. Instead, Hackman had him on the verge of a nervous breakdown, giving him an anxiety attack where one morning he woke up and couldn't walk and the room was spinning. They clashed from the first day of shooting, when they filmed a scene that was cut, where Norman was driving to Hickory and he stops to get gas. Anspaugh shot the master five or six times with Hackman and the gas station attendant—simple stuff that didn't require a lot of acting. When he felt he had what he needed, he told the cameraman to move for another setup but Hackman called Anspaugh out in front of the whole cast and crew: "You've got no taste, your head's completely up your ass, and you're a phony." Anspaugh thought he was joking at first but then he realized he wasn't. The crew went dead quiet and he went up to the actor and admitted to being a little nervous on his first day, saying he should have asked Hackman if he wanted to film another take. Anspaugh agreed to go back and do it again and shot five or six more takes, and there was not one slight divergence in what Hackman did from take to take. Then he walked up to him and asked if there was anything he wanted to try and the actor replied, "Why? What the hell was wrong with it?" On another day he refused to come out of his trailer until his lines were rewritten as he was unhappy with them. After a scene was filmed, Hackman commented, "You're satisfied with that? You really thought that was good?" Barbara Hershey also irked the filmmakers by turning to Hackman and not Anspaugh after wrapping a scene and asking the actor how it was, feeling she had decided to side with Hackman in his feud with the director.

Anspaugh reported that of the 39 days of shooting, probably 35 of them were like that first one, saying it was a little better after Dennis Hopper arrived since Hopper stole everyone's heart. Anspaugh didn't understand that Hackman liked to work on a set that had high anxiety because that was how he got his juice. Towards the end of the shoot, the director said that after Hackman had been yelling at him for an hour, he made an admission. He knew he behaved like a child sometimes but he wanted to make a good movie, but just didn't feel comfortable making movies where he felt comfortable. Anspaugh also speculated that although Hackman knew what he was getting into having to work with the boys, he didn't think the reality hit him until he got there.

The director thought every day on the film was going to be his last because Hackman's agent was trying to get him fired. What saved his job were the dailies: The agent saw that what they were making was actually pretty good. However Hackman insisted on viewing the movie before he agreed to go in to re-record some of his audio, and the feeling was that he wouldn't show up at the studio if he didn't like it. But Hackman did show up. He walked into the room, took his glasses off, looked at Anspaugh and said, "How the fuck did you do that?"

The experience was pretty rough, but Anspaugh felt Hackman's work was flawless. He rationalized that when the actor was being standoffish, that helped the character because in the movie the townspeople never really embraced Norman until the end, so this strategy worked. Anspaugh learned a lot from him and incorporated what he learned into his directing. Dennis Hopper said that Hackman was wonderful in the film and very funny, complaining that they were always shooting the boys playing basketball and not "the money," referring to himself.

Chelcie Ross, who played George Walker, observed the trouble Anspaugh had with Hackman, describing it as a head-on *mano a mano* working relationship that the director had to deal with. Ross could not pretend to analyze or explain Hackman but felt he was one of the best film actors ever, and he learned more from him than from anyone else he had ever worked with. He thought there were two obvious things at work. Hackman was an Oscar-winning actor working with a first-time director and didn't think he needed direction because he knew what he was doing. Secondly, Anspaugh was the default authority figure and the actor had to make it clear only he was in charge of himself.

David Neidorf reported that it was intimidating working with Hackman because he was pretty intense; he tried to be helpful but it was not in his nature. Neidorf described him as a curmudgeon who would sometimes get frustrated and lose his temper, but an acting genius. After the workshops, Hackman was no longer friendly with the boys and the young actor wondered if he was trying to keep some distance because he was playing the coach and didn't want to be too friendly. He would intentionally not learn his dialogue until 15 minutes before shooting so that Hackman would come from a highly agitated place and have some sense of excitement that he would totally screw up, which he never did. Neidorf reported that one time the actor asked if Anspaugh had watched what he had done, saying, "I need someone to pay attention. Not that I need you to tell me what to do, but I need to know you're paying attention." Steve Hollar, who played Rade Butcher, reported that Hackman was a no-bull guy who wouldn't get mad if you messed up—he would just give you a stare.

On Thanksgiving Day, Hackman, Hopper and other cast and crew members joined Angelo Pizzo and his family in Bloomington for dinner. Although he had often clashed with Pizzo and Anspaugh early in the movie's production, by that point the tension between him and the filmmakers had diminished considerably. An extra, Roger Hamilton, Jr., didn't receive any pay for his role as the boy shooting baskets in the empty gym in the last scene. But after the scene was filmed, Hackman took a $20 bill out of his wallet, autographed it and handed it to Roger. At the wrap party, Hackman gave each Husker a plaque.

On the February 10, 1986, *Late Night with David Letterman*, Hackman said that people came up to him on the street and told him that he looked better in person that on film, but he didn't know if that was a compliment. He spoke about *Scarecrow*, being a New York doorman in the 1950s, *Hoosiers* and *Power*. He also reported that he was talking to some people about doing a Broadway musical, though he was unsure he could sing.

He also reportedly expressed interest in returning to the stage in *The Iceman Cometh* and *Long Day's Journey Into Night* but chose instead to do a film: In the spring, he began work on *No Way Out* (1987). Originally entitled Deceit, the action crime drama was a remake of the Paramount film noir *The Big Clock* (1948) and the French-West German thriller *Police Python 357* (1976). The film was shot from April 7 to June 1986 in Washington, Maryland, Virginia, Canada and New Zealand, and at Orion's studios in Hollywood. The new screenplay was by Robert Garland based on his screen story and the Kenneth Fearing novel *The Big Clock*, and the director was Roger Donaldson. The plot centered on a cover-up for married Washington Secretary of Defense David Brice (Hackman) who accidentally kills his mistress, Susan Atwell (Sean Young). Hackman plays a supporting role and is billed 2nd before the film's title and after Kevin Costner who plays Commander Tom Farrell. He is clean-shaven and his costumes by an uncredited designer include glasses and one particularly ugly tie. Hackman gives a mannered performance, but we also see him dance, drive a car, and slap Susan. His best scene is perhaps when David confesses to his General Counsel Scott Pritchard (Will Paton) that he has killed Susan, although the camera is too far away from Hackman to see if his crying incorporates tears.

The film was released on August 14, 1987, with the taglines "A tightly wound and engrossing thriller!" and "Is it a crime of passion, or an act of treason?" *Variety* wrote that Hackman glided through his role. Vincent Canby in *The New York Times* said that the actor was leaner, sharper, better than he had been in years. It was a box office success.

Kevin Costner said that Hackman was the best actor he ever worked with, and cited a scene that was written to take place around a desk. Costner wanted it to be done differently with the men standing away from the desk, and he butted heads with Roger Donaldson as Hackman listened. When the director asked what the actor would do, Costner said that he would figure it out because he was really good. They shot the scene. As the actor was walking out to his car on the lot, Hackman called him over, and Costner assumed that Hackman was going to abuse him. Instead Hackman told him that he had been through a divorce, he had been doing a lot of questionable films of late, and when he saw Costner fighting for what he wanted, it reminded him of how he used to feel about acting. Hackman said it was good what he did, and then he got into his car and drove off.

7

Superman IV: The Quest for Peace

The actor returned to the Superman franchise with *Superman IV: The Quest for Peace* (1987). This was shot from August 1986 to January 29, 1987, on locations in England and the U.S. The screenplay was by Lawrence Konner and Mark Rosenthal, based on a story by Christopher Reeve, Konner and Rosenthal, and the director was Sidney J. Furie. The story had Superman (Reeve) again battling Lex Luthor (Hackman), who had created Nuclear Man (Mark Pillow but voiced by Hackman), a clone made from Superman's hair cells. Hackman, second-billed after Reeve, does not use the bald cap, instead having a strand of hair on his forehead and the rest brushed back. Hackman's clothes are by John Bloomfield and include a black-checked jacket suit with a white ruffled shirt and bow tie, and a particularly ugly silver-brown jacket. He gets to whistle Mozart's "Eine kleine Nachtmusik" and smoke a cigar. In Hackman's best scene, he introduces Superman to Nuclear Man, since the actor uses a surprisingly conversational tone rather than a threatening one.

The film premiered in London on July 23, 1987, and opened in the U.S. on July 24. Janet Maslin in *The New York Times* wrote that Hackman was a treat. But it *Variety* said that he got a few laughs, but had less to work with than before. The film was a box office failure and received Razzie Award nominations for Worst Supporting Actress (Mariel Hemingway) and Worst Visual Effects. In yet another sequel, *Superman Returns* (2006), Lex was played by Kevin Spacey.

The film was cut from 134 to 89 minutes. Hackman appeared in some of the deleted scenes. These include Lex creating the prototype (Clive Mantle) for Nuclear Man which Superman destroys (Lex vacuums up the ashes), talking to the Russians and the U.S. Senate about the arms race with a photograph of him in The Daily Planet showing him arrested for unlawful trading with the enemy, and leaving his New York apartment to go underground but confronted by Superman during the red alert. Co-screenwriter Mark Rosenthal reported that other scenes that included Lex were in the screenplay but may not have been filmed. These had him using the money he had obtained to create a false scare of a nuclear launch which caused a panic in New York City. Lex then looted the city and was seen with a supermarket cart filled with Old Masters from the Metropolitan Museum and going on a 5th Avenue shopping spree. Rosenthal said a lot of the wonderful comedy of Hackman's performance was lost in the cuts.

After *Superman II*, the actor had vowed never to play Lex again, tired of playing him the way he was. Hackman wanted more control over the character to bring him up-to-date with how audiences saw him as a hero for the '80s, and to do this he had to have a hand in developing the storyline. The actor enjoyed the creative input, and this was one of the conditions on which he agreed to reprise the role. He enjoyed himself and had stopped worrying about what people thought about his doing it a long time ago. It was the kind of role that lent itself to a lot of action and scope, and when you got to an age when you were cast in older-man type roles, there was a lot of energy inside him that he felt he wanted to get out. Hackman liked playing Lex because he could use up some of that energy. Christopher Reeve observed that this time the actor really enjoyed himself.

Sidney J. Furie reported that early in the filming, he and Hackman had built a solid rapport. The director said Hackman was a mensch, but midway into shooting when he came to shoot a scene where Lex had a speech about the "primeval swamp," Hackman erupted. There was no swamp on the set and Furie asked Hackman to imagine one. He said, "You call yourself a director?! How am I supposed to play this scene without seeing the primeval swamp?" Furie defended himself by asking, "Isn't that what actors do?" and told him that if anyone could fake it, he could. It is not known whether the scene was shot (it doesn't appear in the completed film), but Furie reported that their relationship was never the same.

Jon Cryer, who played Lenny, said that he loved working with Hackman, who did wonderful improvisational stuff. In his memoir *So That Happened*, Cryer called Hackman genial and happy to chitchat. Hackman told him his favorite role was the one in *Young Frankenstein* since it was the most fun to do, and his favorite film was *The Conversation*. The younger actor said that the actor was workmanlike: He would show up, do what was asked of him, maybe have a little fun with it, and then totally put it out of his mind. For Hackman it was all about the golf he was going to play after he was through for the day, and he couldn't have cared a whit about the movie. Cryer felt that he probably noticed the corner-cutting and saw it as the writing on the wall.

Mark Rosenthal commented that Hackman was one of our greatest actors. He was always able to add a comic tone to his dramatic roles and add edge to his comic roles, which made him wonderful as Lex. Rosenthal reported that Hackman was initially reluctant to do the film since he disliked *Superman III* but he found the actor to be a very skilled comedian and his Lex to be charming and funny in his arrogance. Rosenthal likened him to Phil Silvers in his ability to play a character within a character, as in the scene where Lex pretends to be an officer at the missile launch.

On the November 3, 1986, episode of the BBC talk show *Wogan*, Hackman

7. Superman IV: The Quest for Peace

Poster for *Bat*21* (1988).

spoke about playing Lex Luthor and joked that it was public knowledge that Christopher Reeve used *his* (Hackman's) body to play Superman. Hackman told of his origins in acting, quipping that he got into because he thought it would keep him from working and it was a way to meet girls, though it hadn't worked out that way since acting was a lot of hard work. He talked about his friendships with Dustin Hoffman and Robert Duvall. He said he worked for the art and the money was secondary, but had decided that he could do work where he was paid well for a big-budget film and was cast for his name and it could also be fun.

The New York Times of February 11, 1987, reported that Hackman had been in Washington to promote *Hoosiers*. Motion Picture Association officials took him by the White House in case President Reagan was free for a personal greeting. They kept reassuring Hackman that the president was "one of us, an actor." But when he emerged from the Oval Office, Hackman was still somewhat shaken. He said he didn't care if he came from Hollywood: When Reagan was behind the desk in that room, he was the president of the United States, and he hadn't been that nervous in twenty years.

Hackman commented that he didn't think he would ever do anything else but act and he didn't think he could so successful in anything else. When he retired, he saw himself painting on a small farm in Connecticut. Asked what his consummate performance was, the actor said there were a few moments in *Scarecrow*, and in *The Conversation*, and the withdrawal scene in *French Connection II*. But Hackman had never come away from seeing one of his films without thinking he could have given more, saying he had yet to give it all. He confessed that he was working on the fear of committing himself to something too much.

The actor expressed interest in playing alcoholic drifter Frank Phelan in the drama *Ironweed* (1987). However author and screenwriter William Kennedy wanted Jack Nicholson, who was cast and who received a Best Actor Oscar nomination for his performance. His next film was the action drama *Split Decisions* (1988). Originally titled *Kid Gloves*, it was shot in New York from April to June 1987. Written by David Fallon and directed by David Drury, it told the story of New York City amateur boxer Eddie McGuinn (Craig Sheffer), who avenged the death of his brother Ray (Jeff Fahey), a professional boxer who was killed because he wouldn't take a dive. Hackman played the part of Eddie's father Dan, a widowed policeman and trainer. Hackman gets a funny line in the climactic boxing match between Eddie and Julian "The Snake" Pedrosa (Eddie Velez). After a round, Eddie comments that Pedrosa hits hard, and Dan replies, "He hits hard, yeah. Welcome to the real world." His best scene is perhaps the silent one where Dan cries in reaction to the death of Ray.

The film premiered in Japan on November 5, 1988, and opened in the U.S. on November 11 with the tagline "A son's murder. A father's revenge. A brother's triumph." It was not a box office success.

7. Superman IV: The Quest for Peace

Hackman drove in the 1987 Toyota Pro-Celebrity Grand Prix Classic at the Long Beach Raceway on April 4, 1987.

His next film was the war drama *Bat*21* (1988), shot on location in Sabah, Borneo—Eastern Malaysia. The screenplay was by William C. Anderson and George Gordon, based on Anderson's book *Bat 21*, and the director was Peter Markle. Based on a true story, it centered on 53-year-old USAF missile intelligence expert Lt. Col. Iceal Hambleton (Hackman), whose aircraft is shot down over enemy territory during the Vietnam War; a frantic rescue operation ensues. Hackman is clean-shave and his hair is in a shorter military-style cut. The actor gets to do stunt work, including hanging from a parachute. Hackman's best scene is perhaps Iceal's regret over having to kill the Vietnamese man (Rev. Michael Ng) and the pain that he suffers from a leg wound incurred in the struggle.

The film premiered in Taiwan on August 6, 1988, and opened in the U.S. on October 21 with the tagline "Trapped behind enemy lines. A whole army after him. And only one man can save him." Janet Maslin of *The New York Times* wrote that Hackman's quintessential decency and ordinariness had never seemed more affecting. He took the film role for the money. On the October 19, 1988, *Late Night with David Letterman*, Hackman recommended that Letterman not go to Malaysia. The weather was 100 degrees with 100 percent humidity and there were a lot of ugly things crawling around. Hackman confessed that the film turned out to be nice so the discomfort was worth it.

His next film role was in the romantic comedy *Full Moon in Blue Water* (1988), shot on locations in Texas. The screenplay was by Bill Bozzone and the director was Peter Masterson. Hackman played Floyd, owner of Floyd and Dorothy's Blue Water

French promotional photograph for *Night Moves* (1975).

Grill in Bayside County, Texas, who owes $5280 in back taxes and considers selling the run-down bar. Hackman is clean-shaven and he has mainly one costume by Rondi Davis, a red t-shirt with blue jeans. The actor uses a Southern accent and is seen dancing, playing the violin and punching real estate salesman Charlie (Kevin Cooney) in the nose. He is reunited with Teri Garr from *The Conversation* who plays his girlfriend, school bus driver Louise Taylor. He gives an understated performance, perhaps because Floyd is depressed over the disappearance of his wife Dorothy (Becky Gelke), but he makes Floyd's anger at bar worker Jimmy (Elias Koteas) funny. His best scene is perhaps when Floyd considers sleeping with Louise: The actor reacts to Garr with a giddy horniness.

Released on November 23, 1988, it got a mixed reaction from Roger Ebert, who wrote that Hackman created an authenticity despite the ridiculous events he was called upon to experience. The film was not a box office success.

Hackman said that the film was worth doing for the big argument scene he had with Garr where Floyd chased her around and called her a "whoor." He loved working with Garr. Hackman added that Burgess Meredith, who played the general, was a great character actor.

The actor played a small supporting role in the drama *Another Woman* (1988). Written and directed by Woody Allen, it was shot from the fall of 1987 to January 1988. Gena Rowlands played Marion, 50-year-old New York director of undergraduate studies in philosophy at a women's college on a leave of absence to write a book. Hackman played magazine writer and novelist Larry Lewis, who had an affair with Marion before she married Ken (Ian Holm). Hackman is clean-shaven and gives a mostly controlled performance. The actor's best scene is perhaps the silent one when Larry and Marion run into a Central Park underpass and kiss and he reacts to her "screening him out with a wall."

The film was released on October 14, 1988, with the tagline "Relationships and the choices we make in life." Roger Ebert wrote that Hackman was precisely cast. Pauline Kael in *The New Yorker* said that the actor was in tip-top form and sneaked in a hint of eroticism. The film was not a box office success.

One source claims that Ben Gazzara was first cast as Larry and another says he was first cast as Ken. Hackman reported that Woody Allen was not a real funny guy on the set, though he did say one funny thing: Mia Farrow (who played Hope) was pregnant during filming, and when he asked the director when she was due, he replied, "Maybe today. Yeah, I might have to go home to deliver it." Hackman did what Allen had mapped out in his head, as opposed to coming in and rehearsing and making suggestions. Because he didn't have a very big part, he didn't have a tremendous sense of responsibility about holding the shooting up, so it was a nice experience.

Allen said that the scenes between Rowlands and Hackman, particularly in the

7. Superman IV: The Quest for Peace

flashback of the party, were electrifying. He described the actor's ability as reserve power. You felt he was cruising at 80 miles an hour and being brilliant and that if he stepped on the gas there was still another 300 miles an hour he could do. Allen felt the depth of his power and said when he yelled it was not just surface—you felt it go all the way down through him. He was intimidated by Hackman as he did not want to make a fool of himself in front of him.

In 1987, the actor decided he wanted to direct a remake of director Claude Miller's crime drama *Garde à vue* aka *The Inquisitor* (1981). In that film, a police inspector suspects an attorney of two child sex murders, and has him held for a questioning session that goes on for hours. Hackman had seen the film at the Beverly Center in Los Angeles when it opened. He loved it because he liked the idea of the tension between the three main characters—there was a lot of high theater and the tension of the mystery which was fascinating. It was a story about perceptions, misperceptions and prejudices against people who had money, who were poor, and who were in various positions in life. He went back to see it the next day and he would see it again a dozen times. He got a copy of it, then had an English translation written to send to prospective backers. Hackman wanted to make his directorial debut with this small-budget film, concentrating on the performances, but he failed to get a Hollywood studio interest in backing the project. There was perhaps a lack of confidence in another actor trying to direct, but also the subject matter was tricky since it was about a suspected pedophile. When Hackman tried to option the material, it was too expensive—they wanted a million dollars. When he did get his hands on it, he sent it to Arthur Penn whom he trusted, and who worked on the project with a writer for a long time. But they couldn't lick it and Hackman tabled the project.

He was also attached to the film version of the Ernest Hemingway novel *Across the River and Into the Trees*. Previous attempts had been announced with William Holden and then Burt Lancaster slated to star, and John Huston directing. John Frankenheimer was now to direct the story of a veteran of two world wars staving off death in Venice with one last fling with a child-woman, 19 years of age. However the film would not be made.

Another project was *The Silence of the Lambs*. Hackman bought the screen rights to the 1988 Thomas Harris bestseller with the intention of directing. He loved the book, feeling it was one of the most cinematic he had ever read, and the characters were different from what had been seen before. He wanted Michelle Pfeiffer to play FBI trainee Clarice Sterling and John Hurt to play the insane psychiatrist Hannibal "The Cannibal" Lecter. The actor intended to play Sterling's superior, Jack Crawford. Orion Pictures reported that he was also going to produce the film and play Hannibal Lecter.

But before Hackman could begin work on the film, he was committed to another, *Mississippi Burning* (1988). The film was shot from March 7 to May 14, 1988, in Mississippi and Alabama. The screenplay was by Chris Gerolmo and an uncredited Alan Parker, inspired by actual events that took place in the South during the 1960s, and the director was Parker. The story centered on FBI agents Rupert Anderson (Hackman) and Alan Ward (Willem Dafoe), who in 1964 go to Jessup County, Mississippi, to investigate the disappearance of three civil rights activists. Hackman is clean-shaven and looks physically heavier in the role. His hair is maybe a little too long at the back for period, and Hackman's receding hairline gets a joke in the narrative: After he asks how he can get a better look, a woman at Jilly's Beauty Parlor says his only hope is a wig since they aren't going to be able to do much with his "cue ball." The actor uses a Southern accent since Rupert hails from Thornton, Mississippi, and the role allows him to sing, slap Alan and intimidate Frank Morgan (Michael Rooker) by grabbing his testicles. Hackman has some funny lines. Rupert identifies a group of local men as KKK members in civilian clothes and says, "No pointy hats but plenty of pointy heads." He calls baseball "the only time a black man can wave a stick at a white man and not start a riot." But he also has the gnomic line, "Rattlesnakes don't commit suicide." The actor's best scene is perhaps when Rupert forcibly shaves and beats up Deputy Pell (Brad Dourif).

The film premiered on December 2, 1988, in Washington, D.C., had a limited release starting on December 9 and opened wide on January 27, 1989, with the tagline "1964. When America was at war with itself." Vincent Canby in *The New York Times* wrote that Hackman had possibly the best-written role of his career and was sensational. *Variety* said that Hackman stole the film; Pauline Kael in *The New Yorker* wrote that Hackman was vivid and played with humor and buried rage. The film was a box office success and Hackman received an Academy Award nominations for Best Actor. There were also nominations for Best Picture, Director, Cinematography, Supporting Actress (Frances McDormand, who played Mrs. Pell), Sound and Film Editing. It won for Best Cinematography.

Hackman saw himself as a serious artist and it felt right to do something of historical import. He said it was an extremely intense experience, both the content of the film and the making of it in Mississippi, since it was hot, even in the middle of the night. Hackman was dubious about shooting it there, but Alan Parker kept an edge on the project that was very valuable. Racism was still thriving in the South, which was apparent when Hackman popped into the local cleaners and was startled by the man behind the counter, who identified him as "the actor that's in that nigger movie they're making down here."

He had some initial reservations about the original script, fearing the incident on which it was based was exploited, but before accepted the project, much of that was fixed. Hackman felt it was really the story of how two guys from totally different backgrounds who worked out their relationship in the process of solving a problem:

7. Superman IV: The Quest for Peace

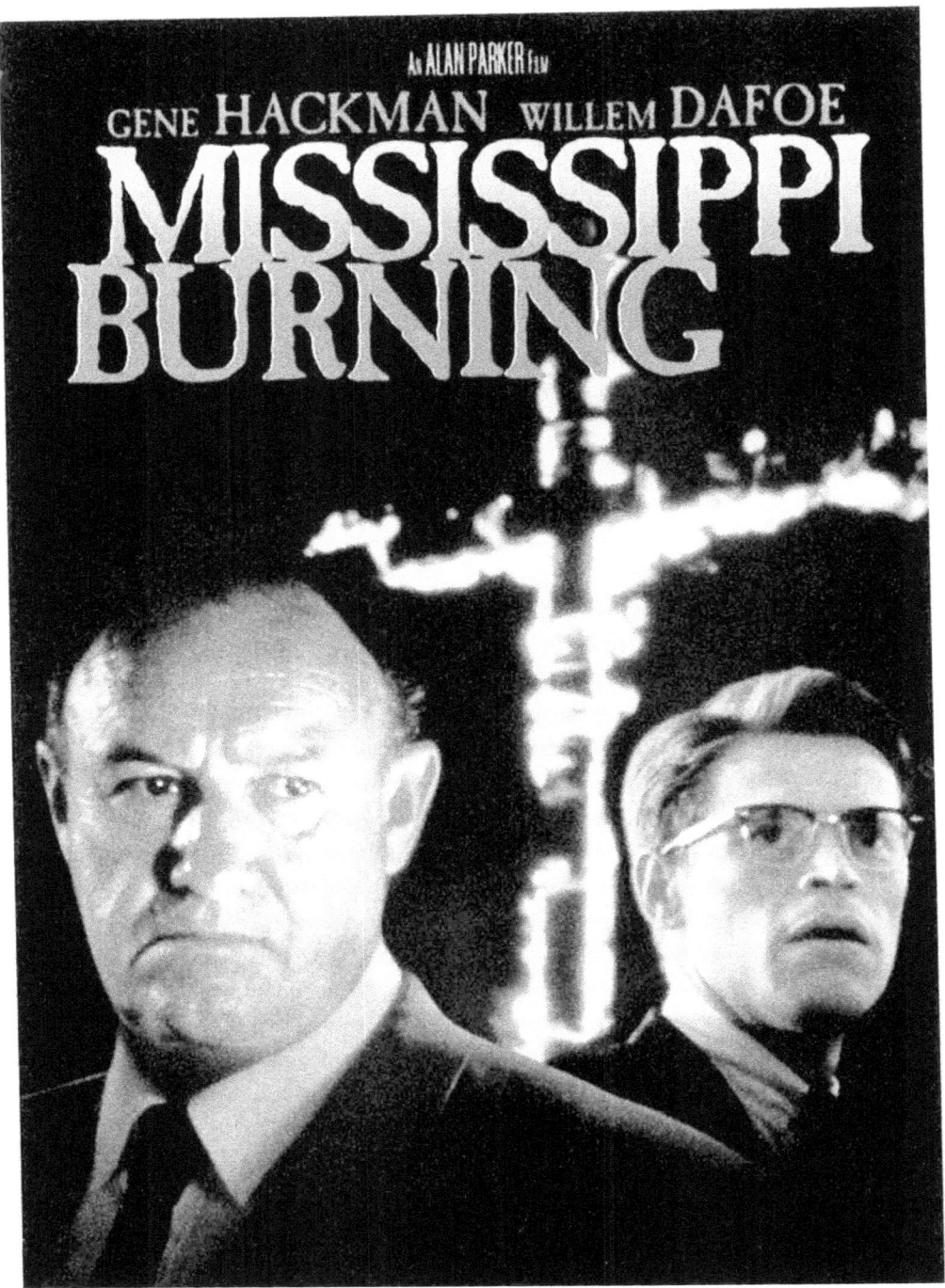

Poster for *Mississippi Burning* (1988).

the violation of civil rights, and a murder. The script just had a few biographical-type lines about the character and the actor built the rest along with the director. Hackman read about that period and the incident, including the book *Three Lives for Mississippi*. He also got a lot of insight from a book called *The Selling of Marcus Dupree*, which paralleled the life of a black football player born near the day of the murders. He didn't spend much time on the accent because he did not want it too strong—country rather than Southern.

The script had a scene where Rupert made love to Mrs. Pell on the floor of her house after she told him the whereabouts of the bodies. Hackman found it be to excessive and said it would distract from her as a human being and from her courage. He and Parker finally agreed that the lovemaking would be left out, but Hackman said an ambiguity remained in the scene, perhaps from Parker's wanting some of that feeling to remain.

Parker said the actor was always the front runner for the part of Rupert and Orion Pictures certainly wanted him, although another source claims they wanted Clint Eastwood. Brian Dennehy may have been briefly considered. Parker reported that Warren Beatty told him before they started shooting that Hackman was the finest American movie actor, and the director would come to agree. Working with him was how it must have like working with the greats like Spencer Tracy and Humphrey Bogart. When you had done 60-odd films, great films and awful films, good directors and bad directors—and were been good in all of them—you had to have something special. Parker didn't become "pals" with him (Hackman retained his privacy and distance from everyone) but the director found him to be a very nice man. He described him as an intuitive and instinctive actor and his brilliance was that he worked with extraordinary economy. He could look at a scene and cut through to what was necessary to make the point that needed to be made.

Hackman did have some complaints. He disliked having to walk into the location swamp which had leeches and an alligator in the scene when the officers go looking for the car of the missing boys. He recalled how such a location could have been done on a studio backlot with more comfort. Parker said they had one argument and it lasted two and a half minutes. He said it was Hackman's idea for Rupert to grab Frank's crotch as opposed to a more conventional fight scene. Hackman was on the cover of the January 9, 1989, *Time* magazine, whose cover story was "*Mississippi Burning*. A new movie's searing view of racism sits a debate over fact vs. fiction."

The actor's next film was the comic crime actioner *Loose Cannons* (1990). It was shot from July 17 to October 23, 1988, on location in Washington D.C. and New York, and at the North Carolina Film Studios. Its working title was *The Von Metz Incident*. The screenplay was by Richard Christian Matheson, Richard Matheson and Bob Clark, and it was directed by Clark. Hackman is MacArthur "Mac"

Stern, a D.C. vice squad and homicide detective paired with Ellis Fielding (Dan Aykroyd), a detective who has split personality disorder. Hackman looks thinner here and he gets to punch in a fight in an S&M club, fire guns and sing. He gets one funny line when he tells a fellow detective (Leon Rippy), "I don't want to use the five points of I.Q. it would take to have a battle of wits with you." Hackman is funny; his best scene is perhaps when he tells Ellis that he needs his help and recites Dylan Thomas.

The film was released on February 9, 1990, with the taglines "Detective Mack Stern is facing the greatest challenge of his career... his new partner!" "Gene Hackman is a cop who's lost his patience. Dan Aykroyd is his partner who's lost his mind" and "A comedy with personality.... Lots of them!" Vincent Canby of

Hackman in *Loose Cannons* (1990).

The New York Times wrote that Hackman deserved much better, giving a thoroughly professional performance that was consistently undercut by the direction of Clark. The film was not a box office success.

The New York Times reported on September 9, 1988, that Hackman had supplied a voice-over for the GTE Corporation's new television commercial. A June 20, 1993, *Times* article on stars who reaped additional benefits from commercials shown in foreign countries included the fact that he had received $1 million to represent Kirin beer in Japan.

Hackman was back on *Late Night with David Letterman* on October 19, 1988, reporting that he was still driving race cars though no longer competitively. He likened the sport to acting where there was a certain amount of concentration involved and where he really put himself out there. He also spoke about being a Marine and told the story of how he was not invited back to the Pasadena Playhouse after his first year. At this time Hackman was in disbelief that he had five new films which included *Bat *21*, *Another Woman* (which he had yet to see) and *Full Moon in Blue Water* which he called *Full Moon Over Blue Water*.

In 1988, Sue Mengers tried to get Hackman to come back as her client (he had left her in 1983), but he declined. He was now represented by Creative Artists Agency. On January 1, 1989, *The New York Times* ran an interview with Ralph Donnelly of Merrick, New York, who was considered one of the pre-eminent experts on the art and science of showing motion pictures. Asked about bankable stars, he said that Hackman was wonderful but his presence didn't guarantee box office success.

The crime drama *The Package* (1989) was shot from January 1989 on locations in Illinois and at the Soviet War Memorial in Berlin, Germany. It had a screenplay by John Bishop. Hackman starred as U.S. Army Sergeant Johnny Gallagher, who must escort a prisoner, Colonel Thomas Boyette (Tommy Lee Jones), from Berlin to the U.S. His costumes by Marilyn Vance-Strakes include a black leather jacket with a black suit. The role allows Hackman to speak German, fire several guns, be handcuffed to a pole, and punch a Marine. He gives a more controlled performance here, and he is funny. Director Andrew Davis gives Hackman a car chase that recalls his famous one from *The French Connection,* and he has a good rapport with his *Under Fire* co-star Joanna Cassidy, who plays his wife Eileen. Hackman's best scene is perhaps his reaction to being accused of negligence by Colonel Glen Whitacre (John Heard) after terrorists attack the Berlin army base.

The film was released on August 25, 1989, with the taglines "He's one man racing against time to stop the most explosive conspiracy in history" and "Gene Hackman is up against Tommy Lee Jones. Let the best man win!" Roger Ebert wrote that Hackman was very good in one of those man-of-action roles he seemed to play more convincingly than ever. Vincent Canby in *The New York Times* said it was the worst film the actor had ever made. It was not a box office success.

A cut scene had Gallagher at the Templehof airbase in Berlin. Cast in the film as Michael, one of Gallagher's Field Soldiers, was Michael Tomlinson, the son of a man Hackman had been friends with in the Marines. Director Davis described Hackman as an Everyman who people felt was not a glamorous movie star but a real person who happened to be a great actor. Davis reported that he was going through a lot of personal stuff at the time and wasn't real patient with anybody, but he had a great experience with Hackman. He was professional and committed to keeping it real. Hackman was also very game to be running around in the Chicago cold. Davis reported one awkward moment when he watched the actor in closeup on a monitor because logistically he could not get physically close to him. Hackman asked why he wasn't watching him in person, and he replied that he could see him much better this way. The actor hated monitors and he wanted the director to be next to the camera to support him. When Davis commented that Francis Coppola used monitors, Hackman replied that he was no Francis Coppola. At one point, Hackman was required to fire nine shots at a pursuer but he argued that his character, an expert marksman, would not miss a target nine times in a row. Davis tried to rationalize it but the actor would not budge, saying he knew the idea worked on paper but it didn't work when he was trying to do it. Hackman was accused of being rigid but he said it was just part of the creative process.

The actor admitted to being a pain and impossible but compromise did not come easy to him, which is why he had recently had his problems with directors. It had become tougher for him to be directed. He didn't feel he knew everything but he just found himself being frustrated and Hackman prayed for the day when someone told him he was finished in Hollywood.

There were occasions when his sense of humor and good humor was seen on the set. He joked and did card tricks for the crew, held doors for extras and waited in line behind Teamsters at the lunch wagon. He said that an actor who dined in his trailer could lose his grip on the folks who bought movie tickets. Hackman complained about the lukewarm coffee along with everyone else, and passed the time between takes making charcoal sketches of crew and cast members, then offered these as mementos to his subjects. When bystanders wandered onto the set and accosted him for an autograph, the actor thanked them.

Davis reported that Hackman and Tommy Lee Jones respected each other but their relationship was not always harmonious since the dynamic of two alpha males paralleled the relationship of their characters in the film. Jones was particularly irked when his co-star wanted to cut Boyette's lines, and this resulted in them not even saying goodbye when shooting wrapped.

Hackman appeared as a guest on the January 16, 1989, episode of the talk show *ABC News Nightline* to talk about *Mississippi Burning*. He was unaware that another guest was to be former Georgia State Representative Julian Bond, who he considered a legend of the civil rights movement. He said if he had known he wouldn't have agreed to attend, since it was unfair to be asked to defend the film, though he didn't mind defending his character.

Hackman attended the 46th Golden Globe Awards on January 28, 1989, at the Beverly Hilton Hotel. He was nominated for Best Actor for *Mississippi Burning* but lost to Dustin Hoffman for *Rain Man* (1988).

According to Peter Biskind's book on Warren Beatty, Hackman turned down another chance to work with the director. This time Beatty wanted him for the part of crime boss Alphonse "Big Boy" Caprice in the action comedy *Dick Tracy* (1990). Hackman said that he loved Beatty but he just couldn't do it. *Variety* had reported that Al Pacino was Beatty's first choice and that Robert De Niro was also under consideration. Pacino was cast and received a Best Supporting Actor Academy Award nomination. Another source reported that Hackman was wanted for the part of Lips Manlis, but he couldn't bear being directed by Beatty again after his experience on *Reds*. Paul Sorvino, who was cast as Lips, was also directed by Beatty in *Reds*.

In February 1989, Hackman was at DePaul University on Chicago's North Side. In a basement room beneath the school gym he fielded theater student questions about his methods and his movies. He was said to have turned in another barn-burning Hackman performance: candid, funny, and naturally, without a hint of show biz glitz.

He was interviewed by Michael Norman in the March 19, 1989, *New York Times*. Norman described him as formidable but not overpowering, fit but not athletic, his look and the way he carried himself and spoke giving him a quality of being uncommonly common. After a 30-year career, celebrity discomfited him, not only going against his grain, but running counter to his method of working. He felt that if you looked at yourself as a star, you had already lost something in the portrayal of any human being. Hackman needed to wear that hair shirt and to keep himself on the edge and stay as pure as possible. He needed to remember that he was not a movie star, he shouldn't be too happy, and he should never take anything for granted.

The actor was tired. Arthur Penn and friends said the gregarious man they knew had become somewhat withdrawn and distressed. Norman theorized that perhaps this was due to the fact that Hackman was 58 and had made 19 films in the last eight years. Another reason could be that he had a stalker haranguing him, calling on the phone, and leaving letters in his apartment house lobby. The actor had been stalked before by a quick-draw artist with loaded revolvers in Alamagordo, New Mexico; a Las Vegas drunk brandishing a .357 magnum; and a rifleman in Seattle who left his gun case at the cast's hotel. But this new man was unusually persistent and he forced Hackman to move out of his Chicago apartment where he stayed as he filmed *The Package*, and into a hotel.

Norman found Hackman to be open and amiable, but also a loner. He could not provide a list of friends and his acting teacher George Morrison said that the actor didn't want them. He was easy to be with, but hard to get close to. Morrison considered himself as good a friend as Hackman had from the old days, but it made him mad that when he came through town, Hackman would not call. The actor struggled to hold onto his privacy, but he did admit for the last five years he had lived quietly with the 28-year-old Betsy Arakawa, the classical pianist he met while she was working part-time in a California fitness center. They shared a two-bedroom adobe house on a wide brown plain outside Santa Fe, New Mexico. Hackman had the solitary hobbies of painting and sketching, and he tooled around in one of his two pickup trucks. His children were grown now; two were college students and the other wrote computer software. Like all parents, the actor wanted to see more of them than he did.

7. Superman IV: The Quest for Peace

Hackman believed the pinnacle of his acting career in terms of character development, to date, was in *The Conversation*. The actor said he was cast so close to type now that he asked, "How many varieties of Everyman were there?" He told his agents he wanted to start playing more sophisticated characters, bankers in expensive suits, just to examine that part of life.

He and Willem Dafoe were reunited as presenters for the 61st Annual Academy Awards, held on March 29, 1989, at the Shrine Auditorium. They presented the award for Best Art Direction and Set Decoration to Stuart Craig and Gerard James for the romantic drama *Dangerous Liaisons* (1988). Hackman was in the audience when his nomination for Best Actor for *Mississippi Burning* was announced by Michael Douglas but the award went to Dustin Hoffman for *Rain Man*. Hoffman kissed Hackman and shook his hand on his way to the podium. There he thanked the other nominees including Hackman for their "wonderful work, even if they didn't vote for me," because he said he didn't vote for them either.

Hackman was not disappointed about losing the award, saying the value of it was how much it would add to the gross of a film and to his fee for his next one. He felt it was great to win awards but you had to put them in perspective. He wasn't competitive and he didn't want to beat other actors. He just wanted to do good work.

In his March *Times* interview, the actor commented on his *Silence of the Lambs* plans, saying he didn't know how far he was going to go with it. Hackman wanted the experience of directing, but he thought it was just the other side of the coin with much of it having to do with ego and filling that great need to be successful. Screenwriter Ted Tally later reported that the actor began writing the screenplay himself but found it challenging, so Tally met with him to give Hackman a pep talk. The writer described Hackman as smart and quirky, though he had some strange ideas about the film which were revealed in their second meeting, included the image of Clarice Starling being visualized across the sky. Tally thought the actor's vision was obscured by his back pain which had caused him to lie on the floor the entire time.

In the *Times*, Tally reported that Hackman said that maybe "Bobby" would play Hannibal Lecter, instead of John Hurt as originally planned. He didn't have the nerve to ask who Bobby was. One could assume that Hackman meant his old friend Robert Duvall, but Tally thought it could have been Robert Redford or Robert De Niro. Then he decided against doing the film—Hackman would no longer make violent films after seeing a brief and violent clip of his performance in *Mississippi Burning* at the Oscars. He found the Thomas Harris book wonderful but said it was one thing to read it and another to show the violence that occurred in it, and there was too much violence in the world. Other sources claim that it was one of his daughters, horrified by the novel's grisly content, who convinced him to drop

Silence. The rights were then bought back by Orion Pictures, and Jonathan Demme was hired to direct. Hackman opted not to play Jack Crawford, a role then taken by Scott Glenn.

In an April 3, 1989, interview, Hackman said that he regretted some of the choices he had made in his career. He didn't do well enough in some roles and took others for the wrong reasons though they seemed like good ideas at the time. He also regretted some pictures he turned down though sometimes he saw that the actors who did them were better than he would have been. He liked acting now better than he did at the beginning of his career but he liked the business much less. Hackman said one of his favorite actors was Ralph Richardson and he hoped to be the kind of actor Richardson was in his last years.

The May 10, 1989, *New York Times* reported that he was one of the Hollywood stars that Don King was trying to persuade to fight in exhibitions on the undercard of a possible Mike Tyson–Jose Ribalta bout in Los Angeles. The promoter would give a portion of the proceeds to help the homeless, and Hackman was known to be a boxing aficionado.

8

Narrow Margin

Hackman's next film was the thriller *Narrow Margin*. Shot from June 12 to October 1989 on locations in Canada, it was a remake of the RKO Richard Fleischer–directed film noir thriller *The Narrow Margin* (1952). The new film was directed and written by Peter Hyams, based on the earlier movie. Los Angeles Deputy District Attorney Robert Caulfield (Hackman) is sent to protect publisher Carol Hunnicut (Anne Archer), who accidentally witnessed a Mafia murder. Hackman, top-billed, is clean-shaven and wears glasses and only has one outfit, a mismatched jacket and pants and mismatched shoes. The actor gets to act with a child (Codie Lucas Wilbee who plays Nicholas) and fights in a men's room with fake Detective Loughlin (Lon Katzman), and appears to do some of his own stunts as he climbs on the top and side and fights on the top of a moving train with Nelson (James B. Sikking). Hackman has some funny lines. Robert tells Chief Deputy District Attorney Martin Larner (J.A. Preston), "I realize television cameras are somewhat of an aphrodisiac to you," and comments to Sgt. Dominick Benti (M. Emmet Walsh) in a helicopter about Carol's remote cabin: "Do you realize when we go down, no one's going to be able to find us except some fucking moose?" He is funny as Robert bides his time by telling a story to Nicholas' mother (Barbara E. Russell). Hackman's best scene is perhaps when Robert deliberately enters the wrong train compartment so as to avoid the men following him.

The film was released on September 21, 1990, with the taglines "Sometimes the difference between life and death can be a Narrow Margin," "One witness. Two determined killers. The ultimate thrill ride," "It's the difference between living and dying" and "It will take you to the edge of suspense." *Variety* said that Hackman added panache to a one-dimensional role. Caryn James of *The New York Times* wrote that the actor was immeasurably better than his material but managed to invent some intriguing quirks in his role. *Rolling Stone*'s Peter Travers said that even in reduced circumstances Hackman was a resourceful actor, and gave the character an awkwardness that added a satisfying edge to his heroics; he was the only element in the film that was not disposable.

The idea for Robert to wear glasses came from Hackman. He liked the idea of playing a lawyer and not necessarily a man of action put in a position of jeopardy and had to use his wits to get out of it and not have to shoot anyone. The actor also liked how there was something dramatic and old-fashioned about a train. He did some of the stunt work, deciding what he could do after the stunt men showed him what was required. Hackman felt that with his limited strength and age he could do things that might take courage but not a lot of skill, and he only felt scared after he had done the stunt and thought about what he had done. The actor received careful guidance from experts and thin safety cables for the scenes when he was on top of and on the side of the train. The most difficult scene was when Hackman was dangling off the side of the train, hanging onto the legs of James B Sikking, and it was safe and thrilling. He also helped convince Anne Archer to do some stunt work which Peter Hyams said it was necessary for her to do, and told others that he only agreed to do his stunts because she had agreed to do hers. Archer confessed that they hadn't talked about it together, but since they thought the other was willing, they felt they had to. Hackman said Robert's chat scene with the bad guy in the train was the most fun for an actor. It was what you were taught to do at acting school, not swinging from trains or jumping off cliffs, which required skills you had to pick up elsewhere.

Interviewed in his caravan while on location, Hackman confessed there was a lot of stress involved in filmmaking, as he had to meet a whole new group of people every two or three months because the actor made two or three films a year. Doing it didn't come naturally to him so it was stressful to have to continually find a way to work since everyone worked differently. His directors had trepidation about whether he was going to behave like a big star, and Hackman had to work through that, and worry that the director would ask him to do things he didn't want to do and whether they would trust him. But the actor enjoyed his work no end, largely because it was an

Hackman in *Narrow Margin* (1990).

outlet. He was an introvert who had this painful thing to go through to find a way to express himself. Hackman continued to work so hard because he had been doing it for so long that he didn't know what else to do. He had numerous houses in the U.S. and across Europe, but found it difficult staying in one place for any length of time, constantly moving from one movie to the next.

On the set, Hackman liked to use charcoal to sketch faces of the cast and crew. He preferred oils to watercolor when he painted, though he didn't plan any exhibitions. When free of work, he spent time with his children. Hackman was very close to his two daughters and his son.

Narrow Margin producer Jonathan Zimbert said they thought Hackman would be great for the part, but they feared it would never happen. However, as soon as Hackman read the screenplay, he asked for a meeting. By a strange chance, the actor and Peter Hyams accidentally bumped into each other at a driving range a few days later, so they had their meeting while whacking balls. Hackman was one of the first actors Hyams thought of since he was the one Hyams most wanted to work with. Hackman was the very definition of a star, as well as one of the greatest actors in the English-speaking language and the kind that seemed right for anything. Hyams said he was probably the most limitless actor around, with this uncanny ability to make things look effortless. The actor was physically graceful and subtly funny, and understood the power of the face and the power of honest behavior. When they shot, Hackman made it look like he wasn't doing anything but when the director looked at the footage, he was shocked. The actor didn't like to do a lot of takes but Anne Archer did, so it was sometimes a juggling act to accommodate both actors.

Archer reported that she was very excited to do the film because she was a fan of Hackman's. She knew it would be a wonderful experience. Archer found Hackman to be a sweetheart and very supportive, and the experience did not disillusion her about him. James B. Sikking said that he also looked forward to working with Hackman, whom he considered to be one of the finest actors in the country.

Next for Hackman was director Mike Nichols' *Postcards from the Edge*, based on the widely praised Carrie Fisher novel about a mother-daughter relationship set against the backdrop of Hollywood. The comic drama began filming on August 14, 1989, and went until October 16. Fisher's screenplay focussed on Suzanne Vale (Meryl Streep), a substance-addicted actress forced to move back in with her actress mother Doris Mann (Shirley MacLaine). There is a "Special Appearance by" Hackman as Lowell, the director of the film Suzanne is making when she overdoses. His wardrobe by Ann Roth has him always in white pants accompanying different colored shirts and jackets. In his best scene, Lowell warns Suzanne not to "fuck up" his movie after he learns she has taken drugs in her trailer.

The film was released on September 14, 1990, with the tagline "Having a wonderful time, wish I were here." Pauline Kael of *The New Yorker* wrote that Hackman managed to give his lines a personal rhythm and he made his scenes halfway credible. A box office success, the film received Academy Award nominations for Best Original Song and Streep for Best Actress.

Hackman based his performance on real-life director Richard Donner. He said he got to do a good part with a good cast and he didn't have the burden of the film on him. Shirley MacLaine didn't share any scenes with Hackman but she wrote about him in her memoir *My Lucky Stars*. She had met the actor at a party some years prior and told Hackman she found him romantically attractive. There was a captivating sexuality about the way he had walked into the room and come over to her. MacLaine wrote that sometimes a man's walk spoke volumes more than his words.

Carrie Fisher called him a good actor with an incredible way of talking that made you sit forward to listen to him. She reported that she ran into Hackman in Hawaii circa 1992. Fisher had just had her daughter Billie Lourd, and felt she looked dreadful because of her weight. She approached him on the walkway of a hotel and told him that she had written the film's screenplay. He responded by saying, "Oh, did you really?" Fisher realized that the actor didn't recognize her, and worse, thought she was a psychotic fan coming up to him. This became a running joke during his stay at the hotel.

Hackman's next film was the thriller *Class Action* (1991), shot from December 6, 1989, to February 14, 1990, in San Francisco. The screenplay was by Carolyn Shelby, Christopher Ames and Samantha Shad, and the director was Michael Apted. Hackman is attorney Jedidiah "Jed" Tucker Ward, who comes up against his estranged attorney daughter Maggie (Mary Elizabeth Mastrantonio) in a case involving Argo Motors being sued over a safety problem. He is clean-shaven and his hair by Manny Miller is a little longer in the back and with gray strands. His face is on a *Newsweek* cover and there is a photograph of the young Hackman as a Marine. The role allows him to dance, sing, wear an apron when cooking, speak with a French accent and cry. The actor's mannerisms perhaps have a context when Jed performs in court. Otherwise he is still when Jed delivers a speech at the funeral of his artist wife Estelle (Joanna Merlin), when listening to Maggie apologize for being angry at him, and when he tells her about seeing her as a baby. Hackman's best scene is perhaps when Jed listens to Maggie's apology.

Released on March 15, 1991, the film had the tagline "A father and a daughter, divided by a case, endangered by the truth." Vincent Canby of *The New York Times* wrote that Hackman had punch and drive, and Peter Travers in *Rolling Stone* said that the actor gave a passionate, riveting performance. The film was a box office success.

Paul Newman, Clint Eastwood, Charles Bronson, Dustin Hoffman, Harrison Ford, Michael Douglas, James Caan, Tommy Lee Jones and Jon Voight were considered to play Jed. Hackman took the opportunity to go to court in San Francisco before the film's rehearsals. He watched Tony Serra, the criminal-law attorney, give his opening statement for two and a half hours in a murder trial. Serra did it without notes, which impressed the actor.

Mastrantonio said that she was more excited than nervous about working with the actor and found him to be very bright, and he did not patronize her because she was younger. The actress reported that Hackman worked differently to the way she did. He could come in and be ready to go and be balanced, whereas she had to bounce off the walls a bit to find her center.

The December 15, 1989, *New York Times* reported that director Ron Shelton, who had written *Under Fire*, had cast Hackman as Louisiana governor Earl K. Long, in the biographical drama *Blaze*. Paul Newman had been offered the part and declined, but then he changed his mind so Shelton went with him. Hackman narrated the Guggenheim Productions documentary short *Island of Hope, Island of Tears* (1989). Directed by Charles Guggenheim, it told the story of the single largest migration of immigrants to Ellis Island between 1890 and 1920. The actor was offered the part of writer Paul Sheldon in the Rob Reiner–directed thriller *Misery* (1990) and declined. James Caan accepted it.

Hackman starred in writer-director Nicholas Meyer's comic action film *Company Business* (1991), shot from March 12 to May 17, 1990, in Washington, D.C., Maryland, Paris, Berlin and Anguilla, British West Indies. The film had the working title *Dinosaurs*. Hackman played Sam Boyd, a retired CIA agent who is recruited to participate in a prisoner exchange with the Russians over KGB mole Pyotr Grushenka (Mikhail Baryshnikov). Hackman wears a mustache, which is a plot point: When Sam must change his identity, he suggests shaving the mustache but Pyotr comments that would be expected. We hear CIA member Elliot Jaffe (Kurtwood Smith) predict that Sam will shave the mustache, though he does not. There is a further plot point when Pyotr wears a fake mustache and Sam laughs at him. Hackman's costumes by Yvonne Blake include glasses and a notable blue-gray checkered cap, and a black ninja outfit. The role allows the actor to smoke a cigarette and cigar, drive cars and a train, ride a bike, fire guns, hide in a Murphy bed, be on the summit of the Eiffel Tower, and speak Russian. Hackman has a post-coital scene with a woman (actress unknown) which he hadn't done on screen for a while, and goes to an East Berlin drag bar. There were no great acting challenges for him in the film.

Company Business was released on September 6, 1991, with the taglines "It's not the company you keep. It's the company that keeps you" and "You can't judge a man by the company that keeps him!" Vincent Canby in *The New York Times* wrote that Hackman had played this role before and was sturdy if a little tired. The film was not a box office success.

It was originally intended as a vehicle for Richard Dreyfuss and Elliott Gould, but both dropped out before production began. After signing to do the film, Hackman tried to back out, saying he was exhausted from shooting three films back to back (*Postcards from the Edge*, *Narrow Margin* and *Class Action*). Fearing a lawsuit, the actor grudgingly stayed on.

In his memoir *The View from the Bridge: Memories of* Star Trek *and a Life in Hollywood*, Nicholas Meyer said his bouts with Hackman just about wrecked him. Meyer wanted Hackman in the role of Sam, considering him the preeminent film actor of his generation. When he tried to meet with him, Hackman was always busy. When Meyer learned that Hackman was exhausted but couldn't get out of the film, he knew this did not bode well for their collaboration. The director couldn't think of a comparable star who would be available on such short notice, and when they finally met, the actor was not happy. He said the script contained too much violence. When Meyer defended it as a spy thriller in which such behavior was typical, Hackman glared at him and said, "You know, you and I don't get along." This was only after talking for five minutes, and they would continue to go toe to toe. As the result of his inability to work in harmony with Hackman, the director lost 20 pounds and lived on Valium. At one point the pair found themselves sitting together in a jail cell in Maryland, waiting for the crew to show up to do a scene. Hackman confessed that he had behaved badly on other films, but this one took the cake. Mikhail Baryshnikov commented that working with Hackman was an extraordinary experience.

The July 6, 1990, *New York Times* reported that Hackman had narrowly avoided a heart attack. On July 4, while vacationing on the Oregon Coast, the 60-year-old actor checked into Portland's St. Vincent Hospital and Medical Center complaining of chest pains. Dr. Herbert Semler said that he thought they got Hackman in the nick of time: He was treated for partial blockage of a coronary blood vessel, after suffering from a narrowing of an artery leading to the heart. The doctor inserted a balloon catheter to reopen the artery. Hackman was released on July 6. It was said that his heart was not holding up under the strain of his life. He was working too much and his generally restless nature and fluctuating weight were contributing factors to the condition.

Hackman now had to watch his diet, cut down on drinking, and work less. He continued to fly and in October 1990, there was an incident. The actor was test-flying a single-engine plane that he was considering buying when, 2500 feet up, the engine suddenly cut out. Hackman worked to restart the engine for ten seconds before it came back to life. It was a scary experience but since he had had a pilot's license for about 20 years, he reportedly stayed calm. He decided against buying that particular plane.

Now Hackman took a break. He said he was painting, working on a full-size plane, and enjoying himself. On October 8, he played in the Pro-Celebrity Golf Tournament Charity Benefit at North Ranch Country Club in California. He felt that taking time off would give him a truer perspective on his career, but after being away for a while, the need for excitement waned and Hackman could be more objective about what was attractive about filmmaking.

In a June 18, 2015, article on the *Uproxx* website, Drew McWeeny reported that he met the actor at this time when he, McWeeny, was a theater manger in Sherman Oaks. He wrote that Hackman, who lived within walking distance, would come every Friday morning to see a film. The second time he showed up, McWeeny gave him an employee ticket, refusing his cash when he offered it. Hackman tried a few times to pay, and McWeeny just smiled and gave him the free ticket, and that became the Friday morning tradition. Sometimes they would chat for a few minutes. The pair would talk about the movies opening each week since Hackman, a genuine movie fan, would try to see everything. What impressed McWeeny the most was watching what happened when people approached him, and he would sign autographs and pose for pictures. When it was someone who had previously worked with the actor, he would immediately know who they were every time, what film it was, what they did on it, and often even details like family members and their names. They looked stunned at just how sharp Hackman's recall was, and many of them were visibly moved at how nice he was.

The actor also decided to give up the idea of directing for now. The screenplay for *Open and Shut* was one he still wanted to do as an actor but he hoped another director would take it on. There was another screenplay Hackman liked which he hoped he could do with Dustin Hoffman and Robert Duvall. And there was also the idea of remaking the French-Italian comedy *La Cage aux Folles* (1978). He was attracted to the part of Renato Baldi (played by Ugo Tognazzi), the gay husband of the queen Albin Mougeotte dit Zaza Napoli (Michel Serrault), seeing it as a new challenge. Hackman believed that he wasn't going to get leading roles any more but he felt there was still work for him, and he didn't think he had reached his best or highest point yet. In 1990, he donated his collection of long, slender wooden East African memorial totems (known as vigango) to the Denver Museum of Nature and Science.

Hackman was considered for the parts of Jim Garrison and Guy Bannister in the Oliver Stone–directed thriller *JFK* (1991). Kevin Costner and Ed Asner were cast instead.

Hackman's next film was director Clint Eastwood's Western *Unforgiven* (1992), shot from August 26 to November 12, 1991, on location in Canada and at a California ranch. The screenplay was by David Webb Peoples. Eastwood starred as retired gunslinger and widowed pig farmer Bill Munny, who reluctantly takes on one last job, abetted by his old partner Ned Logan (Morgan Freeman) and the

"Schofield Kid" (Jaimz Woolvett). Second-billed Hackman played Little Bill Daggett, sheriff of Big Whiskey, Wyoming, where three gunslingers come to get the bounty for the facial slashing of prostitute Delilah Fitzgerald (Anna Thomson) by two cowboys. Hackman is clean-shaven and wears reading glasses. The role allows him to punch and kick English Bob (Richard Harris) and Munny, slap Strawberry Alice (Frances Fisher) and whip Ned, and he has a death scene which is empathetic, despite Bill's bad deeds. Hackman also gets a funny line: Talking about shaving his chin whiskers, he says, "I was tasting the soup two hours after I ate it." The actor uses a stillness when having stand-offs with gunfighter Bob and his biographer W.W. Beauchamp (Saul Rubinek) and Munny. In Hackman's best scene, Bill offers Bob and Beauchamp a gun to shoot him with and waits to see if they use it.

The film premiered on August 3, 1992, and opened on August 7 with the tagline "It's a hell of a thing, killing a man." Todd McCarthy (*Variety*) wrote that Hackman deliciously realized the two sides of the sheriff's quicksilver personality, the folksy raconteur and the vicious sadist. The film was a box office success and received Academy Award nominations for Best Picture, Director, Actor (Eastwood), Supporting Actor (Hackman), Editing, Original Screenplay, Cinematography, Art Direction–Set Decoration and Sound. The winners included Hackman and Eastwood (as Best Director and for Best Picture).

Clint Eastwood had known the actor for many years but they had never worked together, and had to really talk him into playing Bill. Hackman didn't want to do anything with violence in it after he had been involved in a lot of violent films and felt that there had been enough on the screen. The actor was a liberal-minded man and didn't particularly want to contribute to people's notions of idle violence being good entertainment. Eastwood thought they could make a statement against violence and killing if they did it right. Convinced by his agent Fred Spector, Hackman accepted the part and became fascinated. The actor felt it was no accident that the script had the elements of anti-violence and women's rights, and it was a wonderful overview of what things could have been like if there were more people like Munny and people who were willing to stand up for the right things. Even though Eastwood had done a lot of violent films, Hackman found him a very gentle soul.

Bill was a man who hid under a good nature and bonhomie the reality of the brutal nature of social control. Hackman believed that there was both good and bad in everybody and the character had that balance between what he did and said and the ultimate results of those things. The actor equated Bill's violence with how he enjoyed watching actors who had a dangerous quality to them, though they didn't have to have a gun in their hand or anything else. There were women who also had that dangerous quality, where you never knew quite what they were going to do next and that was always interesting in an actor.

Hackman worked three weeks on the film. He arrived on set and left each day on horseback, which was done by the rest of the cast and crew in order to keep the historic atmosphere in the constructed town of Big Whiskey with no vehicles allowed. Hackman found Eastwood's style of directing to his taste. The scenes were blocked in terms of knowing where the actor was going and what props were handled, but most of that was for the camera operator's benefit. Then Hackman was left to his own devices, which was real fun filmmaking because he wasn't sure what was going to happen, and neither were the other actors. Eastwood set up an atmosphere for an actor to have the freedom and confidence to do a character fully. He was a great actor's director because he was also an actor.

For the scene where Bill beats up English Bob, Hackman prepared by doing an affective memory exercise, a Stanislavsky-derived technique that involved reliving a past experience to infuse a moment with emotional truth. He said Richard Harris, with whom the actor had appeared in *Hawaii*, unwittingly provided the key. They had a long conversation and there was a moment where Hackman felt that he didn't remember having worked with him. Harris said he did and the actor said he tried to fake his way through it. Hackman wasn't really angry with him—he loved Harris and thought he was terrific—but he thought he could use the feeling of disappointment and did a kind of transference.

The mood on the set was more light-hearted than usual so the actor was free of any battles, and he joined in with the occasional gentle horseplay between takes. Hackman entertained Frances Fisher, who was also Eastwood's girlfriend, by performing a piece from *Henry V* in the style of Marlon Brando on her camcorder.

Eastwood said Hackman was the only choice for Bill. The director needed someone who had great charm *and* the sinister aspect. He asked the actor to model his character on Los Angeles Police Chief Daryl Gates, who had been criticized for a heavy-handed, militarized and racist approach to policing. This approach came to a head with the Rodney King beating in March 1991, followed by the acquittal of the officers and the riots. Hackman didn't know Gates and found he was a man who felt very strongly about law and order, but he didn't need to go into his personality or anything else. He saw parallels between Gates and Bill, especially since the character most abused by Daggett was the black Ned, and referred to the scene where Bill whipped Ned as his Rodney King scene. Eastwood said the actor was an intense worker and totally professional. He was very fast so the director always had to be ready to roll with him.

Morgan Freeman said that Hackman was so believable that when he turned it on, it was completely on. In the whipping scene Freeman had a visceral reaction so he didn't have to worry about trying to act. He believed, and that was the power Hackman had.

The New York Times of November 8, 1991, reported that Hackman planned to fly to London in the next week to see the Royal Court Theatre production of the

Ariel Dorfman play *Death and the Maiden* because Mike Nichols wanted him for a Broadway production of the three-hander. The show was about a woman who has been tortured and plots her revenge. Juliet Stevenson, the English actress doing the role in London, was sought for the Broadway version. Richard Dreyfuss had been approached for the third role.

The *Times* of November 15, 1991, reported that a Hackman painting was on display in New York's luxury restaurant Les Celebrites in the Essex House on Central Park South. On November 29, a story identified Hackman as one of the stars who did voiceovers for commercials: Starting in 1987, Hackman had worked for the Leo Burnett Company, who advertised United Airlines. His voice asked viewers to "Come fly our friendly skies," accompanied by "Rhapsody in Blue" by George Gershwin, a piano-playing parrot and a computer-savvy mouse.

On December 1, 1991, Hackman married Betsy Arakawa. The couple had dated for seven years. On January 10, 1992, the *Times* reported that Glenn Close had been cast instead of Juliet Stevenson in *Death and the Maiden*, which was to open in late March. Actors' Equity had decided that Stevenson was too obscure an actress to merit a work permit for Broadway, although later it was also said that it was because a troupe of Hispanic actors protested the casting of non–Latin actors in the three roles. Hackman was to play the doctor that Paulina Salas, the former political prisoner, believed raped her and supervised her torture. He said he saw less ambiguity in the whodunit aspect of the play and portrayed the doctor as if he was innocent, making that determination because it wouldn't have been interesting if he wasn't. Roberto Miranda was described as a doctor around the age of 50.

There were 33 previews from February 18, 1992. On March 8, 1992, the *Times* published an Al Hirschfeld caricature of the cast, with Hackman dressed in his underwear and tied to a chair as Glenn Close holds a gun to his head. The show opened on March 17 at the Brooks Atkinson Theatre and ran until August 2. Frank Rich of the *Times* wrote that Hackman, an actor abundantly capable of conveying menace (and most anything else), was gregarious and good-natured and never seemed remotely guilty of having been a sadistic Dr. Mengele. David Richards wrote more about the production in the March 22 *Times*, saying that he was slippery, unsavory and thoroughly unsettling. Glenn Close received a Tony nomination for Best Lead Actress in a Play. On April 1, 1992, there was a loudspeaker announcement before the show that at that evening's performance, Close, Dreyfuss and Hackman would all be unable to appear. After considerable groaning, the loudspeaker came back on and the actors spoke together to say, "April Fools!"

He was a presenter at the 46th Annual Tony Awards, held May 31, 1992, at the Gershwin Theatre in New York. Hackman and Richard Dreyfuss were introduced by the show's host Glenn Close as "delicious," and after Dreyfuss presented the

8. Narrow Margin

Tony for Best Lead Actor in a Play to Judd Hirsch for *Conversations with My Father*, he presented the Tony for Actress in a Play to Close for *Death of a Maiden*. Hackman commented, "There'll be no living with her now," before he read her name. Close stated that she would not have the award if it wasn't for the inspiring collaboration of the two other extraordinary actors.

Hackman was not cast in the 1994 film version of *Death and the Maiden,* which was directed by Roman Polanski. Ben Kingsley took the part of Dr. Roberto Miranda.

The actor's voice was heard as a reader in the documentary *Earth and the American Dream* (1992), written by Bill Couturie and Ken Richards and directed by Couturie. It was lambasted by Walter Goodman in *The New York Times*. The film was Emmy-nominated for Outstanding Individual Achievement–Informational Programming for direction and editing.

The mystery thriller *The Firm* was shot from November 9, 1992, to March 20, 1993, in Massachusetts, Washington, Tennessee, Arkansas and the Grand Cayman Islands. The screenplay was by David Rabe and Robert Towne and David Rayfiel, based on the book by John Grisham, and the director was Sydney Pollack. Tom Cruise stars as Mitch McDeere, a Harvard Law graduate who joins a prestigious Memphis law firm only to discover that it has a sinister dark side. Hackman, second-billed, played Avery Tolar, Mitch's mentor in the firm. The role allows Hackman to dance and scuba-dive. He gets some good lines when Avery tells Mitch's wife Abbie (Jeanne Tripplehorn), "I run around ... because my wife understands me. She's lost interest in me. I know I have." In his best scene, Avery is drugged by Abbie, where his reaction ranges from desire, anger and succumbing to the drug without indicating that he is aware that he has *been* drugged.

The film premiered in New York on June 23, 1983, and was given a wide release on June 30 with the taglines "Power can be murder to resist" and "They made him an offer he should have refused." Todd McCarthy of *Variety* wrote that Hackman turned in another sterling performance. Vincent Canby in *The New York Times* wrote that Hackman had reached that plateau in his career where he could play almost any kind of part in a way that gave it both credibility and humanity. Peter Travers in *Rolling Stone* said that the actor gave his role a romantic grace that was eminently watchable. The film was a box office success and there were Oscar nominations for Best Supporting Actress (Holly Hunter) and Best Score. There was a Canadian-American television spin-off, the action mystery series *The Firm* that ran from January 8 to June 30, 2012.

Pollack originally intended Avery to be a woman and to be played by Meryl Streep or Glenn Close, which would have allowed the Mitch character to have an affair with her. Hackman said that Pollack was the kind of guy that hired people he knew could do a role and he just let you do it. He didn't recall anything the director ever said to him.

Daniel Lenihan taught the actor to dive. Lenihan lived in Santa Fe, worked for the parks department, and was a diving writer in scientific magazines. He later collaborated on books with the actor.

It was reported in the *Los Angeles Times* on June 27, 1993, that Hackman's name did not appear on the release poster due to Tom Cruise's deal that only *his* name could appear above the title. Hackman also wanted his name to appear above the credits, but when this was refused he asked for his name to be removed. His spokesman Dick Guttman advised that he came to the project late, after they had started filming, and was offered his role after a marketing plan had been built around Cruise. Another source claims that the actor asked for his name to be removed from both the film poster and the credits because he didn't want the public to have the impression it was a buddy movie. His name is in the film's opening credits.

9

A Second Academy Award

On January 23, 1992, Hackman attended the 50th Annual Golden Globe Awards, held at the Beverly Hilton Hotel. *The New York Times* reported that he was in a bad mood since as he entered the ballroom at the start of the evening, he was asked if he had been to previous Golden Globes ceremonies and replied tartly, "Too many times." Asked if he enjoyed them, Hackman said, "I'd rather be home." His dour mood lifted when he won Best Supporting Actor for *Unforgiven*, presented by Christian Slater and Teri Garr. In his speech, he thanked Clint Eastwood, who convinced him that the film was going to be real serious and it was, and quipped that because of its lack of violence Eastwood would probably never work again (though he didn't think we had to worry about him). A few months later, he won the British Academy of Film and Television Arts award for Best Supporting Actor for *Unforgiven*.

The Times reported that Hackman attended Super Bowl XXVII in Pasadena, California, on January 31, 1993. He begged Dallas Cowboys quarterback Troy Aikman to look his way and was heard to say, "Wish I had paper for an autograph."

The actor was considered for the role of Samuel Gerard in the action drama *The Fugitive* (1993). Hackman turned it down, and the role went to his co-star in *The Package,* Tommy Lee Jones. The *Times* reported on February 11, 1993, that he was on the board of directors of a non-profit organization created to help former fighters who were in financial need, the Beneficial Organization for Ex-Fighters.

He was a presenter and nominee at the 65th Annual Academy Awards, held on March 29, 1993, at the Dorothy Chandler Pavilion. With Morgan Freeman, Hackman presented the award for Best Cinematography to Philippe Rousselot for *A River Runs Through It* (1992). The award for Best Supporting Actor was presented by Mercedes Ruehl to Hackman for *Unforgiven*. Hackman gave a "quick thanks" to producer David Valdez, writer David Peoples, all the wonderful actors and especially to Clint Eastwood, who made it all possible for him and for everyone else in the film. He said it was a wonderful experience, and he wanted to dedicate his part of the evening to his uncle Orin Hackman, who was a wonderful guy.

Hackman had earlier vowed to call it a day if he won, but now he told the press room he had withdrawn his resignation. He explained that the 88-year-old Orin Hackman had passed away the previous night, and he had just learned about it that day. He was a newspaperman in Rochester, New York, a painter and a "really interesting guy." Hackman later commented that while he liked the Oscars, he didn't believe acting awards had any real weight.

Poster for *Unforgiven* (1992).

9. A Second Academy Award

Hackman's next film was the Western *Geronimo: An American Legend* (1993), shot from May 3 to July 29, 1993, in Moab, Utah, and at the Sony Pictures Studios in Hollywood. The screenplay was by John Milius and Larry Gross (based on a story by Milius) and the director was Walter Hill. The story focussed on the Chiricahua Apache chief (Wes Studi) and his armed resistance to the U.S. government's subjugation of his people. Hackman played U.S. Army Brigadier General George Crook, stationed at the San Carlos fort. The white-bearded Crook is in charge of breaking the Indian resistance and housing them at the Turkey Creek reservation. The role has Hackman ride a horse and he has three scenes with his friend Robert Duvall, who plays Al Sieber. The actor provides stillness in the scene where Crook negotiates peace with Geronimo in the Canyon de los Embudos. His best scene is perhaps one with Duvall; the pair has a cinematic frisson as acting veterans when they smile at each other.

The film premiered on December 2, 1993, and opened on December 10 with the taglines "A Warrior. A Leader. A Legend" and "His name would never be forgotten." Todd McCarthy in *Variety* wrote that Hackman managed to escape the dour straitjacket tone with his irony and seasoned humanity. Janet Maslin in *The New York Times* said that Hackman's role was one not even he could breathe much life into. The film was not a box office success. The box office suffered because a rival Geronimo film was released at the same time, a made-for-TV movie broadcast on TNT on December 5, 1993.

Hackman signed on for the film when he learned that Duvall would be in it. Although he had a heart condition, the actor bore up well under the rigors of location shooting, and in between scenes he retreated to his trailer to escape the intense heat and enjoyed the companionship of Duvall. Duvall reported he hadn't seen Hackman in 15 years, but they picked up where they had left off.

Hackman's next film was the Western *Wyatt Earp*, shot from July 19 to December 15, 1993, in Washington, South Dakota, New Mexico and at the Warner Brothers Burbank Studios. The screenplay was by Dan Gordon and Lawrence Kasdan and the director was Kasdan. The title character (Kevin Costner) is one of the West's most famous individuals and Hackman played lawyer Nicholas Earp, Wyatt's father. Billed third after Costner and Dennis Quaid (who played Doc Holliday), he wears a mustache in some scenes and a beard on others, and has two dialogue scenes with Costner which sees the actors reunited after *No Way Out*. The role allows Hackman to ride a horse and a horse-drawn buggy, and smoke a pipe. His best scene is the breakfast table scene where he tells how the family is going to California.

The film premiered in Los Angeles on June 18, 1994, at Mann's Chinese Hollywood Theater with Hackman in attendance. It was released on June 24 with the tagline "The epic story of love and adventure in a lawless land." Caryn James (*The

New York Times) wrote that Hackman was given another chance to show he could do anything. The film was not a box office success, perhaps because it came after *Tombstone* (1993) which told the same story. *Wyatt Earp* received an Oscar nomination for Best Cinematography.

Hackman was in a cut scene: At the wedding reception of Wyatt and Urilla (Annabeth Gish), Nicholas talks to Urilla and jokes to Wyatt that his brother Morgan (Linden Ashby) is trying to convince the bride that she is making a terrible mistake. He also tells Wyatt that he wouldn't leave her alone for too long if he were him.

When Hackman was approached by Kasdan and Costner about the film, he felt less inclined to work, perhaps because he had won his second Oscar, had turned 60 and had a heart condition, and he felt he had reached a new stage in his life. Usually when he got up to go to work in the morning, he would say that this was the last one he was doing. But then knowing himself, he would probably miss it. The part only required him to work a couple of weeks, and there was little in the way of violence for the character. It also helped that everyone felt that the film would be a box office hit. So Hackman accepted and the experience proved to be a happy one.

The romantic action thriller *The Quick and the Dead* was shot from November 21, 1993, to February 27, 1994, in Tucson and at the Old Tucson Studios. The screenplay was by Simon Moore and the director was Sam Raimi. The Lady aka Ellen (Sharon Stone), a gunfighter, returns to the frontier town of Redemption where a quick-draw competition is being held. She enters in an effort to avenge the death of her marshal father (Gary Sinise). Second-billed Hackman played John Herod, the owner of the town, who also enters the contest. He wears glasses, has stringy dyed hair, and his costumes by Judianna Makovsky include a black-purple suit with matching bowler hat and gloves. The role allows Hackman to fire guns, smoke cigars, rip off the collar of preacher Cort (Russell Crowe), slap Ellen with a glove and play a death scene. He gets some funny lines, as when he asks Ellen, "Do you have some particular problem with me?," and when he tells Cort, "You put a fox in the henhouse, you're gonna have chicken for dinner every time." Hackman plays the role in both the period time of the narrative and in flashbacks when Ellen is a girl (and played by Stacy Linn Ramsower). He gets a movie star entrance, with a camera tilt up the length of his body, closeups and several extreme closeups. His best scene is perhaps Herod's dinner scene with Ellen, the actor peeling an apple as he speaks.

The film was released on February 10, 1995, with the taglines "In this town, you're either one or the other," "Think you're quick enough?" and "You can't ignore her. You can't beat her. You can't resist her. You can't win…" Janet Maslin in *The New York Times* wrote that nobody played a bile-dripping villain to quite the same slinky effect as Hackman. Roger Ebert said that Hackman survived the material, and Peter Travers in *Rolling Stone* wrote that he was mostly reprising his Oscar-winning villain role in *Unforgiven* minus the extras of substance and nuance—but he remained a keen presence even in these reduced circumstances. Todd McCarthy in *Variety* said that Hackman had taken his Oscar-winning *Unforgiven* characterization as the mean-spirited sheriff and magnified the evil tenfold, to near-lampoon effect. The film was not a box office success.

Hackman disliked the script for its violence. He felt the need to relax after the rigors of making his last two films, but he was seduced by TriStar, Raimi and Stone. (One of the film's co-producers, Stone was aggressive in making sure they did their best to get the actor.) According to *Variety*, location filming moved from Durango, Mexico, to Tucson to accommodate him, and he was given a house in Tucson to live in throughout the production. The days on location were baking hot and the nights were sub-zero. Hackman said of Herod that if played a monster and showed some humanity and convinced people that there are people like that, then you had done something as an artist.

Screenwriter Moore said Hackman was probably his favorite film actor of all time and he was excited that he was doing the film. During a read-through in a Los Angeles hotel, Hackman stopped every five minutes to say, "That's a terrible line," "God, that line stinks" or "We've got to change that." Herod's slap to Ellen was not in the script, it was improvised by Hackman. All the actors were instructed in the art of the quick draw by a stunt coordinator. Hackman had the most opportunity to prepare his quick draw and as a result was the fastest actor on the set.

Sam Raimi reported that the actor was very tough but tough for the right reasons, because Hackman was very interested in delivering the very best performance that anyone could. In his book *If Chins Could Kill: Confessions of a B Movie Actor*, Bruce Campbell said he played Wedding Shemp in the film but his scenes were deleted. According to Campbell, on the first day of shooting, Raimi asked Hackman to say a line that wasn't scripted, after tipping his hat to a man across the street and sitting in a chair. At first Hackman refused to do any of it but Raimi persuaded him to do all three.

Russell Crowe said that he preferred to work with someone who was mean and nasty and tough who did a great job than someone who was really nice and sweet and was boring to watch. In his unauthorized biography of Crowe, James L. Dickerson wrote that Hackman kept his distance from the young actor on the set, because he couldn't think of any reason to pal around with someone whom he'd never heard of before. In Martin Howden's biography of Crowe, he also wrote about Hackman's less than cordial relationship with the actor, and mentioned that Crowe made fun of the older actor's "permed" hairstyle. But the young actor felt that it wasn't a bad thing that the pair weren't the best of friends since they played sworn enemies in the film.

Lance Henriksen, who played Ace Hanlon, called Hackman someone he had wanted to work with for 20 years. He believed that the actor *was* his character. In their first scene together, Raimi put the camera on the ground and told Hackman to step up in front of the lens with his legs spread so that through them, you could see Ace standing there, taking a bow. The idea was that Herod would walk to Ace, but Henriksen suggested that Ace should walk to him because it made Herod stronger. At the end of the day, Henriksen felt badly that he had told Gene Hackman what to do, but the actor was not bothered, and accepted it as a good idea. Henriksen admired his lack of ego but said he would have understood if Hackman had reacted by telling him to fuck off.

The actor had now stopped watching his films, saying he thought of himself as being much younger than he was and to see this old guy with the bald head and the paunch was depressing. Hackman was considered one of America's greatest actors, but the box office failure of his latest films made him an un-bankable star on his own.

On March 8, 1994, Hackman attended the 20th Annual People's Choice Awards. He accepted the award for Favorite Dramatic Motion Picture for *The Firm*, with Tom Cruise and Jeanne Tripplehorn. At the 66th Annual Academy Awards (March 21, 1994), Hackman presented the Best Supporting Actress award to Anna Paquin for the musical romance *The Piano* (1994). Before Hackman announced the winner, he quipped, "When I open this envelope, four gifted nominees will engage their considerable talents to convince us they're happy a fifth nominee is taking home the Oscar."

Hackman was referenced in the 1994 comedy *PCU* aka *Politically Correct University* aka *PCU Pit Party*. In the film, Port Chester University student Pigman (Jody Racicot) is writing his senior thesis to prove no matter what time it is, 24 hours a day, you can find a Michael Caine or Hackman movie playing on television. His theory ends when he finds both actors are in *A Bridge Too Far*. Lambasting the film in *The New York Times* of April 29, 1994, Janet Maslin wrote that it might have helped if either of those actors had been in this film.

The actor turned down the part of Deacon in the science fiction adventure *Waterworld* (1995). It was taken by Dennis Hopper. He appeared in NBC's documentary *100 Years of the Hollywood Western* (1994) broadcast on on August 10, 1994. This was written by Jack Haley, Jr., Phil Savenick and Aubrey Solomon and directed by Haley, Jr. The show featured three Westerns that the actor had appeared in: *Unforgiven*, *Wyatt Earp* and *The Quick and the Dead*.

When screenwriter Michael Schiffer scripted *Crimson Tide*, he reportedly wrote the part of Ramsey specifically for Hackman. One source claims that Al Pacino was first offered the part. Another says that the producers wanted Hackman but the studio wanted Warren Beatty. Beatty worked on the script before falling by the wayside. As the studio still didn't want Hackman, the producers then offered the part to Pacino. He said yes but then changed his mind. Hackman's agent reminded them that his client was still interested, but the studio continued to balk, especially at the actor's asking price of $4 million. Tommy Lee Jones was reportedly offered the part and declined. Producers Don Simpson and Jerry Bruckheimer finally persuaded the studio to accept Hackman.

The action thriller was shot from August 15 to December 1, 1994, with additional shooting in late February 1995, in California and France. The screenplay had uncredited rewrites from Quentin Tarantino, Robert Towne and Steve Zallian, based on a story by Shiffer and Richard P. Henrick. Hunter (Denzel Washington), an officer in the U.S. nuclear missile submarine *Alabama*, located off the Russian Peninsula, stages a mutiny to prevent Capt. Ramsey (second-billed Hackman) from launching his missiles without confirming his orders to do so. His costumes by George L. Little includes a red cap that is a nod to director Tony Scott, who reportedly always wore a pink baseball cap on set. Ramsey smokes cigars, pets a Jack Russell, aims a gun at the heads of Wepps (Viggo Mortensen) and Petty Officer Hilaire (Scott Grimes) and punches Hunter. During the two weeks of rehearsals, Scott came up with the idea that Ramsey should have the Jack Russell, who was a male named Woody. Scott gives Hackman many closeups and some extreme closeups. The actor has a good moment after he tells Hunter that he seems to have the pulse of the men, where his expression changes from a smile to anger. In Hackman's best scene, he charges Hunter with mutiny and Hunter has *him* removed as the ship's commander.

The film was released on May 12, 1995, with the taglines "Danger runs deep" and "On the Brink of Nuclear War, Two Men Clash Over the Fate of the World." In *The New York Times*, Janet Maslin wrote that Hackman did everything possible to make the eyeball-to-eyeball confrontations look like something more than the synthetic, empty exercises they actually were. A box office success, the film was Oscar-nominated for Best Sound, Best Film Editing and Best Sound Effects Editing.

Two scenes with Ramsey were cut. One had him asking Hunter to speak to Cob (George Dzundza) about his weight. The other showed Ramsey being called into the Naval Enquiry as Hunter waits.

Hackman reported that it was very intense on the set. Scott ran a very tight set and shot with long lenses which made it difficult doing intimate scenes when the camera was 20 or 30 feet away, since the actor was used to it being right on him. He accidentally punched Denzel Washington in one scene, which created tension but it was good for the film. Another moment of tension arose in the scene when Lt. Bobby Dougherty (James Gandolfini) came to remove Hunter from the conning tower. Gandolfini grabbed Washington more fiercely than had been done in rehearsal, and Washington pushed him back, which resulted in a shoving match.

Scott called for a break to allow the actors to cool off but when they came back it happened again before they broke into laughter. Neither Scott nor Hackman were aware that the two had plotted a prank. One day Quentin Tarantino came to the set and met with Hackman in the parking lot. He told him about the script for the action romance *Top Gun* (1986), which Scott also directed, and his theories about its homosexual subtext. Hackman chuckled, adding that the airplanes were penises. He said he enjoyed meeting Tarantino, who was a terrific movie fan, and said that chatting with him was like talking to a movie encyclopedia. Hackman commented on the suicide of director Tony Scott on August 19, 2012, by saying, "Tony was always sensitive to the needs of an actor. We've lost a wonderful, creative talent."

On May 17, 1995, Hackman returned to *The Tonight Show with Jay Leno* after having been on November 10, 1992, and July 23, 1993, and told an embarrassing story. After having been stung by a film reviewer who suggested he was too old to play the nuclear submarine captain in *Crimson Tide*, a young retail clerk waiting on him offered a 20 percent senior citizen discount with his purchase.

Hackman, perhaps jokingly, downplayed his acting at this time in his career as his having gained a certain poise. He found playing the role easy mainly because the film was the type where he always had a goal and a place he had to go, a high and a low. Hackman also commented on working with the Jack Russell. He fed the animal pieces of hot dog and had to get his hand out in a hurry to avoid being nipped. The actor happily signed autographs for students when the company filmed at the Chapman University in Orange County. He was heard to hum "Anchors Aweigh" as he walked back to the set, ready to do another scene with Woody, happy that his work on the film was by then almost over.

Denzel Washington said that he was entranced by his co-star's presence, and he found himself open-mouthed and staring blankly at Hackman in one scene. He was excited to do the film because Hackman was such a fine actor who gave him extra energy. Washington always wanted to come prepared because Hackman always was. In Hackman's position, it would have been easy to be lazy or to slow down but instead he was very, very professional.

After filming, the actor took a break at one of his European hideaways. He was protective of his private life, but said the press generally left him alone. He admitted he really wasn't that fascinating a personality so there was little about him for people to know about. He guessed that being so normal was what made him successful as an actor, since audiences responded to the proletarian man they saw in him.

Hackman was considered for the part of veteran detective Somerset in the crime mystery *Se7en* (1995) but director David Fincher cast Morgan Freeman instead. He was interviewed for the documentary *Shurtleff on Acting* (1994), written and directed by Michael Gabourie. Shurtleff was a casting agent, author and acting guru and Hackman had been one of his students. The film did not get a theatrical release and premiered in Canadian television in 1994 and then went to DVD in the U.S. in 1995.

His next film was the comic crime thriller *Get Shorty* (1995). It was shot from February, though one source gives the start date as January 17, to April 18, 1995, on locations in California, Florida and Nevada and at the Sony Pictures Studios in Hollywood. The screenplay was by Scott Frank, based on the novel by Elmore Leonard, and the director was Barry Sonnenfeld. John Travolta stars as Chili Palmer, a Las Vegas loan shark who travels to Hollywood to collect a debt from B-movie producer Harry Zimm (second-billed Hackman) of Zimm Filmz. He wears a mustache, gray goatee and false teeth, and his costumes by Betsy Heimann include a noteworthy red turtleneck sweater. Hackman looks facially thinner and the role allows us to see him in his underwear, being beaten by Ray "Bones" Barboni (Dennis Farina) and wearing a neck brace and hand casts. He also has a sexual partner in actress-producer Karen Flores (Rene Russo), but she also sleeps with Chili and with Doris Saphron (an uncredited Bette Midler). Hackman gets a funny line when Harry tells Karen about Chili: "The guy's been in town two days and already he thinks he's David O. Fucking Selznick." His mannerisms have a context for Harry as a Hollywood phony, and he is also funny in the role. His best scene is perhaps when Harry is beaten up by Bones because the actor is usually the perpetrator of such physical violence. The film credits Hackman's stand-in as Gregory B. Goossen, who previously appeared in *The Package, Loose Cannons, Class Action, Unforgiven, The Firm, Geronimo: An American Legend, Wyatt Earp* and *The Quick and the Dead*. The film was a reunion for Hackman and James Gandolfini, who had previously appeared in *Crimson Tide*.

Hackman attended an October 18, 1995, screening at New York's Museum of Modern Art. The film went into wide release on October 20 with the taglines "Drug smuggling. Racketeering. Loan sharking. Welcome to Hollywood!" "Attitude Plays a Part" and "The Mob Is Tough. But It's Nothing Like Show Business." Todd McCarthy in *Variety* wrote that Hackman scored, and Peter Travers in *Rolling Stone* said that the actor did a classic sendup of scum with ambition. The film was a box office success. In the sequel *Cool* (2005), the character of Harry was not reprised. There was also a crime comedy television series created by Davey Holmes but again there was no Harry.

Hackman had turned down the part because he didn't usually do comedies and feared embarrassing himself trying to be funny. Barry Sonnenfeld said that was exactly the attitude he wanted from the actor: to play it straight and let the audience decide if it was funny. Hackman said while he didn't have much ambition left, his choice of film was very much dictated by the chance to work with good people who were also hot at the time. He based Harry on an agent who was the phoniest man Hackman had ever known. He warmed to the film's broad comedy and on set he was modest, with the actor saying he didn't think he did anything great—his stuff was easy. The writers and directors had the hardest part of bringing the story alive and Hackman was just a hanger-on. Another source reported that he spent most of the shoot fuming over Sonnenfeld's direction, and confided to him at the premiere that the entire time he was working with him, Hackman didn't think Sonnenfeld had a clue. He felt the scene where Chili recited lines from the film noir *Touch of Evil* (1958) while watching it in a cinema was one of the most engaging things he had ever seen in a film.

In *The Life*, Nigel Andrews' book on John Travolta, he writes about the young actor's bad hair mornings and how one time he walked into the makeup trailer to find Hackman. Hackman, shocked at how bad Travolta looked, exclaimed, "Oh God, makeup and hair do wonders for you."

At this time, Hackman said he had achieved very few of his ambitions. He still wanted to direct though he was now doubtful that it would ever happen. There were just too many hassles about it, and his heart problem supposedly made directing now out of the question. It was also unlikely Hackman would return to the stage, but his plans to remake *La Cage aux Folles* came to fruition. He wouldn't get to play his dream role since at the age of 65 he was clearly too old for it, and Hackman wouldn't direct the film. But he got Mike Nichols interested in the project; it helped that Nichols had enjoyed working with him on *Postcards from the Edge*, and he had been looking for a more substantial part to offer the actor.

The comedy *The Birdcage* (1996) was shot under the working title *Birds of a Feather* from April 24 to July 24, 1995, in New York, California and Florida and at the Greenwich Studios in Florida and the Paramount Studios and Ren-Mar Studios in Hollywood. The screenplay was by Elaine May, based on the stage play *La Cage aux Folles* by Jean Poiret and the script written by Francis Veber, Édouard Molinaro, Marcello Danon and Poiret. Armand Goldman (Robin Williams), a gay South Beach, Florida, nightclub owner, and his drag queen companion Albert Goldman aka Starina (Nathan Lane) agree to put up a false straight front so that their 20-year-old son—Armand's by his one heterosexual fling—Val (Dan Futterman) can introduce them to his fiancée Barbara's (Calista Flockhart) right-wing moralistic parents. Hackman, second-billed, played Senator Kevin Keely, the father of 18-year-old Barbara and the vice-president of the Coalition for Moral Order, who is campaigning for re-election. This was the part played by Michel Galabru in the original film. Hackman's costumes (by Ann Roth) includes a spectacular white dress and white wig for Kevin's escape from the nightclub in drag. The role allows him to perform farcical actions like climbing a ladder and climbing into a window and dress in drag, and he also sings and dances. Hackman gets some funny lines. He refers to the Goldman servant Agador (Hank Azaria) as a "beige savage," and complains when he is in drag, "No one will dance with me. I think it's the dress. I told them

9. A Second Academy Award

Poster for *The Birdcage* **(1996).**

white would make me look fat." Kevin being an ugly woman also gets a line when, after he escapes from the club, he tells his chauffeur (Kirby Mitchell) to meet him in 20 minutes. The driver replies, "Not for a million dollars." Hackman's best scene is perhaps when he is in drag in the club since it is such a new look for him; director Nichols provides him with a turn-around reveal.

The film was released on March 8, 1996, with the taglines "Come as you are" and "What could possibly come between a match made in heaven? The parents. Dinner. And a nightclub called...The Birdcage." Todd McCarthy in *Variety* wrote that Hackman neatly essayed his role. Janet Maslin in *The New York Times* said that he played with deadpan wickedness. A box office success, it was Oscar-nominated for Best Art Direction–Set Decoration.

The actor said it was a wonderful part, since Kevin was central to the story but Hackman was able to leave it to the younger actors to do all the energetic stuff. Nathan Lane and Robin Williams commented on Hackman, perhaps jokingly. Lane said that he was such a man's man and then Hackman would always surprise him, saying that had just been listening to Barbara Cook in his trailer. Williams thought the actor was amazing. His nicknames for Hackman in drag were "Betty White on steroids" and "Dragzilla." Williams found the actor funny and said his speech about the leaves in New England was one of the funniest, driest pieces of comedy he had ever seen.

Hackman was considered by director Oliver Stone for the title role in the biographical historical drama *Nixon* (1995), the story of the U.S. president Richard Milhous Nixon. Anthony Hopkins was cast instead and received a Best Actor Academy Award nomination. He was offered the part of Dan De Mora in director Carl Reiner's romantic comedy *That Old Feeling* (1996) but declined and Dennis Farina was cast. In a *New York Times* interview (June 16, 1996), Burt Reynolds said that Hackman was wanted for the part of Congressman David Dilbeck in the comedy crime drama *Striptease* (1996). But Hackman declined and Reynolds took it.

Asked in the *Times* (October 15, 1995) why he wasn't playing romantic leads, Hackman said those roles just weren't offered. At his age, there were not that many pictures of a romantic quality, and Sean Connery got most of them. He would love to do one because they were very intense which was the ideal thing for an actor, but maybe it was just not in the cards.

Hackman next appeared in the crime drama *The Chamber* (1996), shot from February 5 to May 6, 1996, in Chicago, Mississippi (the execution scene was filmed in the Parchman Penitentiary gas chamber) and on the Universal backlot. The film had a screenplay by William Goldman and Chris Reese, based on the novel by John Grisham, and it was directed by James Foley. It centered on 26-year-old attorney Adam Hall (Chris O'Donnell) who in 1996 lodges an appeal for Sam Cayhall (Hackman), who has been on Mississippi State Penitentiary's Death Row for 16 years for a bombing murder in 1967 in Indianola. Hackman is seen in both present time and

9. A Second Academy Award

flashback. For the other flashback scenes, Hackman wears a mustache and long sideburns, and for the present scenes a gray beard and his hair is longer in the back. Hackman's makeup, which includes yellowed teeth, is by Kevin Haney and designed to give him a decimated look. His notable costumes by Tracy Tynan include a red prison jumpsuit and a black beanie. The role allows Hackman to use a Southern accent, smoke, sing, and have a death scene. Hackman is funny, particularly in the way he pronounces "bullshit." Hackman has one scene with Faye Dunaway which is a reunion for the actors after they appeared together in *Bonnie and Clyde* though at the age of 55 it is unbelievable that she could play the daughter of a man who is 66. His best scene is perhaps when he tells Adam about the botched execution of the inmate Teddy Meeks. Hackman uses pauses and physicality to express the prisoner beating his head against a metal pole inside the gas chamber. Greg Goossen, Hackman's stand-in, also played J.B. Gullitt.

It premiered in Hollywood on October 2, 1996, with Hackman in attendance, and was given a wide release on October 11 with the tagline "Time is running out." Emanuel Levy in *Variety* wrote that Hackman gave a riveting, highly modulated performance, Janet Maslin in *The New York Times* said he demonstrated beautifully understated acting without a trace of the self-congratulatory. The film was not a box office success, and Dunaway earned a Razzie Award nomination for Worst Supporting Actress.

Hackman in *The Chamber* (1996).

Dennis Hopper was considered for the role of Sam but producer Brian Glazer said that Hackman was perfect casting. He lost 30 pounds for the role and said he wanted to bring something fresh to the character. Hackman viewed several documentaries set on Death Row and researched accents and worked with dialect coach Francine Brown to accurately duplicate the idiosyncrasies of Mississippi's vivid Delta vernacular. The actor said Sam was a fascinating character to play. He was a terrible man but Hackman thought it would be interesting to play as much of the human element of the man as he could so that you saw behind this "monster." Hackman didn't want the audience to have sympathy for him, but there was a human being there, a man who might have been decent had he not been so dreadfully conditioned. He was so full of anger and hatred, but also had a repressed feeling of love for his family that he couldn't admit. By the time he did, it was too late. John Grisham disliked the film and said that Hackman was the only good thing in it.

Faye Dunaway said she had only seen Hackman one or two times since *Bonnie and Clyde* and their scene was her first day of shooting on the film. It was an incredible experience when she turned around and saw him come through the door. Dunaway felt it brought everything back. She and Hackman spoke about it later. He felt the same because the earlier film was his first big role. Dunaway believed that the actor had an unerring sense of what was real and true, and he played his *Chamber* role with economy and clarity when he could have easily gone over the top with it. Hackman was one of her favorites and he was a master and the ultimate craftsman.

Hackman was considered for the part of police officer Tom O'Meara in the action-filled crime drama *The Devil's Own* (1997). When it was decided that he was too old for the part, Harrison Ford was cast.

10

Extreme Measures

Hackman's next role was in the crime mystery *Extreme Measures,* shot from February 26 to May 13, 1996, in New York and Ontario and Toronto, Canada. The screenplay was by Tony Gilroy based on the book by Michael Palmer and the director was Michael Apted, who had previously directed him in *Class Action*. Hugh Grant stars as Guy Luthan, a British doctor working at New York's Gramercy Hospital. He starts making inquiries when the body of a man who died in his emergency room disappears. Second-billed Hackman played 68-year-old Lawrence Myrick, the neurological head of Triphase, a medical center using the kidnapped homeless as human subjects to grow nerves. He wears a mustache and his hair is again worn long in the back. Hackman's costumes by Susan Lyall include some bow ties. The role gives him another death scene, which director Apted shoots with an extreme closeup. His best scene is perhaps when Myrick speaks to Guy over the center's loudspeaker system to get him to come out of hiding.

The film was released on September 27, 1996, with the tagline "Not all surgery is intended to cure. Don't move a muscle." Janet Maslin in *The New York Times* wrote that Hackman brought a cool proficiency to something other than a standard villainous role. Leonard Klady in *Variety* said that one feels the actor's efforts to bring nuance and texture to a cardboard scoundrel. Peter Travers in *Rolling Stone* wrote that Hackman played on the fragile line between genius and cuckoo. The film was not a box office success.

Hackman was attracted to the role despite Dr. Myrick being the film's heavy, saying he was not a particularly evil man but a good doctor deep down and one of the world's great medical minds.

Hugh Grant was jubilant when Hackman took the part, but said from then he was gibbering at the prospect of having to play against this man who always looked like he was furious. As it turned out, the actor couldn't have been less like that. He was very much an actor's actor and all he wanted was to do the job, though Hackman did lunch with the crew.

Hackman said he planned to take the rest of 1996 off, adjusting his work schedule so he would only make one film a year. He felt he had fallen somewhere between star and character actor, but he didn't look back too much and mourn or cheer over the best roles. Hackman just looked towards the future.

The actor returned to work sooner than he had planned. The action crime dama *Absolute Power* (1997) saw him again working for director Clint Eastwood. It was shot from June 3 to August 15, 1996, in Washington, Maryland and Los Angeles. The screenplay was by William Goldman, based on a book by David Baldacci. Eastwood also starred as Luther Whitney, a career jewel thief who witnesses a horrific crime in Washington involving U.S. President Richmond (Hackman, second-billed). The role sees him in a love scene with kissing and implied oral sex which turns rough with slapping, pulling hair, ripping clothes, punching and strangling. Richmond dies off-screen. Hackman expresses funny controlled anger in the president's dance with his chief of staff Gloria Russell (Judy Davis). The actor's best scene is perhaps the love scene and murder of Christy Sullivan (Melora Hardin) as his anger is frightening. Richmond's scream after she is shot by his bodyguards and his crying show a weakness of character, where he is more concerned with what has happened as opposed to any concern over the dead woman. Hackman has no scenes with Eastwood.

The film premiered in Westwood, California, on February 4, 1997, and was given a wide release on February 14 with the tagline "Corrupts Absolutely." Todd McCarthy in *Variety* wrote that Hackman had little to do as the prez but be odiously duplicitous. Janet Maslin in *The New York Times* said he languished in the smallish role of a White House buffoon.

His next film was the crime drama–mystery *Twilight*. It was shot under the working title *Magic Hour* from November 11, 1996, to March 1997. The screenplay was by Robert Benton and Richard Russo and the director was Benton. Paul Newman stars as Harry Ross, a retired Los Angeles private detective. Hackman played Jack Ames, a former Hollywood actor, who is Harry's employer and landlord. Hackman is billed third after Newman and Susan Sarandon who plays Jack's wife, former actress Catherine. The actor's makeup is credited to Ellen Wong and his hair is by Ronald Scott. There is also an Al Hirschfeld caricature of him, a credited still from *I Never Sang for My Father*, and a scene from *Downhill Racer* on television that Jack watches. The role allows Hackman to play cards, lie on the floor after a heart attack, and punch Catherine. He uses stillness in what is perhaps his best scene, when he confesses to Harry that he knows about the death of actor Billy Sullivan 20 years prior.

The film was released on March 6, 1998, with the tagline "Some people can buy their way out of anything. Except the past." Todd McCarthy wrote in *Variety* that Hackman's performance was the most tenacious and underhanded, and Roger Ebert said that the film gave him few opportunities. The film was not a box office success.

10. Extreme Measures

Hackman said everything about Paul Newman was real, but he worried about his own casting in the film. He was very pleased to do it but he didn't really know how to play a movie star. Director Benton felt that Hackman was not only a great actor, but also one of the loveliest people he had ever met.

In his book *Superhero: A Biography of Christopher Reeve*, Chris Nickson writes that HBO wanted Hackman for the part of Martin, the father of a man dying of AIDS, in the made-for-TV movie *In the Gloaming* (1997), directed by Reeve. David Strathairn was cast instead. Hackman was considered for the part of William Parrish in the fantasy romance *Meet Joe Black* (1998). He was attached but then backed out and replaced by Anthony Hopkins. The actor was also considered by screenwriter-director Quentin Tarantino for the part of Max Cherry in the crime drama thriller *Jackie Brown* (1997), but Robert Forster was cast.

Hackman's next film was the action-crime-mystery *Enemy of the State*. It was shot from November 5, 1997, to April 6, 1998, in Washington, Maryland and California. The screenplay was by David Marconi and the director was Tony Scott. Robert Clayton Dean (Will Smith), a Washington labor lawyer, accidentally receives key evidence to a politically motivated crime. He is targeted by Reynolds (Jon Voight), the White House special advisor to the Deputy Director of Operations and his National Security Agency goons. Hackman played Brill aka Edward Lyle, a former NSA communications analyst who now works underground as one of Dean's contacts. He plays a supporting role and there is a still of him from *The Conversation*. Hackman is clean-shaven, he has short-cropped hair and he wears horn-rimmed nerd glasses. The role allows the actor to chew gum (which becomes a plot point), run, punch Smith, carjack and get shot in the hand. Hackman is funny in the movie. His best scene is perhaps his one with Voight. Although the two actors are separated by a wire fence, they bring movie star presence to Brill's demand for money in exchange for the incriminating evidence. Greg Goossen was Hackman's stand-in and Doc Duhame his stunt double.

The film premiered in New York on November 18, 1998, and opened wide on November 20 with the taglines "Invasion of Privacy," "It's not paranoia if they're really after you," "In God we trust. The rest we monitor" and "The only privacy left is inside of your head." Roger Ebert wrote that Hackman seemed utterly confident of everything he said. Peter Travers of *Rolling Stone* said that the actor's effortless authority and control were a pleasure to watch, and considered him the best character actor in the business. Emanuel Levy in *Variety* said that Hackman endowed his role with subversive edge and humor. The film was a box office success. *Variety* reported in 2016 that an ABC-TV series would be based on the film but so far there's been nothing.

Sean Connery was considered for the part of Brill. Hackman had turned down the film several times, but was ultimately convinced by director Scott, with whom he had made *Crimson Tide*. The actor liked Scott and producer Jerry Bruckheimer since they didn't make any bones about doing an action film or a thriller, without saying it was some sort of social commentary. The pair wanted it to be commercially viable, and Hackman said that was honest. He also liked the idea that Will Smith was going to do this straight dramatic role with some comedy in it.

Bruckheimer reported that the actor was always on the top of the list because they had had such a good working relationship on *Crimson Tide*, which the producer had also made. He said Hackman was a wonderful actor and he raised everyone else to his level. Scott said the actor declined the role initially because he didn't like the first draft of the script, but accepted a redraft. The director felt the dynamic and contrast between Hackman and Smith was good, because Smith was so sweet and affable and Hackman was so angry and such a bear.

Smith took the role because he wanted to work with the actor. He said that in the scene where Dean is told by Brill that his life is over, when he was sitting across the table from someone with that kind of intensity and years of fire and passion, it just drove him as an actor. Smith felt that he got a lifetime's worth of experience working with that level of a performer.

"Gene Hackman" was the title of a song by Australian rock group Hoodoo Gurus on their album "Electric Chair," released on April 28, 1998. The song describes him as versatile and the leading actor by a country mile, and references *Superman*, "Popeye" Doyle and his Oscars.

Hackman was part of the voice cast of the animated film *Antz*, about rebellious ants in New York's Central Park. The adventure comedy had a screenplay by Todd Alcott, Chris Weitz and Paul Weitz with uncredited input from Woody Allen, and was directed by Eric Darnell and Tim Johnson, with additional sequences directed by Lawrence Guterman. The story centered on Z (voiced by Allen), an orange ant who works as a soil relocation engineer on the colony's Mega Tunnel. Z tries to break from his totalitarian society and win the affection of Princess Bala (voiced by Sharon Stone), whom he loves. Hackman voiced the part of General Mandible, the red ant leader of the army, who is also engaged to Bala. Mandible is distinguished by wearing a diagonal green leaf sash and a shoulder buckle and a brown leaf helmet. The character is punched by Cutter (voiced by Christopher Walken) and he has a death scene.

The film premiered at the Toronto International Film Festival on September 19, 1998, and opened in the U.S. on October 2 with the taglines "Best Friend. The General. The Hero. The Princess," "See the world from a whole new perspective," "From the studio that brought you *Shrek*," "Every ant has his day" and "Actual size of the next big star." Todd McCarthy in *Variety* wrote that Hackman excelled. The film was a box office success. A direct-to-video sequel was planned but eventually cancelled. Footage of Hackman recording his part is seen in the DVD Behind the Scenes featurette and the documentary *The Secret World of* Antz (1998).

10. Extreme Measures

Mandible's name was originally Formica. The character's designs were by Raman Hui. The voice actors were filmed so that their movement could be incorporated into the animation. Hackman said that it was great fun to do; he said he could be very broad and do things that he just couldn't get away with in live action. It was the kind of work he imagined acting was going to be like before he got into the industry.

Co-director Tim Johnson commented that it was a tribute to the actor that he could make Mandible's four speeches so energetic. Hackman's voice made the villain incredibly effective. He had an amazing power and just listening to him created an imposing physical presence. When the actor delivered a speech, everybody in the sound booth was silent for two minutes afterwards. Hackman was so commanding in the role that they were ready to follow him off to battle or do whatever he told them. Co-director Eric Darnell reported that the actor and Sylvester Stallone attended a screening of the scene where Mandible interrogates Weaver. The film was a reunion for Hackman and Sharon Stone, his co-star from *The Quick and the Dead*.

According to the *New York Times* of October 20, 1998, Hackman was on the dinner committee for the first United States Marine Corps Birthday Ball aboard the aircraft carrier *Intrepid*. The event was to be held on November 10 to commemorate the birth of the Corps on November 10, 1775. Hackman narrated the biographical documentary "Hitchcock, Selznick and the End of Hollywood," the October 23, 1998, episode of the TV series *American Masters*. It was written and directed by Michael Epstein. In 1998, he appeared in the biographical documentary *The Directors: The Films of Richard Donner* and the documentary *The Best of Hollywood* aka *50 Years: The Best of Hollywood*. His next film was *Under Suspicion* (2000), the remake of *Garde à vue* that Hackman had wanted to make; he and Morgan Freeman were credited as executive producers. It was shot from February 1999 on location in Puerto Rico. The screenplay by Tom Provost and W. Peter Iliff was based on the *Garde à vue* screenplay by Claude Miller, Jean Herman and Michel Audiard, which was based on the book *Brainwash* by John Wainwright. Hackman starred as Henry Buchanan Hearst, a 57-year-old San Juan tax attorney and photographer suspected of the rape and murder of two girls by Police Captain Victor Benezet (top-billed Freeman). Hackman's clothes are by Hugo Boss. The actor's hair is by Deena Adair and includes a hair piece which is a plot point, and he wears a goatee. The role allows Hackman to smoke, speak Italian, take photographs, be pushed by Detective Felix Owens (Thomas Jane), fall down a stairwell, be drunk, have sex with a prostitute, and be seen in his underwear.

Henry gets some funny lines. When Felix asks how he writes Tango as the name of his dog, he is told, "How else would you write it? Like waltz or foxtrot?" Henry tells Felix that smoking marijuana "might help your sunny disposition," and he says that his niece Camille (Isabel Algaze) "was high on a sugar rush from pumpkin pie." Director Stephen Hopkins uses unflattering extreme closeups of Hackman, and the actor's performance is mostly spoiled by his mannerisms. However, he is funny and he has some still moments in the interrogation room when Henry talks about his marriage. The actor also impresses in showing Henry's mood swings, going from arrogant bravado and anger to fear, vulnerability and embarrassment. Thomas Jane does a funny impersonation of Hackman speaking. Keith Siglinger is credited as Hackman's stunt double, and Greg Goossen was his stand-in.

On May 11, 2000, the film premiered at the Cannes Film Festival; Hackman attended. It opened in the U.S. on September 22 with the taglines "Everyone has secrets. Some of them are crimes," "In a world of secrets, the truth is never what it seems" and "A hidden past, a secret life, witness or suspect, guilty or innocent?" Peter Travers in *Rolling Stone* wrote that Hackman (and Freeman) pinned you to your seat. Derek Elley in *Variety* said that Hackman came off best but rarely got under the skin of his character's private disappointments and desperation. The film was not a box office success.

This was a reunion for Hackman and Freeman, who had previously appeared in *Unforgiven*. Hackman said the new film was very special because it had been a labor of love. The connection between Henry and William Randolph Hearst occurred to him when considering his character, but it was a subliminal connection that the writer enjoyed and that maybe one or two reporters might pick up. What attracted Hackman to the role changed over the time it took to make the film. At one point he would have been frightened to do it, in terms of baring one's soul, but that was the kind of part that actors begged to do. Hackman doubted that the French would like the remake because the original was such a huge success there. They had Americanized it; Americans didn't want subtlety, so it was broader and much more class-based, and his character had a sense of entitlement about him. Ultimately he felt they hadn't changed it a great deal so it was still very true to the original in most ways.

Freeman reported that when the two were making *Unforgiven*, they said they had to find another project to do together. In another interview he said that the subject came up when the actors ran into each other at a hotel in Los Angeles. Hackman mentioned the project as a possible vehicle for them, and he had a tape he wanted to send. Freeman liked the idea and both were drawn to the roles they would play in the film. Hackman said he would play either role, but he was praying Freeman didn't want "the good part." The film was made by Freeman's production company, Revelations Entertainment, who was better at business, though the process was particularly complicated as it took seven parties to approve the rights deal. The deal was signed on the first day of the 1998 Cannes Film Festival.

Hackman said he loved Freeman as an actor because he was a worthy adversary, and as a human being, and he had great fun working with him. It was an opportunity to do a film with a black actor and a white actor where there were no racial overtones at all, since everybody was equal in those terms. Hackman didn't know if audiences would accept a character-driven thriller, one with no explosions or spaceships, but he wanted to think so. Most of the films Hackman had done recently had been character-driven and it was satisfying since he could expound on what he knew as an actor. It was also less physical than other parts the actor had played and the character was even a bit of a coward, which Hackman liked.

Freeman said working with Hackman was wonderful. He didn't find it too hard working with an icon he so respected after he had learned how to deal with that from working with José Ferrer Off Broadway in 1978. He respected Hackman because he brought such depth to his work.

Stephen Hopkins reported that working with Hackman was a bit intimidating because he (Hopkins) was such a fan. He was such a great actor because he was also a great filmmaker and made it look really easy. Thomas Jane advised that he when he was offered the film, he jumped at the chance because Hackman (and Freeman) were masters of their craft. They made it look so easy at first glance, but they were the hardest working actors he had yet to come across. To get to work in the same room with them and actually trade a few punches was priceless. Jane reported that Hackman was a very instinctual actor, working from his gut, with a sense of logic.

Hackman was interviewed on the set of the film by *Venice* magazine's Alex Simon. Hackman had no favorite film of those he had done. When he thought back, he thought more about the people that he had worked with and the group that he was with. Many times the film wasn't successful, but Hackman had a great time on it because the acting was so good. He advised struggling artists to concentrate and persevere, and to try to work at your craft as much as possible. It was not always easy, but even a workshop or Off Off Broadway play gave you experience and poise. Concentration was key, even when there was so much distraction when you made a film. You had to keep yourself in a place so that when he was called upon to perform, you were ready to go.

The New York Times reported on March 15, 1999, that a novel by Hackman would be published later in the year by Newmarket Press. He had spent the last three years working with Dan Lenihan on *Black Star Rising,* about pirates and shipwrecks of the early 1800s and the requisite wood-splintering storm. They had divided up the writing so the actor worked from the beginning and Lenihan worked from the end. By the time it was published (September 30, 1999), it had been retitled *Wake of the Perdido Star,* subtitled *A novel of shipwrecks, pirates and the sea.* Hackman and Lenihan discussed their novel on the November 3, 1999, episode of the talk show *The Charlie Rose Show.* The pair had been neighbors for more than ten years and Hackman said the collaboration came about when they were sitting in a restaurant having coffee, talking about what kind of things they liked to read. They decided they would like to write a novel they would both like to read. Lenihan reported the idea was Hackman's, and that Hackman went home that night and started writing an audition chapter. After two weeks he had ten pages which he gave to Lenihan, who felt it would work; the audition chapter remained in the book. They exchanged ideas when they met once or twice a week and critiqued each other's chapters, and talked about the arc of the story. The novel had to be about the sea because it was something that Hackman was fascinated by and Lenihan's expertise since he was one of the world's leading underwater archaeologists. The actor had also spent time sailing and was familiar with motorboats. The pair was intrigued by the literature of the sea, like Jack London and Melville and Mark Twain. They had met when he and his wife were looking to become certified divers. Lenihan took them on a dive off Key West or Fort Jefferson to look at a ship in a wreckage field. Lenihan had also filmed them diving in Truk Lagoon in the South Pacific, where Hackman had touched downed Japanese Zero planes. They settled on the novel being set from the 18th to the 19th century with the main character being Jack O'Reilly, who moved with his family from Connecticut to Cuba, on the ship that went down. The pair had also talked about doing another novel with the same characters.

Hackman spoke about living in Sante Fe, saying the main reason he ended up there was for his painting and drawing. The actor liked to do landscapes and the colors and the light were beautiful, though he had been trying to move from representational to abstract. He described himself as self-educated in art, not wanting to bother anybody with trying to teach him to do it, though he had been painting since his early days in New York in 1950 when he went to the Art Students League. The actor always drew and he had a talent for it but didn't feel that he could keep with it for the rest of his life. Even his feeling about painting changed, as once it didn't have enough energy for him, so he tried other hobbies like flying and racing cars. Hackman didn't give up racing so much as it gave up him because he couldn't put a season together since he was then working constantly and couldn't drop everything to learn the craft properly. Hackman hadn't flown for a couple of years, though he still had the planes, and was now back to being excited about his painting.

The actor felt he had had a great life, being really privileged to have been given the opportunity to do some of the things that he had done. He wished that in the late '70s and early '80s he had moved back to New York so he could have kept more in touch with the theater. Hackman was open to going back now and do something like *Death of a Salesman* if it was the right project, depending on what he was offered. It wasn't too late but he admitted that he liked to be comfortable, having lived the soft life for so long. The actor equated camping out in New York as cockroach time. On the same night, Hackman was celebrated at a book party at Elaine's in Manhattan.

Hackman's next film was the sports comedy *The Replacements*, shot from August 9 to November 3, 1999, on location in Maryland and Virginia. The screenplay was by Vince McKewin and the director was Howard Deutch. The story centered on the 1987 professional football players' strike where replacements were brought in for the Washington Sentinels to try to make the playoffs. Hackman played Jimmy McGinty, the new coach of the team, who insists on having retired player and boat scraper Shane Falco (Keanu Reeves) as the quarterback. The actor, second-billed (after Reeves), wears a mustache and has gray hair. The only unusual part of his wardrobe by Jill Ohanneson is the black-banded straw hat he wears during the games. Hackman gets to imitate the Welsh accent of player Nigel Gruff (Rhys Ifans) and throw a ball during practice. The film offered nothing challenging in terms of acting, but Hackman supplies some sharp looks of anger and director Deutch gives him a long closeup in reaction to the team's victory in the climactic game.

The film premiered on August 7, 2000, and opened on August 11 with the taglines "Pain heals, Chicks dig scars…. Glory lasts forever," "Pros on strike. Everyday guys get to play," "Throw the ball. Catch the girl. Keep it simple" and "Hit hard." Joe Leydon in *Variety* wrote that you gained additional respect for Hackman's ability to infuse a paper-thin role with gravitas and authority. Elvis Mitchell in *The New York Times* said that the actor seemed to be repeating lines he used in *Hoosiers* and old United Airlines commercials.

Hackman commented that he liked football and he loved the idea of playing a coach. He also liked stories where there was a little guy overcoming something, and there was enough of that in this story to make it fascinating. Deutch reported that a scene was cut: Jimmy telling player Clifford Franklin (Orlando Jones) to never let go of the ball off the field because he was always dropping it.

Deutch had an amazing experience with the actor. Hackman was his favorite guy in the world and working with him was like having King Arthur sprinkle fairy dust on the set. He was helpful to everybody and everyone's work was elevated when they worked with him. Deutch felt Hackman was a great actor, who was equally good at daring comedy and drama. He demanded as much from everybody else as the actor gave of himself, and since Hackman knew how to do everyone else's job, he would let Deutch know if someone wasn't doing theirs. His availability and generosity to Keanu Reeves proved that the more experienced you were, the more flexible and open you were. Deutch reported that the actor directed the long scene of the team's first practice on the field, since Hackman was unhappy with what he proposed. Hackman had hung around real coaches and picked up their lingo, attitude and energy and used this to improvise lines. A lot of his scenes had him simply watching the games and reacting; Deutch said that Hackman made that convincing and believable in the moment, which was hard to do.

Keanu Reeves commented that he was a fantastic actor. Hackman was very cool to everyone and that acting with him made one better. His craft, charm and technique made him a consummate actor.

Hackman had been considered to replace Marlon Brando as William Randolph Hearst in the biographical drama *RKO 281* when it was planned as a theatrical film. He lost interest when the project was scaled down to be a made-for-TV movie and the part was taken by James Cromwell. The actor next did a cameo in the comic crime adventure *The Mexican*. This was shot from April 17 to July 2000 in Mexico, Nevada and Los Angeles. In the J.H. Wyman screenplay, Jerry Welbach (Brad Pitt) is sent from Los Angeles to Mexico to retrieve a pistol called The Mexican for his boss Margolese (Hackman). Hackman is billed eighth in the end credits and only appears in one scene. He wears a mustache and speaks Spanish.

The film was released on March 2, 2001, with the tagline "Love with the safety off." The film was a box office success. Director Gore Verbinski reported that Hackman went to Mexico for two days to shoot his part, doing it as a favor though he (Verbinski) couldn't remember who for. The director understood that the actor never did cameos so they were very lucky to have him. Verbinski felt the part was like Sydney Greenstreet in the film noir mystery *The Maltese Falcon* (1941), and he needed someone of Hackman's caliber to keep the audience focused.

On April 28, 2000, Hackman and Daniel Lenihan were at a Chicago Borders book store to sign copies of *Wake of the Perdido Star*. One person had him sign a *French Connection* poster and another had him sign a chair. Hackman was wanted for the part of President Franklin Delano Roosevelt in the historical actioner *Pearl Harbor* (2001) but Jon Voight was cast instead. The actor turned down the part because he didn't want to offend his wife, who was born in Japan. Her mother was in Tokyo when the raids happened and the children were chased up into the hills. It was traumatic for them and they asked Hackman not to do the film.

His next was the crime-comedy-romance *Heartbreakers,* shot from April 24 to August 1, 2000, under the working title *Breakers* in Florida and California. The screenplay was by Robert Dunn, Paul Guay and Stephen Mazur. The con team of Max Conners (Sigourney Weaver) and her daughter Page (Jennifer Love Hewitt) seduce, marry and scam wealthy men. Hackman played William B. Tensy, a Palm Beach tobacco billionaire who becomes one of their victims. The actor wears his mustache, his hair is a comb-over, and his makeup includes a red nose and liver spots and dentures yellowed by smoking. His costumes include a particularly garish-colored golf outfit. The role allows Hackman to chain-smoke and to have a smoker's cough, repeated slapstick hits on the head from Max, tea spilled on him and a member massage from Page and a fall onto a statue (the penis is lodged in his mouth).

10. Extreme Measures

After William's maid Miss Madress is arrested for theft, the actor gets a funny line when he asks the police sergeant (Ken Magee), "If it's at all possible, could you slap her around a little?" Director David Mirkin supplies an extreme closeup of Hackman, as seen from Max's point of view through her door peephole. William's hacking cough is a funny running gag. Hackman's best scene is perhaps his attempted seduction of Max.

The film was released on March 23, 2001, with the taglines "Caution: Dangerous Curves Ahead," "They Will Love You for Richer. And Leave You for Poorer" and "This is not a simple work. This is a family business!" A.O. Scott in *The New York Times* wrote that Hackman was gleefully repulsive, and Roger Ebert said the actor performed in an astonishing combination of the gauche and the obnoxious. Peter Travers in *Rolling Stone* said that Hackman made the best argument against smoking that Hollywood had ever offered. Todd McCarthy in *Variety* said that the actor seized his role with gleeful self-deprecation. The film was a box office success. It was remade as the Indian *Bachke Rehna Re Baba* aka *Beware* (2005).

Hackman asked the prop department to get him herbal cigarettes. These did not generate the amount of smoke required so Hackman had to smoke real cigarettes. He said it was hard for him, but the actor would try to find ways to surprise and disgust Sigourney Weaver with the smoking, as when he kissed her while blowing smoke out (she had no idea this would happen). Hackman had a great deal of fun with the role because William was unattractive and did despicable things. He felt that director Mirkin was very good about adding a line or pulling one out of a scene to make it work better, and if he heard him laughing in the background of a take he knew they were on the right track. The actor said the interesting thing about comedy was that usually it was a better set, though you worked just as hard if not harder.

Mirkin reported that Hackman was excited to play William because he liked his nastiness and meanness. He said getting the actor was a dream because not only was he one of the world's best, he was also a brilliant comedian. Hackman was a great sport, willing to be ego-less in his appearance. What was inspiring was that after all the movies he had made, the actor was still excited to go to work and to experiment to make things better. Mirkin felt that Hackman and Weaver were terrific together, enhancing each other's performances. She had told the director that it was going to be hard not to be attracted to the actor because she had such a crush on him for such a long time, but this became easy to get over once she saw how creepy he was in the role.

When Hackman attended the Cannes Film Festival in May 2000 for *Under Suspicion*, he was asked how he managed to avoid attending the festival until now. He grinned and said: "Just lucky, I guess. I'm not sure what it does, but ..." and shrugged. The actor reported that the time when he wanted to direct had passed as he realized he didn't have the patience, and admitted to his reputation for being a curmudgeon on the set. Hackman's Cannes appearance allowed him to be featured in the documentary short *Cannes: Through the Eyes of the Hunter* (2001). Directed by Nicolas Neuhold, this followed Markus, an autograph collector who spends ten days at the festival trying to get the signatures of the famous. Hackman is seen three times: arriving for the press conference for his film, exiting the press room where he signs for Markus, and later signing more autographs. The actor is interviewed and asked if, despite all the tough characters he plays, is he really a softie? He replies, "It's not in me," and denies "needing a nap" as suggested by the interviewer. The film's narrator comments that Hackman "is a great star to get an autograph from, but he's no Elizabeth Taylor" (Taylor is Markus' number one target).

Hackman commented on July 18, 2000, to WENN about his novel by saying he was now a "respected man of letters." He was unlikely to take up an offer of writing a sequel and giving up acting for good. The idea of writing the novel sounded like a recipe for losing a friend, but he and his co-author got along great, though maybe it would have been a better book if they had fought more.

Hackman was interviewed by Michael Ellison for a July 21, 2000, article in *The Guardian*. He spoke about reading the reviews for his novel, which is something he never did for his films. One had described it as immature and another as really good for young adults, which the actor saw as the kiss of death. Hackman and Lenihan had wanted to do a second book but discovered that their new idea had been used in a recent book. Hackman wasn't sure how his work in theater and the movies informed his writing but he agreed that he might have turned to the printed word as a way of validating himself. The actor had always admired writers and their control, and saw no reason why he should be restricted to one means of expression.

11

Heist

The action crime drama *Heist* was shot from August 2000 in New Hampshire and Quebec, Canada. Written and directed by David Mamet, it centered on Joe Moore (Hackman), a career jewel thief who finds himself at odds with his longtime partner Bergman (Danny DeVito). Hackman, top-billed, is clean-shaven and uses a mustache and glasses as disguises. He uses guns, a taser, drives a car and boat, slaps Jimmy Silk (Sam Rockwell), hits the customs officer (Ted Whittal) and punches Bergman; but he is also hit by Jimmy, punched by Bergman's henchmen and shot in the leg. When Jimmy aims a gun at him, he tells Fran (Rebecca Pidgeon), "He isn't gonna shoot me? Then he hadn't oughta point a gun at me. It's insincere." The film doesn't offer him any great acting challenges. Director Mamet gives him a long closeup at the film's end. The actor's stunt doubles are Norman Howell and Jerome Tibeghien and his stand-in is Greg Goossen, who also plays Officer #1.

The film premiered on September 10, 2001, at the Toronto International Film Festival, which Hackman attended, and it opened in the U.S. on November 9, 2001, with the taglines "Love makes the world go 'round. Love of Gold" and "It isn't love that makes the world go round." A.O. Scott in *The New York Times* wrote that Hackman worked by sleight of eye, voice, face and soul. Roger Ebert said that the actor inhabited his characters so easily that he distracted from the plot twists by the simple sincerity with which he confronted them. David Rooney in *Variety* said that Hackman brought the material considerable authority with a subdued, wily turn. The film was not a box office success.

Hackman commented that he had always liked Mamet's writing, how he could create a character like Joe where you never quite knew who he was, with a nice switch at the end. That kind of writing was something really very special. When interviewed for *The New York Times* (December 16, 2001), Hackman commented that doing the film wasn't a lot of fun, and emotionally the toughest shoot he had had in quite a while. He said there was a lot of repetition in the lines and many times they were misdirected or purposely obtuse, which was difficult for him to fill up both emotionally and intellectually. Another source claimed that the actor found the film difficult because he was so much older than everyone involved. He kept much to himself, and in the end managed to draw on that feeling of being an outsider in the group for his portrayal.

Hackman spoke to WENN on August 9, 2000, about how his declining health had made him give up hobbies like car racing. He still painted, which had always been a real love of his, but he didn't like showing his work.

Hackman's next film *The Royal Tenenbaums* (2001) shot from February 26 to May 2001 in New York and New Jersey. It was directed by Wes Anderson and written by Owen Wilson and Anderson. Royal Tenenbaum (Hackman) is a disbarred New York litigator, ex-convict and estranged patriarch who loses his home and learns that his ex-wife Etheline (Anjelica Huston), an archaeologist and bridge class teacher, plans to re-marry after 20 years. Hackman sports his mustache and his hair is gray, combed back off his forehead and long at the back. In early scenes, Royal has brown hair not combed back. The costumes by Karen Patch include pink pajamas and a swimming outfit with a cap. The role allows Hackman to fire a BB gun, get a facial and massage, be hit by Etheline, ride a go-kart, ride on a garbage truck, be stabbed by Pagoda (Kumar Pallana) and have a death scene. The actor is funny, and in his best scene argues with Etheline's business manager (Danny Glover). The actor's stand-in Greg Goossen also plays Gypsy Cab Driver.

Hackman in *Heist* (2001).

The film premiered at the New York Film Festival on October 5, 2001, and premiered in Hollywood at the El Capitan Theater on December 6, with Hackman in attendance. After a limited release starting December 14, the film received a wide release on January 4, 2002, with the taglines "Family Isn't a Word…It's a Sentence" and "You Are Invited to a Remarkable Family Gathering." Peter Travers in *Rolling Stone* wrote that the film was a triumph for Hackman. Travers added that the complex comic gravity of his performance proved that he could do no wrong as an actor.

11. Heist

Poster for *The Royal Tenenbaums* (2001).

Todd McCarthy in *Variety* wrote that Hackman was wonderful and his boisterous presence and refusal to be defeated gave the picture extra energy. A.O. Scott (*The New York Times*) said that the actor's quick precision and deep seriousness nearly rescued the movie from its own whimsy. A box office success, the film was Oscar-nominated for Best Original Screenplay.

Hackman reported that a few years prior, Anderson called his agent and asked to meet him. They had lunch in a New York hotel where the director said he had an idea for a film that he wanted him to be in. Hackman asked Anderson not to do that because he did not particularly like scripts that had been written for him to play someone's idea of himself, preferring to invent things about a character. They had a nice chat and the director went ahead and wrote the script for Hackman anyway. Anderson said the actor didn't want to work 60 days on a movie, and the money was not good. Hackman also hesitated because of a lack of understanding of or association to Royal. (Warren Beatty, Michael Caine and Gene Wilder were then considered.) The actor was also concerned about his family's comfort over him playing such a role and sought their approval, according to Jennifer Warner's book *The Fantastic Mr. Anderson: A Biography of Wes Anderson*. Hackman didn't think he was as bad as the selfish character, but there were times that he had been fairly insensitive with his children and with his ex-wife—so maybe he was more right for it than he realized.

On set, Hackman was not easy to be around. Anderson said Hackman called him a "cunt." Bill Murray (who played neurologist Raleigh St. Clair) would come to the set on his days off to help protect the director, with whom he had previously worked. Murray's presence was a calming one because Hackman had taken a real liking to him, perhaps because Murray had once sublet the actor's old New York apartment. Anjelica Huston reported that she was scared of Hackman and also wanted to protect Anderson. She said he once told the director, "Pull up his pants and act like a man."

Hackman said there was great love on the set, but at the same time he was very conflicted because people were much younger than he was, and the actor felt left out or ignored. He actually knew the latter wasn't true but he used it anyway. Hackman defended his behavior, saying the only valid way he could act was to be faithful and honest for his own sense of performance and he would not change because of the way a director chose to shoot his film or the design of his wardrobe.

Anderson said the actor was great and very exciting to work with but he was separate from everyone else and scary. Anderson almost felt he forced Hackman to do it, wearing down his resistance over a period of a year and a half. Hackman told the director, about two-thirds of the way through filming, that the film would end his career. Anderson said that despite the challenging behavior, he still remembered the experience fondly.

11. Heist

Anjelica Huston reported that the scene where Etheline hits Royal was shot on the first day and was a bit daunting. The script said she was to hit him across the face and in rehearsal she merely hit Hackman lightly on the lapel. When filming, Huston decided to inject some improvisation, because he knew what was coming. In the take, she hit Hackman on the face, leaving a red imprint on his cheek. He was the perfect gentleman about it, though Huston heard him mutter something under his breath.

Gwyneth Paltrow, who played Margot Tenenbaum, commented that she loved working with Hackman. He was a bear of a guy, but she also found something very sweet and sad in there. Paltrow thought the actor was one of the greatest, and to be in his presence and watch him do his thing made it okay that he was in "a bad fucking mood."

Hackman narrated the made-for-TV war documentary *Heroes of Iwo Jima* (2001) which told the story behind the most famous war photograph ever taken. The film was written by Lauren Lexton and Arnold Shapiro and directed by Lexton. On the October 14, 2001, *Inside the Actors Studio*, Hackman talked about what he didn't want in a director, and said that what good directors did was be supportive and encouraging without making it feel like direction. The actor liked to rehearse on the set until he felt very comfortable, and then do few takes. After take three, it was pretty much set, and he had a little guy on his shoulder always with him, saying good or not so good. Hackman never watched dailies, and with the exception of a couple of moments he had done in films, the actor had never really enjoyed watching himself or told himself that he was okay. Hackman said it was important for male actors to show a feminine, sensitive side in a role, as Brando and James Dean and Laird Cregar and Montgomery Clift did; you could do it and still be a man. He had auditioned for the Actors Studio a number of times and was turned down. Ellen Burstyn finally got Hackman in.

The actor talked about *Wake of the Perdido Star*, *The Royal Tenenbaums* and *Heist*. Asked what challenges lay ahead for him, Hackman just wanted to be continued to be offered things that were interesting and somewhat different. His favorite word was action, and least favorite was cut. The sound or noise Hackman loved was the sound of his wife's voice and what he hated was cell phones. Hackman's favorite curse word was motherfucker. The profession other than his he would have liked to have done was to be a successful painter, and the opposite was in the corporate world. If Heaven exists, Hackman would like God to say to him at the Pearly Gates: "Good job" though he thought God would more likely say "comme ci, comme ça."

To create a new film role, Hackman liked to break the script down into several acts, to see where the character's arc fell. He asked himself the simple things, like where he had been, where was he going, and what did he want? The most important thing was how the actor was like and unlike the character. Hackman used effective memory and relaxation and if you did that work and were capable of doing the lines and relating to people all at the same time, something would happen. You may not get the emotional thing you wanted, you may break out into laughter, but something would happen. When the actor first went to California people knew he was from New York, and one time a lighting man asked if Hackman was one of those "Stanislavs," like he was a bug or something. You had to be tough to say that is the way you worked, and if that resulted in losing a job, then you lost a job. But it paid off if you stayed with what you knew because you would have a good time.

The action thriller *Behind Enemy Lines* was shot from October 16, 2000, to January 2001 in Slovakia. The screenplay was by David Veloz and Zak Penn with uncredited work by John Gatens, based on a story by James Thomas and John Thomas. Owen Wilson starred as Chris "Longhorn" Burnett, a Naval lieutenant from the USS *Carl Vinson* whose F-18 plane was shot down in 1995 in Southern Bosnia while flying reconnaissance. Hackman played Admiral Leslie Reigart, the Commander of Adriatic Battle Group. His best scene is when he objects to the orders of Commander of NATO Naval Command Juan-Miguel Piquet (Joaquim De Almeida).

The film premiered in San Diego on November 17, 2001, and went into wide release on November 30 with the taglines "In War There Are Some Lines You Should Never Cross," "Prepare to cross the line," "Mission: to evade and survive" and "His only weapon is his will to survive." Stephen Holden in *The New York Times* wrote that Hackman infused his rather stock character with a complex personal psychology. Robert Koehler in *Variety* said that the actor didn't generate his usual fire for the role that, if written differently, could have been a great one for him. The successful film spawned three direct-to-video sequels, *Behind Enemy Lines II: Axis of Evil* (2006), *Behind Enemy Lines: Colombia* (2009) and *SEAL Team 8: Behind Enemy Lines* (2014), but Reigart was not in them. Hackman was featured in one deleted scene, where Admiral Donnelly (Geoff Pierson) tells Reigart that he is relieved of his duties.

Wilson called Hackman one of those actors who was never less than really good, and the type he dreamed about becoming. When Wilson thought about *Hoosiers*, *Crimson Tide*, *The French Connection* and *Bonnie and Clyde*, he saw those were such different characters; but unlike Al Pacino and Robert DeNiro, Hackman didn't change his appearance with big makeup jobs or rely on different accents.

Hackman said that he didn't go out of his way to play military roles, they chose him. The actor had done a few of them and supposed he looked like one of those guys, which was funny because Hackman had been a bad Marine. The actor believed that he could play anything, though knew every actor said that, but guessed there were certain parts that people didn't think of him for. Hackman tried not to do things he had already done but there were only so many stories out there.

11. Heist

Director John Moore said that the actor was very tough and solid and knew what he was going to do so Moore had to know what to do with him. It was a real pleasure, especially for a first-time director, to get someone of Hackman's magnitude to show him how to do it. His approach was to use the script and if changes were needed, rather than change words he would do it with body language or subtlety. Hackman came up with the idea that Reigart smoked so he would have a weakness.

John Davis had also produced *The Firm*, *The Chamber* and *Heartbreakers* and reported that the actor was the first to be cast with the studio happy with the weight and bearing he would bring to the part. Hackman's name helped green-light the film, especially since he had a foreign audience. Davis got him to accept director Moore and Wilson, whom the actor had also seen in the comic action adventure *Shanghai Noon* (2000), and approved the script changes Wilson made for his character. Davis delayed having the actor and Moore meet, in case Hackman didn't like him. He went away to do another film and when the actor returned it was time to go to Europe for the location shooting. He finally met Moore the day before his first day of shooting. Co-executive Producer Wyck Godfrey reported that Hackman observed the director shooting the mine sequence with explosions going off behind Wilson, and he was impressed with how Moore handled the sequence. The director approached the actor and they spoke for a few minutes, and then Hackman told him to "Get back to work."

Hackman shot for five weeks and was brought back for a few days to shoot on the carrier ship. He had to be landed on a COD airplane that was catapulted off at 130 miles an hour in a couple of seconds, but he handled the stress of the incident. Davis reported that the actor got mad at the producers when they shifted around some lines in a scene, since he had worked hard to get his scenes down days before the shooting. Hackman would arrive on the set a few minutes before he was needed and didn't want to chat but just shoot the scene and then return to his trailer, which was Hackman's idea of being professional. One scene's location was moved to accommodate him. The location of the dialogue scene between Reigart and Piquet was moved from a hangar under the flight deck to the admiral's bridge (on top of the flight tower) because he found the hangar area too noisy.

On November 11, 2001, Hackman was in a chartered plane in Toronto getting ready to take off when the pilot said that there was a hang-up in New York. The 20-minute delay turned into three days. They taxied back to the terminal and saw the television news about the attacks on the Twin Towers. Hackman reacted the same way a lot of people did, initially thinking it was an accident when the first plane hit, and then knowing the second plane's hit was deliberate.

On October 30, 2001, Hackman was involved in a road rage incident in Hollywood. He and another man came to blows after their cars collided on the busy intersection of Sunset Boulevard and Crescent Heights in the West Hollywood area.

The actor admitted he was at fault and got out of his sedan to offer his apologies to the other driver, a 30-year-old man. One source claims that Hackman's car hit the Volvo station wagon when it crossed in front of him unexpectedly. He was waiting in the right lane of a busy junction when the Volvo in the left lane attempted to make a right turn in front of him and hit his car in the back. The drivers went to an island in front of a Virgin Records store, where Hackman tried to exchange insurance information. The other driver and his male passenger began shoving him. Witness Nathaniel Keefer said the Volvo driver was really close to Hackman's face and kept stepping toward him for several minutes but the actor kept his cool until something offensive was said. Another source claims that the man made an anti-gay epithet, and Hackman hit him four or five times. He said he snapped and took both men on because he felt threatened. They wrestled and rolled on the ground. Another witness reported that the Volvo driver pushed and shouted at Hackman, and the second man then leapt out of the car and kicked him in the groin and they wrestled. Hackman had no recollection of being hit in the groin, but he got a couple of good shots in, as one guy had him around the neck. Police arrived to break up the fight, though another source claims that the men were not fighting when police arrived. The men had bruised faces but were not willing to press charges and no one was arrested. Hackman commented that it was an infamous day for him. It was one of those things that happened to people, and the violence escalated because there were so many people around and no one wanted to back down. He forgot his age and it was embarrassing. His publicist Dick Guttman commented that Hackman thought it was funny. Guttman added that as an ex–Marine he could take care of himself, and though the actor was really a very gentle guy, anybody could be provoked and Hackman chose to stand up rather than get knocked down. The actor just hoped that the scene of the incident didn't end up on one of those Hollywood tours.

Hackman performances had volcanic undercurrents. He admitted to being sometimes difficult on set but spoke of his battles regretfully—of the estrangement the actor sometimes felt from his colleagues and the cost to his physical and mental health. Hackman claimed not to relish the chafing against directorial authority, but he was not about to suppress the instincts that had served him so brilliantly. What he mostly fought for was the time and space to relax—to get comfortable enough to revisit those wrenching injuries that drove him to become an actor in the first place.

Hackman planned to take a year off from films and had begun work on a second book with Daniel Lenihan, a less melodramatic yarn. He planned to do more diving and painting. The battles of the last few movies had left him winded. On January 2, 2002, WENN reported that Hackman didn't have a future movie job set up and he was trying desperately to slow down. The actor would wait and see how the three currently in release did and then look around.

11. Heist

He won the Best Actor in a Motion Picture Drama for *The Royal Tenenbaums* at the 59th Golden Globe Awards, held on January 20, 2002, at the Beverly Hilton Hotel, but did not attend to accept it. *The New York Times* reported that Hackman had missed his airplane connection in the Caribbean.

In the February 2002 issue of *Premiere* magazine, interviewee Hackman reported that living in New Mexico meant that he didn't see a lot of people in the business. He got along very well with actors but they were best taken in small doses. John Frankenheimer wanted him for the role of Lyndon Johnson in the biographical made-for TV drama *Path to War* (May 18, 2002). Michael Gambon was cast instead.

His next film was the thriller *Runaway Jury* (2002), shot from September 2002 to January 2003 in Louisiana and California. The screenplay was by Brian Koppelman, David Levien, Rick Cleveland and Matthew Chapman, based on the John Grisham novel. The story centered on Nick Easter (John Cusack), the co-manager of Game Trader and a juror in the New Orleans trial of Celeste Wood (Joanna Going) vs. Vicksburg Firearms over the wrongful death of her husband, stockbroker Jacob (an uncredited Dylan McDermott) two years prior. Second-billed Hackman played Rankin Fitch, the lead jury consultant for the defense. He has a mustache and a gray goatee and his clothes by Canali include a black fedora and long coat. The part allows him to walk in the mud and ride a trolley car. He is funny but also threatening towards Marlee (Rachel Weisz) when he meets her in person. Director Gary Fleder gives him some extreme closeups. His best scene is in the washroom with his old friend Dustin Hoffman, who plays prosecutor Wendall Rohr. It is exciting to see the two veteran actors together.

Hackman attended a press conference for the film on September 19, 2003, at the Wyndham Hotel in New Orleans. The film was released on October 9, 2003, with the tagline "Trials are too important to be decided by juries." Roger Ebert wrote that Hackman gave a consistent performance. The film was a box office success.

Sean Connery was originally cast as Finch when the film was going to be made in 1997. Hackman said to play a character that politically he didn't believe in was what made acting so fascinating. While he and Hoffman were old friends, Hoffman reported that they hadn't spoken much over the years. After Hoffman did a film, Hackman would telephone and say "You were a piece of shit," or "Very interesting. You did it again," or "That was a tough role. Not many actors could have pulled that off and you're not one of them."

For the washroom scene, the actors feared that two old guys talking would bore the hell out of audiences and they wanted a girl to walk through in a bikini saying she thought it was the ladies' room. Hackman agreed to rehearse, since the scene was not in the original script and was created when Gary Fleder learned that the actors were friends. They rehearsed for four to five hours the day before the shooting. After the master shot was done, the pair admitted they feared they wouldn't be able to get through the long scene again without blowing lines. Neither slept the night before. But doing their closer shots, they had a wonderful time and wished it could have gone on and on. Hackman said it was great fun to work with Hoffman because of the kind of actor he was, someone who would pick up on whatever he would say or do and give it back to him. It was like a little ping pong match, which some people could do and some could not. Hoffman also reported that when they got drunk at Hackman's request after the film was wrapped, Hackman told him he feared he was never going to work again. Hoffman now had the desire to do a whole film with him, but to date this has not occurred.

Fleder reported that the actor was so quiet and soft-spoken that it was easy to take an idea he had as a throwaway suggestion, but he learned everything Hackman said had meaning. He didn't want to play the part as rude or mean-spirited and was smart enough to know that when Fitch yelled it was a sign of his weakness and loss of control of his situation. Fleder believed that what made Hackman's performance great was his embracing Fitch's moment of loss in his face, attitude, behavior, and the way his collar choked him. He suggested having Fitch throw up outside the courthouse and the moment was filmed where the actor spilled a mouthful of soup. Fleder felt that it was so grotesque that it is upstaged Fitch's last scene in the bar with Nick and Marlee. For the washroom scene, Hoffman had asked that his close-ups be done first but then Fleder first shot Hackman, who was game that day. Fleder said shooting Hoffman second gave Hoffman the incentive to top Hackman's performance, since although they were friends they were also competitive as actors. Fleder felt the scene was a combination of Hackman's classical, very precise style and Hoffman's style of improvisation and spontaneity. It was like Thelonious Monk vs. Yo-Yo Ma.

John Cusack said that he was very excited to work with Hackman, who had always been a hero to him, and the experience was great fun. It seemed that Hackman came in with a very clear idea of what he wanted to do and he made it look absolutely effortless. Rachel Weisz said that it didn't get more exciting than working with him. He knew how to play villains in the most charming way imaginable and it was almost impossible to dislike Hackman even though his character was so evil and corrupt and nasty. Weisz tried to be tough opposite him but it was hard to out-tough the actor.

Hackman narrated the 2002 documentary *Colors of Courage: Sons of New Mexico, Prisoners of Japan*, directed by Scott Henry and Tony Martinez. It told the story of the ethnically diverse 200th and 515th Coast Artillery Regiments, who fought with great distinction in the Philippines, endured the Bataan Death March and became two of World War II's most decorated military units in.

On January 19, 2003, the 60th Annual Golden Globe Awards were held at the

11. Heist

Beverly Hilton Hotel. For his "outstanding contribution to the entertainment field," Hackman was presented the Cecil B. DeMille award by Michael Caine and Robin Williams. Looking tanned, Hackman commented that he never wanted to be anything but an actor, and quoted George C. Scott's appropriate line in *Patton*: "God help me, I love it." He added that being at the Palace Theatre in his little home town was his favorite time as a young boy. If Hackman had 40 cents he could ride the streetcar back and forth, get a bag of popcorn and see a double feature. The actor would sit in that movie house and the screen would light up and he would be transported to darkest Africa. Hackman would swing from the trees with Johnny Weissmuller, dive to the depths of the ocean with Ray Milland and John Wayne, ride the Santa Fe trail or walk side by side with his favourite, James Cagney. Hackman watched with fascination films like DeMille's *The Buccaneer* and *Union Pacific* as they unfolded before him. Just a couple of miles from where they were that evening, DeMille helped to make *The Squaw Man* in 1914 and that was the beginning of Hollywood feature films. Hackman was honored and proud to receive the award. He finished with a line he had always wanted to say, "Top of the world, ma. Top of the world" (a line from Cagney's *White Heat*, 1949).

Hackman was the narrator of writer-director Larry Kopald's documentary *Hidden City* (2003). It told the story of coral reefs and how essential they were regarding the health of our oceans and our planet. The actor was parodied in "Krazy Kripples," the March 26, 2003, episode of the animated TV series *South Park*. In the episode, written and directed by Trey Parker, he was voiced by Parker and shown to battle with Christopher Reeve (voiced by Matt Stone) over Reeve using fetus stem cells to enable him to walk again. Hackman is shown wearing a gray mustache and gray hair, a red high-necked sweater and dark pants recalling his look from *Get Shorty* and a porkpie hat which recalls *The French Connection*. He appears in three scenes and helps to entrap Reeve in a Phantom Zone like the one in *Superman*.

His next film was the romantic comedy *Welcome to Mooseport*, shot from April 30 to July 2003 in Los Angeles, in Ontario and at the Toronto Film Studios. The screenplay was by Tom Schulman based on a story by Doug Richardson, with uncredited lines by co-star Ray Romano. Monroe "Eagle" Cole (Hackman) is a retired U.S. president who returns to his vacation home in Mooseport, Maine, and runs for mayor against plumber Handy (Romano) of Handy Harrison's Hardware. The role lets him play golf, jog, get accidently punched by his security guard (Karl Pruner) and brawl with Handy, and his face is on a bust. Monroe gets a funny line when he tells vegetarian vet Sally (Maura Tierney) at diner, "I could eat a horse ... radish." He is funny, and his best scene is when Monroe asks Grace (Marcia Gay Harden) not to leave his employ, which includees him kissing her.

The film was released on February 20, 2004, with the taglines "May the best man lose" and "This town isn't small enough for the both of them." Roger Ebert wrote that Hackman could charm the chrome off a trailer hitch. Dave Kehr of *The New York Times* said that the actor filled the role of special guest star, floating above and apart from the rest of the cast, descending occasionally for a verbal wrestling bout or a bit of broad slapstick. Todd McCarthy in *Variety* wrote that Hackman lacked that extra spring in his step and undercurrent of maliciousness that marked his best performances. The film was not a box office success.

Hackman appeared in deleted scenes which included a dropped subplot battling with Irma (June Squibb), speaking in Norwegian for a television car commercial, doing variations on Monroe's fantasies of killing his ex-wife Charlotte (Christine Baranski), etc.

The actor replaced Dustin Hoffman, who bowed out several months before filming. It was a reunion for Hackman and Christine Baranski after they had appeared together in *The Birdcage*. His golf game was improved by pro Chi Chi Rodriguez, who has a cameo as himself. While making the film in Toronto, Hackman stayed out of public places following a SARS virus scare in April 2003.

Director Donald Petrie called Hackman brilliant and said he loved working with him. Petrie said Hackman was brave and could do anything, had the authority and charisma and command of the screen to play the president, and could get believably furious but be funny when doing it. Ray Romano said Hackman upped his (Romano's) game, and when the person you were working off was so *there* and so right and giving you so much, it was easy. Romano was intimidated by him but aside from being a great actor, Hackman made him feel at ease. He gave Romano a compliment early where he told him he liked what he had done, and that made Romano fully committed to the work. Romano observed how a little bit goes a long way on film, as when Hackman improvised a whistle in one scene which made it richer.

In his August 15, 2003, article about the friendship between the actor, Dustin Hoffman and Robert Duvall, Richard Meryman reported that Universal was developing a script to star them. On October 20, *The Hollywood Reporter* said that it was to be called *Bit Players*. The film was not made. *The New York Times* of March 4, 2004, reported that Hackman turned down the chance to return as the narrator of United Airlines TV commercials.

Hackman spoke about Dustin Hoffman in the March 8, 2004, episode of the BBC historical documentary television series *The Hollywood Greats*. Hackman was the narrator of the historical documentary *Imaginary Witness: Hollywood and the Holocaust* (2004). The history of Hollywood's handling of the Nazis and its depiction of the Holocaust, it premiered at the Tribeca Film Festival on May 6, 2004.

St. Martin's Press published Hackman and Daniel Lenihan's second novel *Justice for None* on June 1, 2004. Set in the small town of Vermilion, Illinois, on the brink of the Great Depression, it centered on Boyd Calvin, a troubled World War

11. Heist

I veteran on the run from the law, suspected of murdering his estranged wife and her lover. He joins up with another wrongly accused man, an African-American, and the two begin to face their shadowed pasts.

On the July 7, 2004, episode of *Larry King Live*, Hackman spoke about his dislike of doing interviews and watching his films. One film the actor said he would like to have done was the thriller *The China Syndrome* (1979), and his favorite was *Scarecrow*. He said he didn't consider himself a *star* like Warren Beatty, Robert Redford and Brad Pitt. Hackman would have liked to say that he chose based on the script, but that was not always the case since many times it was a need to work if the actor hadn't done so for a while, and he took things that might have been on the border. Ideally the choice was based on script, director, co-star and location. In the past, he had done things for the money but he would no longer do that. The actor said he was working on another novel, a Civil War yarn tentatively called *The Mississippi Story*. Hackman only feared passing away, which was normal for a person his age, and he wanted to make sure that his wife and family were taken care of.

In her book *Susan Sarandon: A True Maverick* (2004), Betty Jo Tucker wrote that the actress and Hackman might reteam in a film of the Richard Russo novel *Straight Men*, again with director Robert Benton. He would play a professor in the midst of a hilarious midlife crisis. To date, the film has not been made. *The* May 4, 2005, *New York Times* reported that Hackman provided the voiceover for commercials for the Lowe's Home Improvement retail chain. Almost five years later, the February 28, 2010, *Times* revealed that he had been replaced as Lowe's voiceover announcer.

The *Times* of May 9, 2006, wrote the actor was referenced in Kathy Griffin's new television comedy special *Strong Black Woman*. She made fun of gay men who wanted to claim only good-looking actors as gay and said, "Here's what you'll never hear from all the gays. 'Oh, girl, don't be naïve—don't tell me you don't know about Miss Gene Hackman.'"

Hackman narrated four episodes of the sports documentary TV series *America's Game: The Superbowl Champions*, broadcast on the NFL Network and CBS: the January 29, 2007, San Francisco 49ers Super Bowl XIX of 1984; the February 2, 2007, San Francisco 49ers Super Bowl XXIV of 1989; the March 2, 2007, Washington Redskins Super Bowl XXII of 1987; and the March 23, 2007, San Francisco 49ers Super Bowl XVI of 1981. He was a guest on "Big Breakfast," the March 10, 2007, episode of the Food Network's reality show *Diners, Drive-ins and Dives*. The show's host Guy Fieri visited Harry's Roadhouse, a small diner in the middle of Santa Fe, which the actor frequented.

12

Retirement

Hackman told WENN on April 18, 2008, that although he had never announced his retirement, the actor couldn't bring himself to return to Hollywood and play "grandfathers." He guessed you could call it retired. Hackman hadn't worked for four years and didn't miss the business. He missed the process of being on sets with actors when things got cooking but there was so much crapola in order to get there that it was just too painful. Hackman would have preferred to go back to the theater but that was not going to happen. He was pretty satisfied with his life and kept himself busy and his mind active, writing historical fiction novels with Daniel Lenihan. Hackman wrote every day for at least a couple of hours, exercised a little bit, and then "it was time for the old folks to go to bed."

His third book with Lenihan, *Escape from Andersonville: A Novel of the Civil War*, was released on May 13, 2008 by St. Martin's Press. Set in 1864, it told the story of Union officer Nathan Parker, who has been imprisoned at the nightmarish Andersonville prison camp in Georgia along with his soldiers. They hatch a daring plan to escape through a tunnel and make their way to Vicksburg, where he intends to alert his superiors to the imprisonment and push for military action.

Clint Eastwood commented on Hackman's decision to retire, telling WENN on June 25, 2008, that it was a sad thing. Eastwood knew the actor's agent and asked him if he could talk him into coming back, since Hackman was too good not to be performing.

The Hollywood Reporter of April 15, 2009, advised that Hackman would be inducted into the Actors Hall of Fame for career achievement in theater, film and TV. Criteria for nomination include peer recognition and awards, humanitarian contribution to the dramatic arts and education and a demonstrated advancement of the craft of acting. An induction ceremony and celebration was to take place that year in Los Angeles.

The New York Times of September 25, 2009, reported that the Fox Network animated comedy television show *The Cleveland Show* would reference Hackman in its September 27 premiere episode. The title character says to his son Cleveland

12. Retirement

Jr., "Gays are smart. Just look at how many lines Gene Hackman has been able to memorize over the years."

It was reported in April 2010 that director Tony Scott wanted Hackman for the crime drama *Potsdamer Platz* but he was not interested. To date the film has not been made. Hackman was also considered for a part in *Last Vegas*, writer Dan Fogelman's tale of four Baby Boomer childhood friends who reunite decades later to witness the marriage of lifelong bachelor Billy (Jack Nicholson). The 2013 comedy was made by director Jon Turtletaub but neither Hackman nor Nicholson was in the cast.

On August 11, 2010, Hackman spoke out on behalf of 200 chimpanzees. In a letter written to Dr. Collins, head of the federal agency that controlled the fate of the creatures, he said they had been living peacefully in New Mexico for a decade, after spending many years being used in experiments. But if the government's plan moved forward, they would be sent to a facility for use in painful and invasive experiments. Many of these chimpanzees were more than 30 years old, and some would not survive being relocated. Hackman concluded, "These astonishingly intelligent animals had given their lives to research and should be retired."

On September 2010, it was reported that he was to have his first solo novel published by Pocket Books, an imprint of Simon & Schuster. *Jubal's Bounty*, a Western set in late 19th century New Mexico, followed a brave young hero who was forced to take the law into his own hands after the murder of his family. Hackman said the Western territory's rich history inspired him to write the tale of proper justice. He had tried to keep the story fresh and not copy from what had been seen in movies, but inevitably that happened because those scenes were so indelibly written in one's mind. *Jubal's Bounty* was released as *Payback at Morning Peak* on June 7, 2011. The back cover said that Hackman lived in Santa Fe, New Mexico, with his wife and two German shepherds.

The actor was a guest on the December 7, 2010, episode of the Canadian documentary television series *The Role That Changed My Life*. In "I Was an Underdog," it was claimed that he had turned his career around playing a small town Basketball coach in *Hoosiers*. The episode was written and directed by Jason Lewis.

Hackman's stand-in, Greg Goossen, died of a heart attack on February 26, 2011, at the age of 65. In the *New York Times* obituary of March 4, it was stated that Hackman insisted in his contracts that Goossen be his stand-in and bodyguard, and play a minor part in his later films.

Interviewed in the June 1, 2011, *GQ*, Hackman said that he wanted to be remembered as a decent actor who tried to portray what was given to him in an honest fashion. He summed up his life with the phrase "He tried."

Interviewed in the July 13, 2011, issue of *Men's Journal*, the actor said that what he wanted to do before he died was to be a better writer. On October 11, 2011, Colliderwww reported that Hackman was considered for the role of an aging alcoholic father who decides to take a road trip from Montana to Nebraska to collect what he believes to be a million dollar Publisher's Clearing House prize in the comic adventure *Nebraska* for director Alexander Payne. Bruce Dern was cast and earned a Best Actor Academy Award nomination.

The actor was hit by a car around 3 p.m. on January 13, 2012, while he was riding his Trek mountain bike without a helmet in Isla Mirada outside of Miami. A 60-year-old woman in a 2007 Toyota Tundra bumped him from behind. Hackman was airlifted to the Ryder Trauma Center in Florida as he had a large gash on his forehead and injuries to his body. The Florida Highway Patrol conducted an investigation into the cause of the crash. The actor was released from the hospital later that day and insisted he was fine, having just bumps and bruises. He took the mangled bike to the Ley Largo Bike Tours and Adventures shop days after the accident. Its back tire was almost completely folded in half from the impact, and though he asked for the damaged parts to be repaired, the actor also wanted to keep the broken pieces as a memento. On January 23, TMZ released the 911 call made at 2:56 p.m. for the accident. The male caller reported that Hackman was unconscious and had multiple bleeding wounds, but he had a pulse and shallow breathing. The driver of the car was still on the scene. During the call, Hackman regained consciousness and tried to move, though he was told to stay still as paramedics were on the way. An ambulance was heard arriving, and police sources reported that the driver cooperated with authorities.

It was rumored that Hackman would return to films in director Martin Scorsese's biographical crime comedy *The Wolf of Wall Street* (2013). The Terence Winter script called for the film's opening to be voiced by Hackman, but Edward Herrmann was used instead. On October 30, 2012, it was reported that he had pimp-slapped a 63-year-old homeless man named Bruce Becker who physically threatened him and his wife when they were leaving a Santa Fe restaurant in the afternoon. Becker had allegedly approached them in the past and they had given him food and money. This time the couple tried to avoid him and he was said to have approached in a threatening manner, calling Betsy a "cunt" which made Hackman slap Becker across the face. He did so being afraid that they were going to be attacked. Becker called the police, who interviewed Hackman and his wife on the scene and determined the slap was in self-defense. No charges were filed by either side.

He was referenced in the Broadway solo play *I'll Eat You Last: A Chat With Sue Mengers* by John Logan. Running at the Booth Theatre from April 24 to June 30, 2013, it centered on Mengers (Bette Midler) in the living room of her Beverly Hills home in 1981, and among her anecdotes were her efforts to get Hackman cast in *The French Connection* and *All Night Long* and his leaving her agency.

Hackman spoke about Clint Eastwood in writer-director Richard Schickel's documentary *Eastwood Directs: The Untold Story*, which premiered at the Tribeca Film Festival on April 27, 2013. Hackman said that of all the people he had ever met in the business, Eastwood was the closest to being both a creative director and a human being.

Hackman's second solo novel, *Pursuit*, published by Pocket Books on November 26, 2013, told the story of Juliette Worth, a police officer wrongly demoted after a hostage situation gone wrong. She is reassigned to investigating cold-case disappearances, a situation that turns sinister when her own daughter goes missing. The thriller had the front cover tagline "Some cops do what's expected. She does what's right—and puts everything on the line."

In publicist Dick Guttman's memoir *Starflacker: Inside the Golden Age of Hollywood*, self-published in 2015, he dedicated a chapter to his client Hackman, "The Man Who Walked Away." Anecdotes included how Hackman was the prisoner of a civilian on a flight to Buffalo for the premiere of *Superman II*, his practical joke on critic Gene Siskel, the script *Snaproll*, set against the Mojave Air Races, that they wrote together but was never filmed, and his aversion to doing publicity.

In November 2015, it was rumored that Hackman would be in the sequel to the romantic actioner *Top Gun* (1986). This sequel was not made. He narrated the documentary *The Unknown Flag Raiser of Iwo Jima*, broadcast on the Smithsonian television channel on July 3, 2016. He was also the narrator for the documentary short *We, the Marines*, released on July 21, 2017. In addition the actor's name is attached to a biographical documentary on Ted Kotcheff that is still in development. On January 27, 2018, it was reported that Hackman purchased a Trek Dual Sport+ e-bike at The Broken Spoke bike shop in Santa Fe, to mainly ride on bike paths for exercise. A photograph of the actor in front of the shop appeared on the Bicycling.com website.

Hackman is 88 at the time of this writing. According to the Turner Classic Movies website, when Hackman is in New York he teaches at the New Actors Workshop, a two-year professional actor training program.

While we may never see him act again, he has left a sizable body of work that can continue to be appreciated.

Appendix

Stage

Performance dates reflect the actor's participation, not the show's run.

The Curious Miss Caroway (1956) Pasadena Playhouse of Theater Arts.
A View from the Bridge (1957) Bellport Long Island summer stock. Crew: sets, props, lighting. Part: Marco.
Chaparral (September 10–20, 1958) Sheridan Square Playhouse, New York. Part: Dan Steel.
The Saintliness of Margery Kempe (February 2, 1959–?) York Playhouse, New York. Part: John Kempe.
Children from Their Games (April 11–14, 1963) Morosco Theater, Broadway. Part: Charles Widgin Rochambeau.
A Rainy Day in Newark (October 22–26, 1963) Belasco Theater, Broadway. Part: Sidney Rice.
Barefoot in the Park (19??) Biltmore Theatre, Broadway.
Come to the Place of Sin (December 10, 1963) Theatre de Lys, Off Broadway.
Any Wednesday (February 18, 1964–October 28, 1964) Music Box, Broadway. Part: Cass Henderson.
Poor Richard (December 2, 1964–March 13, 1965) Helen Hayes Theatre, Broadway. Part: Sydney Carroll.
Fragments (August 1966) Berkshire Theater Festival Stockbridge, Massachusetts.
The Natural Look (March 11, 1967) The Longacre, Broadway. Part: Dr. Barney Harris.
Fragments (October 2–22, 1967) Cherry Lane Theater Off Broadway. Parts: Zach, Baxter.
Death and the Maiden (March 17–August 2, 1992) Brooks Atkinson Theatre, Broadway. Part: Dr. Roberto Miranda.

Films

Mad Dog Coll (1961). Part: Policeman.
Lilith (1964). Part: Norman.
Hawaii (1966). Part: John Whipple.
Bonnie and Clyde (1966). Part: Buck Barrow.
Community Shelter Planning (1967). Part: Donald Ross.
First to Flight (1967). Part: Sgt. Tweed.
A Covenant with Death (1967). Part: Harmsworth.
Banning (1967). Part: Tommy Del Gaddo.
The Split (1968). Part: Detective Lt. Walter Brill.
The Gypsy Moths (1969). Part: Joe Browdy.
Marooned (1969). Part: Buzz Lloyd.
Riot (1969). Part: "Red" Fraker.
Downhill Racer (1969). Part: Claire.
I Never Sang for My Father (1970). Part: Gene Garrison.
Doctors' Wives (1971). Part: Dr. Dave Randolph.
The Hunting Party (1971). Part: Brandt Ruger.
Cisco Pike (1972). Leo Holland.
The French Connection (1971). Part: Jimmy "Popeye" Doyle.
Prime Cut (1972). Part: Mary Ann.
Scarecrow (1973). Part: Max.
The Conversation (1974). Part: Harry Caul.
Zandy's Bride (1974). Part: Zandy Allan.
Night Moves (1975). Part: Harry Moseby.
Young Frankenstein (1974). Blindman.
Bite the Bullet (1975). Part: Sam Clayton.
French Connection II (1975). Part: "Popeye" Doyle.

Lucky Lady (1975). Part: Kibby.
The Domino Principle (1976). Part: Roy Tucker.
A Bridge Too Far (1977). Part: Major General Stanislaw Sosabowski.
March or Die (1977). Part: Major William Sherman Foster.
America at the Movies (1976). Part: Himself.
Superman aka *Superman: The Movie* (1978). Part: Lex Luthor.
Superman II (1980). Part: Lex Luthor.
Formula 1—Febbre della velocità aka *Speed Fever* (1978). Part: Himself.
A Look at Liv (1979). Part: Himself.
Reds (1981). Part: Pete Van Wherry.
All Night Long (1981). Part: George Dupler.
Eureka (1983). Part: Jack McCann.
Under Fire (1983). Alex Grazier.
Two of a Kind (1983). Part: Voice of God.
Misunderstood (1984). Part: Ned Rawley.
Uncommon Valor (1983). Part: Col. Jason Rhodes.
Twice in a Lifetime (1985). Part: Harry MacKenzie.
Target (1985). Part: Walter Lloyd.
Power (1986). Part: Wilfred Buckley.
Hoosiers (1986). Part: Norman Dale.
No Way Out (1987). Part: Tom Farrell.
Superman IV: The Quest for Peace (1987). Part: Lex Luthor.
Split Decisions (1988). Dan.
Bat*21 (1988). Lt. Col. Iceal Hambleton.
Full Moon in Blue Water (1988). Part: Floyd.
Another Woman (1988). Part: Larry Lewis.
Mississippi Burning (1988). Part: Rupert Anderson.
Loose Cannons (1990). Part: MacArthur Stern.
The Package (1989). Part: Johnny Gallagher
Narrow Margin (1989). Part: Robert Caulfield.
Postcards from the Edge (1990). Part: Lowell.
Class Action (1990). Part: Jedediah Tucker Ward.
Island of Hope, Island of Tears (1989). Part: Narrator.
Company Business (1991). Part: Sam Boyd.
Unforgiven (1992). Part: Little Bill Daggett.
Earth and the American Dream (1992). Part: Reader.
The Firm (1993). Part: Avery Tolar.
Geronimo: An American Legend (1993). Part: Brig. Gen. George Crook.
Wyatt Earp (1994). Part: Nicholas Earp.
The Quick and the Dead (1995). Part: John Herod.
Crimson Tide (1994). Captain Ramsey.
Get Shorty (1995). Part: Harry Zimm.
The Birdcage (1996). Part: Senator Kevin Keeley.
The Chamber (1996). Part: Sam Cayhall.
Extreme Measures (1996). Part: Dr. Lawrence Myrick.
Absolute Power (1997). Part: President Richmond.
Twilight (1998). Part: Jack Ames.
Enemy of the State (1998). Part: Brill.
Antz (1998). Part: Gen. Mandible (voice).
Under Suspicion (2000). Crew: Executive Producer. Part: Henry Hearst.
The Replacements (2000). Part: Jimmy McGinty.
The Mexican (2001). Part: Margolese.
Heartbreakers (2001). Part: William B. Tensy.
Cannes: Through the Eyes of the Hunter (2001). Part: Himself.
Heist (2001). Part: Joe Moore.
The Royal Tenenbaums (2001). Part: Royal Tenenbaum.
Behind Enemy Lines (2001). Part: Reigart.
Runaway Jury (2003). Part: Rankin Fitch.
Colors of Courage: Sons of New Mexico, Prisoners of Japan (2002). Part: Narrator.
Hidden City (2003). Part: Narrator.
Welcome to Mooseport (2004). Part: Monroe.
Imaginary Witness: Hollywood and the Holocaust (2004). Part: Narrator.
I Knew It Was You: Rediscovering John Cazale (2009). Part: Himself
Eastwood Directs: The Untold Story (2013). Part: Himself.
We, the Marines (2017). Part: Narrator.

Featurettes/Video

The Sky Divers (1969)
Return of the Movie Movie (1972)
On the Road with: Scarecrow (1973)
The Day of the Director (1975)
The Making of Superman II (1982)
Ken Adam—Production Designer (1990)
Clint Eastwood on Westerns (1992)
Eastwood & Co.: Making Unforgiven (1992)
Wyatt Earp: Walk with a Legend (1994).
Wyatt Earp: It Happened That Way (1994)
The Making of Crimson Tide (1995)
All Access: On the Set of Crimson Tide (1995)
Eastwood on Eastwood (1997)
The Secret World of Antz (1998)
Backstory: Bonnie and Clyde (2000)
Poughkeepsie Shuffle: Tracing The French Connection (2000)

The Making of HeartBreakers (2001)
HeartBreakers *Laffs and Gaffs* (2001)
Wes Anderson with the Filmmakers (2001)
Behind the Scenes: Behind Enemy Lines (2001)
Cannes: Through the Eyes of the Hunter. (2001)
Taking Flight: The Development of Superman (2001).
Making the Connection: The French Connection *30th Anniversary Special* (2001)
Making the Connection: Untold Stories of The French Connection (2001)
Making Superman: *Filming the Legend* (2001)
Page to Screen: The Silence of the Lambs (2002)
All on Accounta Pullin' a Trigger (2002)
The Making of Runaway Jury (2003)
Off the Cuff: Hackman & Hoffman (2003)
Exploring the Scene: Hackman & Hoffman Together (2003)
The Ensemble: Acting (2003)
Hoosiers History: The Truth Behind the Legend (2004)
Get Shorty: *Wiseguys and Dolls* (2005)
Get Shorty: *Look at Me* (2005)
You Will Believe: The Cinematic Saga of Superman (2006)
All Access: The Showdown of Enemy of the State (2006)
The Making of Enemy of the State (2006)
Revolution! The Making of Bonnie and Clyde (2007)
Hackman on Doyle (2009)

Television

The United States Steel Hour: "The Little Tin God" (April 22, 1959). Part: Joey Carlton.
The United States Steel Hour: "The Pink Burro" (July 15, 1959). Part: Steve.
*Brenne*r: "The Bluff" (July 25, 1959). Part: Officer Richard Clayburn.
The United States Steel Hour: "Big Doc's Girl" (November 4, 1959). Part: Reverend MacCreighton.
The United States Steel Hour: "Bride of the Fox" (August 24, 1960)
Tallahassee 7000: "The Fugitive" (May 16, 1961). Part: Joe Lawson.
The Defenders: "Quality of Mercy" (September 16, 1961). Part: Jerry Warner.
The United States Steel Hour: "Brandenburg Gate" (October 4, 1961.
The United States Steel Hour: "Far from the Shade Tree" (January 10, 1962). Part: Ed.
Look Up and Live: "The End of the Story" (February 10, 1963). Part: Frank Collins.
Naked City: "Prime of Life" (February 13, 1963). Part: Mr. Jasper.
The Defenders: "Judgement Eve" (April 20, 1963). Part: Stanley McGuirk.
Route 66: "Who Will Cheer My Bonnie Bride" (May 10, 1963). Part: Motorist.
That Was the Week That Was: "Pilot" (November 10, 1963). Part: Reverend.
DuPont Show of the Week: "Ride with Terror" (December 1, 1963). Part: Douglas McCann.
East Side/West Side: "Creeps Live Here" (December 23, 1963). Part: Policeman.
Brenner: "Laney's Boy" (May 24, 1964). Part: Policeman.
Brenner: "Unwritten Law" (July 5, 1964). Part: Officer Richard Clayburn.
Neighbors (never broadcast). Part: Chuck Robinson.
The Trials of O'Brien: "The Only Game in Town" (March 18, 1966). Part: Roger Nathan.
Directions: "Marriage" (June 5, 1966).
Hawk: "Do Not Mutilate or Spindle" (September 8, 1966). Part: Houston Worth.
The F.B.I.: "The Courier" (January 15, 1967). Part: Herb Kenyon.
The Invaders: "The Spores" (October 17, 1967). Part: Tom Jessup.
Iron Horse: "Leopards Try, But Leopards Can't" (October 28, 1967). Part: Harry Wadsworth.
CBS Playhouse: "My Father and My Mother" (February 13, 1968). Part: Ned Piper.
I Spy: "Happy Birthday Everybody" (February 26, 1968). Part: Frank Hunter.
The 40th Annual Academy Awards (April 10, 1968). Part: Himself.
Shadow on the Land: (November 4, 1968). Part: Reverend Tom Davis.
Insight: "Confrontation" (May 29, 1970). Part: Holt.
43rd Annual Academy Awards (April 15, 1971). As himself.
The Hollywood Squares (December 20, 1971). As himself.
The Tonight Show with Johnny Carson (January 7, 1972). As himself.
Cinema (January 27, 1972). As himself.
Laugh-In (February 2, 1972). Parts: Drunk, POW, Sheriff.
The 29th Annual Golden Globes Awards (February 6, 1972). As himself.

APPENDIX

Laugh-In (March 13, 1972). As himself.
The 44th Annual Academy Awards (April 10, 1972). As himself.
The Tonight Show with Johnny Carson (December 28, 1972). As himself.
The 45th Annual Academy Awards (March 27, 1973). As himself.
The Tonight Show with Johnny Carson (April 9, 1973). As himself.
The Tonight Show with Johnny Carson (March 21, 1974). As himself.
Dinah! (January 22, 1975). As himself.
The Merv Griffin Show (February 26, 1975). As himself.
At Long Last Cole aka *At Long Last Cole: What a Swell Party It Was!* (April 10, 1975). As himself.
The Mike Douglas Show (August 19, 1975). As himself.
The Mike Douglas Show (September 8, 1975). As himself.
The Mike Douglas Show (September 12, 1975). Part: Himself.
The Mike Douglas Show (November 5, 1975). As himself.
The Tonight Show with Johnny Carson (November 15, 1975). As himself.
Film '72 (January 2, 1976). As himself.
The Merv Griffin Show (January 21, 1976). As himself.
The Merv Griffin Show (October 16, 1976). As himself.
The Mike Douglas Show (May 17, 1977). As himself.
The Mike Douglas Show (July 11, 1977). As himself.
That's Hollywood: "You've Never Seen This Before" (July 13, 1978). Part: Kibby from *Lucky Lady*.
V.I.P.—Schaukel (December 22, 1978). As himself.
Revista de cine (January 1, 1979). As himself.
The American Film Institute Salute to Fred Astaire (April 18, 1981). As himself.
The South Bank Show (May 1, 1983). As himself.
The Tonight Show with Johnny Carson (January 17, 1984). As himself.
The 41st Annual Golden Globe Awards (January 28, 1984). As himself.
The 56th Annual Academy Awards (April 9, 1984). As himself.
Night of 100 Stars II (March 10, 1985). As himself.
Late Night with David Letterman (February 10, 1986). As himself.
The American Film Institute Salute to Billy Wilder (March 6, 1986). As himself.
Wogan (November 3, 1986). As himself.
Late Night with David Letterman (October 19, 1988). As himself.
The Joe Franklin Show (date unknown). As himself.
ABC News Nightline (January 16, 1989). As himself.
The 46th Golden Globe Awards (January 28, 1989). As himself.
The 61st Annual Academy Awards (March 29, 1989). As himself.
Good Morning America (September 9, 1989). As himself.
Today (September 20, 1990). As himself.
CBS This Morning (October 1, 1990). As himself.
Sky Sports World Championship Boxing: "WBA, WBC & IBF World Heavyweight Title: Evander Holyfield vs. George Foreman" (April 19, 1991). As himself.
ABC's Wide World of Sports (April 20, 1991). As himself (audience member).
1992 Tony Awards (May 31, 1992). As himself..
The Tonight Show with Jay Leno (November 10, 1992). As himself.
The 50th Annual Golden Globe Awards (January 23, 1992). As himself.
The 65th Annual Academy Awards (March 29, 1993). As himself.
The Tonight Show with Jay Leno (July 23, 1993). As himself.
The 20th Annual People's Choice Awards (March 8, 1994). As himself.
The 66th Annual Academy Awards (March 21, 1994). As himself.
100 Years of the Hollywood Western (August 10, 1994). As himself.
Biography: "Clint Eastwood: The Man from Malpaso" (December 11, 1994). As himself.
Shurtleff on Acting (1994). As himself.
The Movie Show (February 10, 1995). As himself.
CBS This Morning (May 12, 1995). As himself.
The Tonight Show with Jay Leno (May 17, 1995). As himself.
Showbiz Today (May 15, 1996). Part: Himself.
American Masters: "Hitchcock, Selznick and the End of Hollywood" (October 23, 1998). Part: Narrator.

Appendix

The Rosie O'Donnell Show (November 18, 1998). As himself.
Jet 7 (date unknown, 1998). As himself.
The Directors: The Films of Richard Donner (date unknown, 1998). As himself.
The Best of Hollywood aka *50 Years: The Best of Hollywood* (date unknown, 1998). As himself.
The Charlie Rose Show (November 3, 1999). As himself.
HBO First Look: "The Making of *The Replacements*" (2000). As himself.
Bravo Profiles (August 7, 2000). As himself.
American Masters: "Clint Eastwood: Out of the Shadows" (September 27, 2000). As himself.
Heroes of Iwo Jima (2001). Part: Narrator.
Inside the Actors Studio (October 14, 2001). As himself.
Biography: "Dustin Hoffman: First in His Class" (2002). As himself.
The 60th Annual Golden Globe Awards (January 19, 2003). As himself.
HBO First Look: "Runaway Jury" (2003). As himself.
The Hollywood Greats: "Dustin Hoffman" (March 8, 2004). As himself.
Larry King Live (July 7, 2004). As himself.
America's Game: The Superbowl Champions (January 29, 2007). Part: Narrator.
America's Game: The Superbowl Champions (February 2, 2007). Part: Narrator.
America's Game: The Superbowl Champions (March 2, 2007). Part: Narrator.
Diners, Drive-ins and Dives: "Big Breakfast" (March 10, 2007). As himself.
America's Game: The Superbowl Champions (March 23, 2007). Part: Narrator.
AFI Life Achievement Award: A Tribute to Warren Beatty (June 25, 2008). As himself.
AFI's 10 Top 10: America's 10 Greatest Films in 10 Classic Genres (June 17, 2008). As himself.
The Role That Changed My Life: "I Was an Underdog." (December 7, 2010). As himself.
The Unknown Flag Raiser of Iwo Jima (July 3, 2016). Part: Narrator.

Books

Wake of the Perdido Star (1999). Coauthor with Daniel Lenihan.
Justice for None (2004). Coauthor with Daniel Lenihan.
Escape from Andersonville: A Novel of the Civil War (2008). Coauthor with Daniel Lenihan.
Payback at Morning Peak (2011). Author.
Pursuit (2013). Author.

Bibliography

Abramovitch, Seth. "Police: Gene Hackman Acted in Self-Defense When He Slapped a Homeless Man." *The Hollywood Reporter.* October 31, 2012. Retrieved October 22, 2017 from http://www.hollywoodreporter.com.

Adams, Val. "Leokum's 'Neighbors' About Sale of Home to Negroes." *New York Times.* January 4, 1996. Retrieved Jannuary 17, 2017 from http://www.nytimes.com.

_____. "… No Neighbors." *New York Times.* February 1, 1966. Retrieved January 17, 2017 from http://www.nytimes.com.

Adler, Renata. "Screen: Holdup at a Pro Football Game." *New York Times.* November 5, 1968. Retrieved January 26, 2017 from http://www.nytimes.com.

Alexander, Ron. "Chronicle." *New York Times.* March 23, 1993. Retrieved July 29, 2017 from http://www.nytimes.com.

Allen, Woody, and Bjorkman, Stig. *Woody Allen on Woody Allen.* New York: Grove Press, 1993.

Amburn, Ellis. *The Sexiest Man Alive: A Biography of Warren Beatty.* New York: HarperEntertainment, 2002.

Anderson, Susan Heller. "It's a Bird! It's a Plane! It's a Movie!" *New York Times.* June 26, 1977. Retrieved April 15, 2017 from http://www.nytimes.com.

Andrews, Nigel. *John Travolta: The Life.* New York: Bloomsbury USA, 1998.

Anspaugh, David, and Pizzo, Angelo. Hoosiers (Collector's Edition) DVD Audio Commentary. MGM Home Entertainment, 2005.

Arick, Michael M. *William Friedkin Discusses Deleted Scenes. The French Connection* Collector's Edition DVD. Twentieth Century Fox Home Entertainment, 2001.

Armstrong, Stephen B. *Pictures About Extremes: The Films of John Frankenheimer.* Jefferson, NC: McFarland, 2007.

Arnold, Jeremy. "Articles: A Covenant With Death (1967)." *Turner Classic Movies.* Retrieved January 21, 2017 from http://www.tcm.com.

_____. "Articles: Superman: The Movie (1978)." *Turner Classic Movies.* Retrieved April 9, 2017 from http://www.tcm.com.

Atkinson, Brooks. "The Theatre: 'Chaparral.'" *New York Times.* September 10, 1958. Retrieved January 7, 2017 from http://www.nytimes.com.

_____. "Theatre: Sardonic Humor." *New York Times.* February 3, 1959. Retrieved January 6, 2017 from http://www.nytimes.com.

Axmaker, Sean. "Articles" Scarecrow (1973). "*Turner Classic Movies.* Retrieved February 16, 2017 from http://www.tcm.com.

Bardin, Brantley. "Idol Chatter." *Premiere.* February, 2002. Retrieved November 8, 2017 from http://www.premiere.com.

Barlow, Helen. "Gene Hackman. The former marine famous for his on-screen mean streak shows Empire his soft side." *Empire.* February, 2002. Retrieved November 12, 2017 from http://www.empireonline.com.au.

Barnes, Clive. "Theater: Schisgal's Comic Insights." *New York Times.* October 3, 1967. Retrieved January 21, 2017 from http://www.nytimes.com.

_____. "Stage: 'All Over Town' Proves a Zany Surprise." *New York Times.* December 30, 1974. Retrieved February 28, 2017 from http://www.nytimes.com.

Barron, James. "Boldface Names: A Good Decking." *New York Times.* May 29, 2001. Retrieved September 27, 2017 from http://www.nytimes.com.

_____, with Dewan, Shaila K. "Boldface Names. Drawing By Numbers. " *New York Times.* April 17, 2001. Retrieved September 27, 2017 from http://www.nytimes.com.

Baxter, John. *Hollywood In The Sixties.* London, New York: Tantivy Press, A. S. Barnes & Co., 1972.

Bell, Joseph N. "On Location in Mexico with Liza and Friends." *New York Times.* June 29, 1975. Retrieved March 24, 2017 from http://www.nytimes.com.

Bellafante, Ginia. "No Fun Like Making Fun of Celebrity Waywardness." *New York Times.* May 9, 2006. Retrieved October 15, 2017 from http://www.nytimes.com.

_____. "'Family Guy' Neighbor Shows Off New Address." *New York Times.* February 25, 2009. Retrieved October 16, 2017 from http://www.nytimes.com.

Bennett, Spencer. "Gene Hackman Slaps Homeless

Bibliography

Malcreant." *MIX979*. October 31, 2012. Retrieved October 4, 2017 from http://www.mix979fm.com.

Bergan, Ronald. *The United Artists Story*. London: Octopus Books, 1986.

Bergen, Candice. *Knock Wood*. New York: Simon & Schuster, 1984.

Berger, Phil. "Notebook; Fighting Tyson Intrigues Mandarich." *New York Times*. May 10, 1989. Retrieved July 11, 2017 from http://www.nytimes.com.

Berman, Nat. "Why Did Gene Hackman Up and Vanish from Acting?" *TVOvermind*. June 28, 2017. Retrieved October 31, 2017 from http://www.tvovermind.com.

Bettenger, Brendan. "Writer Dan Fogelman Wants Jack Nicholson to Suffer a hangover while in Last Vegas." *Collider*. April 21, 2010. Retrieved October 17, 2017 from http://www.collider.com.

Biskind, Peter. *Gods and Monsters: Thirty Years of Writing on Film and Culture*. London: Bloomsbury Publishing, 2016.

_____. *Star: How Warren Beatty Seduced America*. New York: Simon & Schuster, 2010.

_____. "Thunder on the Left: The Making of Reds." *Vanity Fair*. January 22, 2007. Retrieved April 20, 2017 from http://www.vanityfair.com.

Bochner, Hart. PCU. 20th Century Fox/Paul Schiff Production, 1994.

_____. PCU DVD Director's Audio Commentary. Starz/Anchor Bay, 2013.

Borgnine, Ernest. *Ernie—The Autobiography*. New York: Citadel, 2008.

Bouzereau, Laurent. *The Making of* "Close Encounters of the Third Kind." CTHV Home Video, 1997.

_____. *The Making of Network*. Turner Entertainment, 2006.

_____. *Revolution! The Making of Bonnie And Clyde*. Warner Bros. Entertainment, 2007.

_____. *Witness To Reds: The Rising/Comrades/Testimonials/The March/Revolution Part 1 &2/Propaganda*. Paramount Pictures, 2006.

_____. *The Silence of the Lambs: The Beginning*. MGM Home Entertainment, 2005.

Brenner, Elsa. "It's Race Weekend At Lime Rock." *New York Times*. September 1, 1985. Retrieved May 27, 2017 from http://www.nytimes.com.

Brooks, Mel. *Young Frankenstein: A Mel Brooks Book: The Story of the Making of the Film*. New York: Black Dog & Leventhal, 2016.

Browning, Mark. *Wes Anderson: Why His Movies Matter*. Santa Barbara, CA: ABC-CLIO, 2011.

Buckley, Tom. "At The Movies." *New York Times*. May 30, 1980. Retrieved April 28, 2017 from http://www.nytimes.com.

Bumbray, Chris. "The Good, the Bad & the Badass: Gene Hackman." *Joblo*. May 28, 2014. Retrieved October 25, 2017 from http://www.joblo.com.

Bumiller, Elisabeth. "Public Lives; Motto for a Movie Tough Guy: Semper Fi." *New York Times*. October 20, 1998. Retrieved August 28, 2017 from http://www.nytimes.com.

Burke, Tom. "How Long Must A Pizza Waiter Wait? Very Long." *New York Times*. March 25, 1973. Retrieved February 16, 2017 from http://www.nytimes.com.

Burstyn, Ellen. *Lessons in Becoming Myself*. New York: Riverhead Books, 2007.

Callan, Michael Feeney. *Robert Redford: The Biography*. London: Simon & Schuster, 2011.

Calta, Louis. "… 'Chaparral' To Close." *New York Times*. September 20, 1958. Retrieved January 7, 2017 from http://www.nytimes.com.

Campbell, Bruce. *If Chins Could Kill: Confessions of a B Movie Actor*. New York: St. Martin's Press, 2001.

Campbell, Christopher. "'The Silence of the Lambs' at 25: Why Gene Hackman Dropped Out and Why Thomas Harris Wouldn't Watch It." *Fandango*. February 19, 2016. Retrieved July 14, 2017 from http://www.fandango.com.

Canby, Vincent. "Screen: 'Hawaii,' Big, Long Film, Has Its Premiere:Story Is Subordinated to Island's Scenery." *New York Times*. October 11, 1966. Retrieved January 19, 2017 from http://www.nytimes.com.

_____. "Screen: Jim Brown Leads Prison Riot." *New York Times*. January 16, 1969. Retrieved January 28, 2017 from http://www.nytimes.com.

_____. "The Screen: Barnstorming Parachutists." *New York Times*. August 29, 1969. Retrieved January 29, 2017 from http://www.nytimes.com.

_____. "Movie Review: Cates's Film, 'I Never Sang for My Father,' Begins Run." *New York Times*. October 19, 1970. Retrieved February 4, 2017 from http://www.nytimes.com.

_____. "Movie Review: 'Cisco Pike': Tale of Has-Been Rock Star Opens at Forum." *New York Times*. January 15, 1972. Retrieved February 11, 2017 from http://www.nytimes.com.

_____. "Screen: 'Prime Cut,' Uneven Gangster Melodrama." *New York Times*. June 29, 1972. Retrieved February 12, 2017 from http://www.nytimes.com.

_____. "Movie Review: 2 Drifters on a Photogenic Landscape: The Cast." *New York Times*. April 12, 1973. Retrieved February 16, 2017 from http://ww.nytimes.com.

_____. "Movie Review: A Haunting 'Conversation': 'Conversation.'" *New York Times*. April 21, 1974. Retrieved February 20, 2017 from http://www.nytimes.com.

_____. "Movie Review: Young Frankenstein." *New York Times*. December 16, 1974. Retrieved February 26, 2017 from http://www.nytimes.com.

_____. "Screen: Popeye Doyle':French Connection II' Is Very Different." *New York Times*. May 10, 1975. Retrieved March 17, 2017 from http://www.nytimes.com.

_____. "Movie Review: Night Moves." *New York Times*. June 12, 1975. Retrieved March 11, 2017 from http://www.nytimes.com.

_____. "The Screen: 'Bite the Bullet' Is a Richard Brooks Error." *New York Times*. June 27, 1975. Retrieved March 15, 2017 from http://www.nytimes.com.

_____. "Film View." *New York Times*. December 14, 1975. Retrieved March 25, 2017 from http://www.nytimes.com.

Bibliography

____. "Screen: 'Lucky Lady' Is Misnomer of Miscast and Mismanaged Comedy." *New York Times*. December 26, 1975. Retrieved March 23, 2017 from http://www.nytimes.com.

____. "Film View." *New York Times*. November 14, 1976. Retrieved April 3, 2017 from http://www.nytimes.com.

____. "Film: Kramer's Falling 'Domino.'" *New York Times*. March 24, 1977. Retrieved March 29, 2017 from http://www.nytimes.com.

____. "Film: It's a Long War In 'Bridge Too Far.'" *New York Times*. June 16, 1977. Retrieved April 2, 2017 from http://www.nytimes.com.

____. "Screen: It's a Bird, It's a Plane, It's a Movie." *New York Times*. December 15, 1978. Retrieved April 9, 2017 from http://www.nytimescom.

____. "Movie Review: Miss Streisand In 'All Night Long.'" *New York Times*. March 6, 1981. Retrieved April 26, 2017 from http://www.nytimes.com.

____. "Movie Review: Beatty's 'Reds,' With Diane Keaton." *New York Times*. December 4, 1981. Retrieved April 20, 2017 from http://www.nytimes.com.

____. "Screen: 'Under Fire.'" *New York Times*. October 21, 1983. Retrieved May 6, 2017 from http://www.nytimes.com.

____. "The Screen: 'Target,' A Spy Thriller By Penn." *New York Times*. November 8, 1985. Retrieved May 21, 2017 from http://www.nytimes.com.

____. "Screen: 'Power,' By Sidney Lumet." *New York Times*. January 31, 1986. Retrieved May 26, 2017 from http://www.nytimes.com.

____. "Film: 'No Way Out,' Washington Drama." *New York Times*. August 14, 1987. Retrieved June 5, 2017 from http://www.nytimes.com.

____. "Review/Film; Allen Directs Rowlands In 'Another Woman.'" *New York Times*. October 14, 1988. Retrieved June 19, 2017 from http://www.nytimes.com.

____. "Reviews/Film; 'Full Moon,' Down Home In Texas." *New York Times*. November 23, 1988. Retrieved June 22, 2017 from http://www.nytimes.com.

____. "Review/Film; Retracing Mississippi's Agony, 1964." *New York Times*. December 9, 1988. Retrieved July 6, 2017 from http://www.nytimes.com.

____. "Review/Film; Hackman And Chicago In 'Package,' A Thriller." *New York Times*. August 25, 1989. Retrieved July 12, 2017 from http://www.nytimes.com.

____. "Reviews/Film; Hackman and Aykroyd in 'Loose Cannons.'" *New York Times*. February 9, 1990. Retrieved July 15, 2017 from http://www.nytimes.com.

____. "Review/Film; Down and Out at the Top in Hollywood." *New York Times*. September 12, 1990. Retrieved July 19, 2017 from http://www.nytimes.com.

____. "Review/Film; Father and Daughter in the Courtroom." *New York Times*. March 15, 1991. Retrieved July 21, 2017 from http://www.nytimes.com.

____. "Review/Film; Ex-Spies in Double Trouble." *New York Times*. April 25, 1992. Retrieved July 22, 2017 from http://www.nytimes.com.

____. "Review/Film: Unforgiven; A Western Without Good Guys." *New York Times*. August 7, 1992. Retrieved July 24, 2017 from http://www.nytimes.com.

____. "Review/Film: The Firm; A Mole in the Den of Corrupt Legal Lions." *New York Times*. June 30, 1993. Retrieved July 30, 2017 from http://www.nytimes.com.

Carvajal, Doreen. "Media Talk; The Celebrity Author Who Sat and Wrote." *New York Times*. March 15, 1999. Retrieved September 5, 2017 from http://www.nytimes.com.

Carr, Jay. "Articles: Lilith (1964)." *Turner Classic Movies*. Retrieved January 14, 2017 from http://www.tcm.com.

Carter, Bill. Reporter's Notebook; With Ratings Slipping, CBS Reaches for Youth. " *New York Times*. January 10, 1995. Retrieved August 8, 2017 from http://www.nytimes.com.

Casty, Alan. *Robert Rossen: The Films and Politics of a Blacklisted Idealist*. Jefferson, NC: McFarland, 2013.

Cedrone, Lou. "'Valor' not uncommon, but highly unlikely." *The Baltimore Evening Sun*. December 23, 1983. Retrieved May 14, 2017 from http://www.news.google.com.

Cerone, Daniel Howard. "The Nice Guy Gets an Edge : Jay Leno Begins His Fourth Year Behind 'The Tonight Show' Desk...and He's Gaining on Letterman." *Los Angeles Times*. May 25, 1995. Retrieved August 13, 2017 from http://www.latimes.com.

Chaiken, Michael, and Cronin, Paul. *Arthur Penn: Interviews (Conversations with Filmmakers Series)*. University Press of Mississippi, 2008.

Chase, Chris. "Love Is Hell, Warren." *New York Times*. June 25, 1972. Retrieved February 15, 2017 from http://www.nytimes.com.

____. "At The Movies." *New York Times*. March 13, 1981. Retrieved April 30, 2017 from http://www.nytimes.com.

____. "At The Movies." *New York Times*. January 8, 1982. Retrieved April 30, 2017 from http://www.nytimes.com.

____. "At The Movies: The filming of New York's youngest." *New York Times*. July 1, 1983. Retrieved May 7, 2017 from http://www.nytimes.com.

Chitwood, Adam. "Paramount Demands Budget Cut for Alexander Payne's Nebraska. " *Collider*. October 11, 2011. Retrieved October 20, 2017 from http://www.collider.com.

Chiu, Tony. "Francis Coppola's Cinematic 'Apocalypse' Is Finally at Hand ..." *New York Times*. August 12, 1979. Retrieved April 16, 2017 from http://www.nytimes.com.

Chiusano, Scott. "'The Birdcage' at 20: Here are 20 things you never knew about the Robin Williams and Nathan Lane comedy laced with giddy ingenuity." *New York Daily News*. March 29, 2016. Retrieved August 12, 2017 from http://www.nydailynews.com.

Collins. Glenn. "A Job Fit for a Living Legend." *New*

York Times. November 5, 1988. Retrieved July 9, 2017 from http://www.nytimes.com.
Collins, Glenn. "'Jelly's Last Jam,' With 11, Leads in Tony Nominations." *New York Times*. May 5, 1992. Retrieved July 29, 2017 from http://www.nytimes.com.
_____. with Nagourney, Adam. "Public Lives ... The Buddy System In Literary Terms." *New York Times*. November 3, 1999. Retrieved September 9, 2017 from http://www.nytimes.com.
Coppola, Francis Ford. The Conversation DVD Audio Commentary. Paramount, 2000.
Cork, John. *Richard Attenborough: A Director Remembers*. MGM Home Entertainment, 2002.
Cousans, Patrick. *Making Frankensense of Young Frankenstein*. 20th Century Fox Home Entertainment, 1996.
Cowie, Peter. *Coppola: A Biography*. New York: Da Capo Press, 1994.
Cowie, Susan D., and Johnson, Tom. *The Films of Oliver Reed*. Jefferson, NC: McFarland, 2011.
Cramer, Jeff. "A Very Candid Conversation with William Norton." January 16, 2010. Retrieved February 6, 2017 from http://jeffcramer.blogspot.com.au.
Crick, Robert Alan. *The Big Screen Comedies of Mel Brooks*. Jefferson, NC: McFarland, 2002.
Crowther, Bosley. "'Nothing but a Man' and 'Lilith' Presented." *New York Times*. September 21, 1964. Retrieved January 14, 2017, from http://www.nytimes.com.
_____. "Screen: Thin Idea in Elaborate Decor: Adaptation of 'Oh Dad' Has Premiere Here Rosalind Russell and Winters in Cast." *New York Times*. February 16, 1967. Retrieved January 21, 2017 from http://www.nytimes.com.
Cryer, Jon. *So That Happened: A Memoir*. New York: Penguin, 2015.
Culhane, Mark. "Film; For Oscar's Producer, the Key Is C." *New York Times*. March 26, 1989. Retrieved July 9, 2017 from http://www.nytimes.com.
Cunningham, Frank R. *Sidney Lumet: Film and Literary Vision*. Lexington, KY: University Press of Kentucky, 2011.
Dafoe, Willem. "Frances McDormand." *Bomb Magazine*. Spring, 1996. Retrieved July 6, 2017 from http://www.bombmagazine.org.
Dalva, Robert. *Close-up on 'The Conversation.'* American Zeotrope, Year unknown.
Daniel, Douglas K. *Tough as Nails: The Life and Films of Richard Brooks (Wisconsin Film Studies)*. London: University of Wisconsin Press, 2011.
Darnell, Eric, and Johnson, Tim. Antz DVD Director's Commentary.
Darnton, Nina. "At the Movies." *New York Times*. May 8, 1987. Retrieved June 12, 2017 from http://www.nytimes.com.
Davis, Andrew, and Cassidy, Joanna. The Package DVD Audio Commentary. Kino Lorber, 2014.
Davis, Dave. "Gene Hackman Is No Longer Acting, But Is Still Working." *Joblo*. September 29, 2010. Retrieved October 17, 2017 from http://www.joblo.com.

Davis, John, and Godfrey, Wyck. Behind Enemy Lines. DVD Audio Commentary. 20th Century Fox, 2002.
Davis, L. G. "Hollywood's Most Secret Agent." *New York Times*. July 9, 1989. Retrieved July 11, 2017 from http://www.nytimes.com.
Davis, Sandy. "Hackman knows the military mind Actor talks 'Behind Enemy Lines.'" *NEWSOK*. November 30, 2001. Retrieved October 2, 2017 from http://www.newsok.com.
Deutch, Howard. The Replacements DVD Audio Commentary. Warner Home Video, 2000.
Dickerson, James. L. *Russell Crowe: The Unauthorized Biography*. London: Schirmer Trade Books, 2011.
Dilley, Whitney Crothers. *Cinema of Wes Anderson: Bringing Nostalgia to Life*. New York: Columbia University Press, 2017.
Donner, Richard. *Superman II: The Richard Donner Cut*. Alexander & Ilya Salkind Production/Richard Donner Film/International Film Production/Warner Bros., 1979, 1980, 2006.
_____, and Mankiewicz, Tom. *Superman II: The Richard Donner Cut*, DVD Audio Commentary. Warner Bros., 2006.
Dougherty, Phillip H. "The Media Business: Advertising; Campaign Make-Over For GTE." *New York Times*. September 9, 1988. Retrieved July 9, 2017 from http://www.nytimes.com.
Dunaway, Faye, and Sharkey, Betsy. *Looking for Gatsby*. New York: Simon & Schuster, 1997.
Eames, John Douglas. *The MGM Story*. London: Octopus Books, 1975.
_____. *The Paramount Story*. London: Octopus Books, 1985.
Ebert, Roger. "Bonnie and Clyde." September 26, 1967. Retrieved January 25, 2017 from http://www.rogerebert.com.
_____. "The Split." October 17, 1968. Retrieved January 26, 2017 from http://www.rogerebert.com.
_____. "Riot." February 20, 1969. Retrieved January 28, 2017 fro http://www.rogerebert.com.
_____. "The Gypsy Moths." November 17, 1969. Retrieved January 29, 2017 from http://www.rogerebert.com.
_____. "Downhill Racer." December 22, 1969. Retrieved February 1, 2017 from http://www.rogerebert.com.
_____. "Marooned." December 25, 1969. Retrieved February 2, 2017 from http://www.rogerebert.com.
_____. "I Never Sang for My Father." January 1, 1970. Retrieved February 4, 2017 from http://www.rogerebert.com.
_____. "The French Connection." January 1, 1971. Retrieved February 8, 2017 from http://www.rogerebert.com.
_____. "Cisco Pike." February 16, 1972. Retrieved February 11, 2017 from http://www.rogerebert.com.
_____. "Prime Cut." January 1, 1972. Retrieved February 12, 2017 from http://www.rogerebert.com.
_____. "The Poseidon Adventure." December 21, 1972. Retrieved February 14, 2017 from http://www.rogerebert.com.

Bibliography

_____. "Scarecrow." April 12, 1973. Retrieved February 16, 2017 from http://www.rogerebert.com.

_____. "The Conversation." January 1, 1974. Retrieved February 20, 2017 from http://www.rogerebert.com.

_____. "Young Frankenstein." January 1, 1974. Retrieved February 26, 2017 from http://www.rogerebert.com.

_____. "French Connection II." January 1, 1975. Retrieved March 17, 2017 from http://www.rogerebert.com.

_____. "Night Moves." June 11, 1975. Retrieved March 11, 2017 from http://www.rogerebert.com.

_____. "Bite The Bullet." June 27, 1975. Retrieved March 15, 2017 from http://www.rogerebert.com.

_____. "Lucky Lady." December 29, 1975. Retrieved March 23, 2017 from http://www.rogerebert.com.

_____. "A Bridge Too Far." June 17, 1977. Retrieved April 2, 2017 from http://www.rogerebert.com.

_____. "Superman." December 15, 1978. Retrieved April 9, 2017 from http://www.rogerebert.com.

_____. "Reds." January 1, 1981. Retrieved April 20, 2017 from http://www.rogerebert.com.

_____. "Superman II." January 1, 1981. Retrieved April 15, 2017 from http://www.rogerebert.com.

_____. "All Night Long." January 1, 1981. Retrieved April 26, 2017 from http://www.rogerebert.com.

_____. "Under Fire." October 21, 1983. Retrieved May 6, 2017 from http://www.rogerebert.com.

_____. "Uncommon Valor." December 19, 1983. Retrieved May 14, 2017 from http://www.rogerebert.com.

_____. "Two of a Kind." December 20, 1983. Retrieved May 8, 2017 from http://www.rogerebert.com.

_____. "Twice In A Lifetime." December 25, 1985. Retrieved May 19, 2017 from http://www.rogerebert.com.

_____. "Power." January 31, 1986. Retrieved May 26, 2017 from http://www.rogerebert.com.

_____. "Hoosiers." February 27, 1987. Retrieved May 29, 2017 from http://www.rogerebert.com.

_____. "No Way Out." August 14, 1987. Retrieved June 5, 2017 from http://www.rogerebert.com.

_____. "Bat*21." October 21, 1988. Retrieved June 14, 2017 from http://www.rogerebert.com.

_____. "Another Woman." November 18, 1988. Retrieved June 19, 2017 from http://www.rogerebert.com.

_____. "Full Moon in Blue Water." November 25, 1988. Retrieved June 22, 2017 from http://www.rogerebert.com.

_____. "Mississippi Burning." December 9, 1988. Retrieved July 6, 2017 from http://www.rogerebert.com.

_____. "The Package." August 25, 1989. Retrieved July 12, 2017 from http://www.rogerebert.com.

_____. "Loose Cannons." *Ebert & Siskel*. February 10, 1990. Retrieved July 15, 2017 from http://www.YouTube.com.

_____. "Postcards from The Edge." September 12, 1990. Retrieved July 19, 2017 from http://www.rogerebert.com.

_____, _____. "Narrow Margin." September 21, 1990. Retrieved July 17, 2017 from http://www.rogerebert.com.

_____, _____. "Class Action." March 15, 1991. Retrieved July 21, 2017 from http://www.rogerebert.com.

_____, _____. "'Unforgiven' ropes honors for Eastwood." March 30, 1993. Retrieved July 26, 2017 from http://www.rogerebert.com.

_____, _____. "The Firm." June 30, 1993. Retrieved July 30, 2017 from http://www.rogerebert.com.

_____, _____. "Unforgiven." July 21, 2002. Retrieved July 24, 2017 from http://www.rogerebert.com.

_____. "Geronimo." December 10, 1993. Retrieved August 1, 2017 from http://www.rogerebert.com.

_____. "Wyatt Earp." June 24, 1994. Retrieved August 2, 2017 from http://www.rogerebert.com.

_____. "The Quick and the Dead." February 10, 1995. Retrieved August 4, 2017 from http://www.rogerebert.com.

_____. "Crimson Tide." May 12, 1995. Retrieved August 7, 2017 from http://www.rogerebert.com.

_____. "Get Shorty." October 20, 1995. Retrieved August 10, 2017 from http://www.rogerebert.com.

_____. "The Birdcage." March 8, 1996. Retrieved August 12, 2017 from http://www.rogerebert.com.

_____. *Extreme Measures*." September 27, 1996. Retrieved August 18, 2017 from http://www.rogerebert.com.

_____. "The Chamber." October 11, 1996. Retrieved August 16, 2017 from http://www.rogerebert.com.

_____. "Absolute Power." February 14, 1997. Retrieved August 19, 2017 from http://www.rogerebert.com.

_____. "Twilight." March 6, 1998. Retrieved August 22, 2017 from http://www.rogerebert.com.

_____. "Antz." October 2, 1998. Retrieved August 27, 2017 from http://www.rogerebert.com.

_____. "Enemy of the State." November 20, 1998. Retrieved August 24, 2017 from http://www.rogerebert.com.

_____. "The Replacements." August 11, 2000. Retrieved September 6, 2017 from http://www.rogerebert.com.

_____. "The Mexican." March 2, 2001. Retrieved September 11, 2017 from http://www.rogerebert.com.

_____. "Heartbreakers." March 23, 2001. Retrieved September 13, 2017 from http://www.rogerebert.com.

_____. "Heist." November 9, 2001. Retrieved September 19, 2017 from http://www.rogerebert.com.

_____. "Behind Enemy Lines." November 30, 2001. Retrieved September 28, 2017 from http://www.rogerebert.com.

_____. "The Royal Tenenbaums." December 21, 2001. Retrieved September 22, 2017 from http://www.rogerebert.com.

_____. "Runaway Jury." October 17, 2003. Retrieved October 9, 2017 from http://www.rogerebert.com.

_____. "Welcome to Mooseport." February 20, 2004. Retrieved October 12, 2017 from http://www.rogerebert.com.

Earnshaw, Tony. "Interview: Denzel Washington."

Bibliography

Yorkshire Post. February 24, 2012. Retrieved August 7, 2017 from http://www.yorkshirepost.co.uk.

Edelstein, David. "Gene Hackman, Hollywood's Every Angry Man." *New York Times*. December 16, 2001. Retrieved October 5, 2017 from http://www.nytimes.com.

Eggertsen, Chris. "The surprising actor who almost played Hannibal Lecter in 'Silence of the Lambs.'" *Uproxx*. February 12, 2016. Retrieved October 30, 2017 from http://www.uproxx.com.

Ellenberger, Allan R. *Margaret O'Brien: A Career Chronicle and Biography*. Jefferson, NC: McFarlane, 2004.

Eller, Claudia. "Getting Over Obstacles for 'Under Suspicion.'" *Los Angeles Times*. June 1, 1999. Retrieved September 3, 2017 from http://www.articles.latimes.com.

Elley, Derek. "Review: 'Under Suspicion.'" *Variety*. May 17, 2000. Retrieved September 1, 2017 from http://www.variety.com.

Elliott, Stuart. "The Media Business: Advertising; Famous Voices in Demand, While the Faces Go Unseen." *New York Times*. November 29, 1991. Retrieved July 28, 2017 from http://www.nytimes.com.

_____. "The Media Business: Advertising; For Leo Burnett, a United review signals unwanted clouds moving into the friendly skies." *New York Times*. July 29, 1996. Retrieved August 21, 2017 from http://www.nytimes.com.

_____. "UAL Dismisses Leo Burnett, Its Longtime Ad Angency." *New York Times*. October 19, 1996. Retrieved August 21, 2017 from http://www.nytimes.com.

_____. "The Media Business: Advertising—Addenda; Lowe's Sets Review, Incumbents Included." *New York Times*. May 4, 2005. Retrieved October 14, 2017 from http://www.nytimes.com.

_____. "Lowe's Puts Its Focus on Knowing the Customer's Wants." *New York Times*. February 28, 2010. Retrieved October 18, 2017 from http://www.nytimes.com.

Ellison, Michael. "Why has Gene Hackman written a novel?" *The Guardian*. July 21, 2000. Retrieved September 18, 2017 from http://www.theguardian.com.

Emery, Robert J. *The Directors: The Films of John Frankenheimer*. Media Entertainment/American Film Institute, 1997.

_____. *The Directors: The Films of Sydney Pollack*. Media Entertainment/American Film Institute, 1997.

_____. *The Directors: The Films of William Friedkin*. Media Entertainment/American Film Institute, 1995.

Epstein, Dwayne. *Lee Marvin: Point Blank*. Tucson, AZ: Schaffner Press, 2013.

Erickson, Hal. *"From Beautiful Downtown Burbank": A Critical History of Rowan and Martin's Laugh-In, 1968–1973*. Jefferson, NC: McFarland, 2000.

Ess, Ramsey. "'That Was the Week That Was' Brings Political Satire to America." *Splitsider*. May 18, 2012. Retrieved March 2, 2017 from http://www.splitsider.com.

Ewbank, Tim. *Olivia: The Biography of Olivia Newton-John*. London: Hachette Digital, 2008.

Farber, Stephen. "Why Couldn't This 'Lady' Have an Unhappy Ending?" *New York Times*. December 14, 1975. Retrieved March 26, 2017 from http://www.nytimes.com.

_____. "TV Is Polishing Ann-Margaret's Image." *New York Times*. July 17, 1984. Retrieved May 19, 2017 from http://www.nytimes.com.

_____. "'Guardian,' A Thriller On Crime." *New York Times*. October 18, 1984. Retrieved May 24, 2017 from http://www.nytimes.com.

Farinolat, Michele, and Freedman, Mimi. *Backstory: The Poseidon Adventure*. Prometheus Entertainment/Van Ness Films/Foxstar Productions/Fox Television Studio/American Movie Classics, 20th Century Fox, 2000.

Farrow, Mia. *What Falls Away*. New York: Doubleday, 1997.

Farrow, Moira. "'Narrow Margin' Finds Its Route." *New York Times*. September 10, 1989. Retrieved July 17, 2017 from http://www.nytimes.com.

Finn, Natalie. "Gene Hackman Admits to Slapping Homeless Man While Defending Wife's Honor." *ENews*. October 31, 2012. Retrieved October 22, 2017 from http://www.eonline.com.

Finstad, Suzanne. *Natasha: The Biography of Natalie Wood*. New York: Random House, 2011.

_____. *Warren Beatty: A Private Man*. New York: Random House, 2006.

Fischer, Paul. "Superstars Face Off." *The Sunday Mail*. October 12, 2003. Retrieved November 8, 2017 from http://www.thesundaymail.com.au.

_____. "Owen Wilson Royal Tenenbaums, Behind Enemy Lines." Femalewww.au. Undated. Retrieved October 2, 2017 from http://www.femail.com.au.

Fischer, Russ. "Tony Scott Will Next Direct Potsdamer Platz, with Bardem, Statham and Rourke." */Film*. April 7, 2010. Retrieved October 17, 2017 from http://www.slashfilm.com.

Fisher, Carrie. Postcards From The Edge DVD Audio Commentary. Mill Creek–Sony Pictures Home Entertainment, 2001.

Fleder, Gary. Runaway Jury DVD Audio Commentary. 20th Century Fox, 2004.

Foshee, Andrea. "Articles: Hawaii (1966)." *Turner Classic Movies*. Retrieved January 19, 2017 from http://www.tcm.com.

Frankenheimer, John. The French Connection II DVD Audio Commentaty. 20th Century Fox, 2002.

_____. The Gypsy Moths DVD Audio Commentary. Turner Home Entertainment, 2002.

Friedkin, William. The French Connection DVD Audio Commentary. Twentieth Century Fox, 2005.

_____. *The Friedkin Connection: A Memoir*. New York: Harper Perennial, 2014.

Friedman, Lester D. *Arthur Penn's Bonnie and Clyde*. Cambridge, UK: Cambridge University Press, 2000.

Friend, Tom. "Super Bowl XXVII: In Pasadena; With

All the Fun That Comes Before, Why Let the Game Begin?" *New York Times*. February 1, 1993. Retrieved July 29, 2017 from http://www.nytimes.com.

Fristoe, Roger. "Articles: Young Frankenstein (1974)." *Turner Classic Movies*. Retrieved February 25, 2017 from http://www.tcm.com.

_____. "Articles: Network (1976)." *Turner Classic Movies*. Retrieved March 30, 2017 from http://www.tcm.com.

Funke, Lewis. "News of the Rialto: Togetherness—A 'Natural Look.'" *New York Times*. November 6, 1966. Retrieved January 17, 2017 from http://www.nytimes.com.

Funke, Phyllis. "How You Gonna Keep 'em Down in Hollywood After They've Seen the Sticks?" *New York Times*. September 22, 1974. Retrieved February 27, 2017 from http://www.nytimes.com.

Gabriel, Trip. "Call My Agent!" *New York Times*. February 19, 1989. Retrieved July 9, 2017 from http://www.nytimes.com.

Gajewski, Ryan. "Gene Hackman Mistakenly Mourned by Twitter After Article Proclaims Him 'Gone.'" *The Hollywood Reporter*. January 29, 2015. Retrieved October 25, 2017 from http://www.hollywoodreporter.com.

Galbraith, Jane. "Film Clips. A look at Hollywood and the movies: 'Firm' Billing: Trust Us—Gene Hackman's in It." *Los Angeles Times*. June 27, 1993. Retrieved July 30, 2017 from http://www.articles.latimes.com.

Garr, Teri, with Mantel, Henriette. *Speedbumps: Flooring It Through Hollywood*. Penguin, 2006.

Geerhart, Ed. "Cold War Short Subjects." Retrieved October 29, 2017 from http://www.conelrad.com.

Gelb, Arthur "… Theatre Tonight." *New York Times*. February 2, 1959. Retrieved January 6, 2017 from http://www.nytimes.com.

Gent, George. "Channel 13 Delays a Race Play To Seek 'Additional Guidance.'" *New York Times*. January 8, 1966. Retrieved Janaury 17, 2017 from http://www.nytimes.com.

_____. "Fiction or Autobiography?" *New York Times*. February 11, 1968. Retrieved January 22, 2017 from http://www.nytimes.com.

Germain, David. "'Heist' Lures Mamet Back to Crime." *Backstage*. November 12, 2001. Retrieved September 20, 2017 from http://www.backstage.com.

Goldman, William. *Adventures in the Screen Trade: A Personal View of Hollywood and Screenwriting*. New York: Warner Books, 1984.

_____, et al. A Bridge Too Far DVD Audio Commentary. MGM (Video& DVD), 2005.

_____. *Four Screenplays with Essays*. New York: Applause Theatre & Cinema Books, 2000.

Gonthier, David F., Jr., and O'Brien, Timothy, M. *The Films of Alan Parker, 1976–2003*. Jefferson, NC: McFarland, 2015.

Goodman, Walter. "Screen: 'Eureka' by Nicolas Roeg." *New York Times*. August 30, 1985. Retrieved May 3, 2017 from http://www.nytimes.com.

_____. "Review/Television; In 90 Minutes, 500 Years' Worth of Destruction." *New York Times*. April 22, 1993. Retrieved July 31, 2017 from http://www.nytimes.com.

Gould, Jack. "TV: Crean's Drama, 'My Father and My Mother.'" *New York Times*. February 14, 1968. Retrieved January 22, 2017 from http://www.nytimes.com.

Green, Penelope. "Oh, the Stars! The Stars!" *New York Times*. October 31, 2004. Retrieved October 13, 2017 from http://www.nytimes.com.

Greenspun, Roger. "Screen: For 'Downhill Racer,' Time Is the Master." *New York Times*. November 7, 1969. Retrieved February 1, 2017 from http://www.nytimes.com.

_____. "Movie Review: Schaefer's 'Doctors' Wives': Dyan Cannon Portrays Unfaithful Spouse 4 Other Features Bow in Local Showings." *New York Times*. February 4, 1971. Retrieved February 4, 2017 from http://www.nytimes.com.

_____. "Movie Review: Love of Rancher's Wife Is Spark for 'The Hunting Party,' a Western." *New York Times*. July 17, 1971. Retrieved February 6, 2017 from http://www.nytimes.com.

_____. "Movie Review: The French Connection." *New York Times*. October 8, 1971. Retrieved February 7, 2017 from http://www.nytimes.com.

Grobel, Lawrence. *Al Pacino*. New York: Simon & Schuster, 2008.

Gussow, Mel. "How 'All Over Town' Got on Boards. *New York Times*. January 2, 1975. Retrieved March 16, 2017 from http://www.nytimes.com.

_____. "Books: Young Artist, 74, Is Basking In Belated Turn In the Spotlight." *New York Times*. February 17, 2003. Retrieved January 6, 2017 from http://www.nytimes.com.

Guttman, Dick. *Starflacker: Inside the Golden Age of Hollywood*. Beverly Hills, CA: R. Guttman Associates, 2015.

Hackman, Gene, and Scheider, Roy. The French Connection DVD Audio Commentary. Twentieth Century Fox, 2005.

Hainey, Michael. "81 Years. 79 Movies. 2 Oscars. Not 1 Bad Performance. " *GQ*. June 1, 2011. Retrieved October 20, 2017 from http://www.gq.com.

Harmetz, Aljean. "The Movies That Draw Hatred." *New York Times*. May 4, 1981. Retrieved April 30, 2017 from http://www.nytimes.com.

_____. "The Life and Exceedingly Hard Times of Superman." *New York Times*. June 14, 1981. Retrieved April 30, 2017 from http://www.nytimes.com.

_____. "How a Hollywood Rumor Was Born, Flourished and Died." *New York Times*. December 12, 1982. Retrieved May 1, 2017 from http://www.nytimes.com.

_____. "David Putnam, A Force In International Films." *New York Times*. May 3, 1983. Retrieved May 7, 2017 from http://www.nytimes.com.

_____. "Shoestring Movies As An Art." *New York Times*. November 28, 1984. Retrieved May 24, 2017 from http://www.nytimes.com.

_____. "American Film Institute Honors Billy Wilder." *New York Times*. March 8, 1986. Retrieved June 3, 2017 from http://www.nytimes.com.

_____. "Vietnam Now Behind It, Hollyood Turns to

the Civil Rights Struggle." *New York Times.* April 19, 1988. Retrieved July 7, 2017 from http://www.nytimes.com.

Hartley, Mark. *Electric Boogaloo: The Wild Untold Story of Cannon Films.* Umbrella Entertainment/Ratpac Documentary Films/Brett Ratner/Wildbear Entertainment/ Melbourne International Film Festival Premiere Fund/ Screen Queensland/ Film Victoria/Screen Australia/Celluloid Nightmares/Mark Hartley Film, 2014.

Harwood, James. "Review: 'Superman.'" *Variety.* December 12, 1978. Retrieved April 9, 2017 from http://www.variety.com.

Havill, Adrian. *Man of Steel: The Career and Courage of Christopher Reeve.* New York: Signet, 1996.

Heath, Paul. "Val Kilmer says he's in Top Gun 2." *The Hollywood News.* November 17, 2015. Retrieved October 28, 2017 from http://www.hollywoodnews.com.

Heller Anderson, Susan. "Chronicle." *New York Times.* July 6, 1990. Retrieved July 20, 2017 from http://www.nytimes.com.

Higham, Charles. "Why Stix Nix Big Fix." *New York Times.* October 12, 1975. Retrieved March 25, 2017 from http://www.nytimes.com.

_____. "Coppola's Vietnam Movie Is a Battle Royal." *New York Times.* May 15, 1977. Retrieved April 6, 2017 from http://www.nytimes.com.

Hiller, Arthur. *The Lonely Guy.* Universal City Pictures, 1984.

Hilton, Beth. "Hackman quits movies for writing career." *Digital Spy.* May 6, 2008. Retrieved October 15, 2017 from http://www.digitalspy.com.

Hirschberg, Lynn. "Deliverance." *New York Times.* June 16, 1996. Retrieved August 20, 2017 from http://www.nytimes.com.

_____. "Screenwriters Are (Obsessive, Creative, Neurotic) People, Too." *New York Times.* November 9, 2003. Retrieved October 12, 2017 from http://www.nytimes.com.

Hirschhorn, Clive. *The Columbia Story.* London: Pyramid Books, 1989.

_____. *The Universal Story.* London: Octopus Books, 1983.

_____. *The Warner Bros. Story.* London: Octopus Books, 1979.

Hogrewe, Jerry. *All on Accounta Pullin' a Trigger.* Warner Home Video, 2002.

Holden, Stephen. "Film Review; Sounds Like Tony Soprano, But Just a Tad Weepier." *New York Times.* March 2, 2001. Retrieved September 11, 2017 from http://www.nytimes.com.

_____. "Film Review; Immersed in War (in Bosnia for a Change) With Gusto and Gadgetry." *New York Times.* November 30, 2001. Retrieved September 28, 2017 from http://www.nytimes.com.

Holtzman, William. *Seesaw: A Dual Biography of Anne Bancroft And Mel Brooks.* New York: Doubleday & Company, 1979.

Horton, Andrew. *The Films of George Roy Hill.* Jefferson, NC: McFarland, 2005.

Howden, Martin. *Russell Crowe—The Biography.* John Blake Publishing, 2010.

Howe, Matt. All Night Long. Retrieved April 28, 2017 from http://www.barbra-archives.com.

Hunter, Allan. *Gene Hackman.* New York: St. Martin's Press, 1987.

Huston, Anjelica. *Watch Me.* Great Britain: Simon & Schuster UK, 2014.

Hyams, Peter. Narrow Margin DVD Audio Commentary. Optimum Releasing, 2007.

Hyden, Steven. "The Greatest Living American Actor at 85: Gene Hackman Is Retired But Still in Charge." *Grantland.* January 27, 2015. Retrieved October 25, 2017 from http://www.grantland.com.

Ihnat, Gwen. "Owen Wilson on getting swallowed by an Anaconda and beaten up by Jim Carrey." *AV Film.* August 31, 2015. Retrieved October 1, 2017 from http://www.film.avclub.com.

Itzkoff, Dave. *Mad as Hell: The Making of Network and the Fateful Vision of the Angriest Man in Movies.* New York: Time Books, 2014.

_____. "Notes of a Screenwriter, Mad as Hell." *New York Times.* May 19, 2011. Retrieved March 30, 2017 from http://www.nytimes.com.

Jackson, Kathi. *Steven Spielberg: A Biography.* Westport, CT: Greenwood Publishing Group, 2007.

Jacobs, Matthew. "June Squibb's Oscar Nomination Means She No Longer Has To Audition For Parts." *HuffPost.* November 14, 2015. Retrieved November 4, 2017 from http://www.huffingtonpost.com.

Jagermauth, Kevin. "R.E.M.'s Michael Stipe Says He Was Offered Kevin Spacey's Role In David Fincher's 'Se7en.'" *The Playlist.* November 9, 2016. Retrieved October 30, 2017 from http://www.theplaylist.net.

James, Caryn. "Review/Film; Strangeness On a Train." *New York Times.* September 21, 1990. Retrieved July 17, 2017 from http://www.nytimes.com.

_____. "Review/Film: Wyatt Earp; Into the Heart And Soul Of Darkness." *New York Times.* June 24, 1994. Retrieved August 2, 2017 from http://www.nytimes.com.

_____. "Film View: The Right Wing As Punching Bag." *New York Times.* April 7, 1996. Retrieved August 20, 2017 from http://www.nytimes.com.

_____. "'A Personal Journey With Martin Scorsese Through American Movies.'" *New York Times.* March 6, 1998. Retrieved August 13, 2017 from http://www.nytimes.com.

Johnson, Dirk. "State Line City Journal; Two States Divided by One Town." *New York Times.* July 23, 1998. Retrieved August 28, 2017 from http://www.nytimes.com.

Johnson, Gayle L. *The Making of Hoosiers: How a Small Movie from the Heartland Became One of America's Favorite Films.* CreateSpace Independent Publishing Platform, 2010.

Johnstone, Iain. *The Making of Superman II.* Alexander Salkind/Dovemead Ltd/International Film Production, 1982.

Kael, Pauline. *5001 Nights at the Movies.* New York: Holt, Rinehart and Winston, 1984.

_____. *Deeper Into Movies.* New York: Warner Books, 1973.

Bibliography

____. *Hooked.* New York: E.P. Dutton, 1989.

____, ____. *Kiss Kiss Bang Bang.* London: Calder & Boyars, 1970.

____, ____. *Movie Love.* New York: Dutton, 1991.

____, ____. *Reeling.* Boston, Toronto: Little, Brown & Company, 1976.

____. *State of the Art.* New York: E.P. Dutton, 1985.

____, ____. *Taking It All In.* New York: Holt, Rinehart & Winston, 1984.

____, ____. *When the Lights Go Down.* New York: Holt, Rinehart and Winston, 1980.

Kapsis, Robert E., and Coblentz, Kathie. *Clint Eastwood: Interviews. Revised and Updated.* Jackson: University Press of Mississippi, 2012.

Karli, Shaun R. *Becoming Jack Nicholson: The Masculine Persona from Easy Rider to The Shining.* Plymouth, UK: Rowan & Littlefield, 2012.

Kaufman, Dave. "Review: 'Bonnie and Clyde.'" *Variety.* August 9, 1967. Retrieved January 25, 2017 from http://www.variety.com.

Kehr, Dave. "At the Movies. Just Grazing With the Stars." *New York Times.* November 9, 2001. Retrieved October 5, 2017 from http://www.nytimes.com.

____, ____. "Film In Review; 'Welcome to Mooseport.'" *New York Times.* February 20, 2004. Retrieved October 12, 2017 from http://www.nytimes.com.

Kellow, Brian. *Can I Go Now?: The Life of Sue Mengers, Hollywood's First Superagent.* New York: Penguin, 2015.

Kent, Leticia. "They Were Behind the Scenes of 'Between the Lines.'" *New York Times.* June 12, 1977. Retrieved April 16, 2017 from http://www.nytimes.com.

Kerr, Walter. "Theater: 'The Natural Look' Is Here; Ad Game Play Opens at the Longacre." *New York Times.* March 13, 1967. Retrieved January 20, 2017 from http://ww.nytimes.com.

____, ____. "Kerr Off Broadway." *New York Times.* October 15, 1967. Retrieved January 22, 2017 from http://www.nytimes.com.

Keyser, Les. *Hollywood In The Seventies.* San Diego and New York: A.S. Barnes & Company; London: The Tantivy Press, 1981.

King, Larry. "Interview with Mikhail Baryshnikov." *CNN.* May 5, 2002. Retrieved July 23, 2017 from http://www.cnn.com.

King, Wayne. "Film; Fact vs. Fiction in Mississippi." *New York Times.* December 4, 1988. Retrieved July 9, 2017 from http://www.nytimes.com.

____, and Weaver, Warren, Jr. "Washington Talk: Briefing; Oval Office Fright." *New York Times.* February 11, 1987. Retrieved June 6, 2017 from http://www.nytimes.com.

Kiselyak, Charles. *Complete Cuckoo a.k.a. the Making of One Flew Over the Cuckoo's Nest.* Quest Productions/The Saul Zaentz Company, 1997, 2002.

Kisselgoff, Anna. "Baryshnikov Quits as Head of American Ballet Theater." *New York Times.* September 29, 1989. Retrieved July 20, 2017 from http://www.nytimes.com.

Klady, Leonard. "Review: Extreme Measures." *Variety.* September 16, 1996. Retrieved August 18, 2017 from http://www.variety.com.

Klein, Alvin. "'Death and the Maiden': Singling Out Ideas." *New York Times.* May 11, 1997. Retrieved August 23, 2017 from http://www.nytimes.com.

Klein, Joshua. "Robert Benton. The magic hour." *A.V. Club.* March 4, 1998. Retrieved August 23, 2017 from http://www.avclub.com.

Klemesrud, Judy. "Movies: ... And the Actor It Makes a Star." *New York Times.* November 21, 1971. Retrieved February 12, 2017 from http://www.nytimes.com.

____. "Costa-Gavras: 'I'm Not Anti-American.'" *New York Times.* April 22, 1973. Retrieved February 20, 2017 from http://www.nytimes.com.

____. "'Rocky Isn't Based on Me,' Says Stallone ...." *New York Times.* November 28, 1976. Retrieved April 3, 2017 from http://www.nytimes.com.

Koehler, Robert. "Film: Review: Behind Enemy Lines." *Variety.* November 21, 2001. Retrieved September 28, 2017 from http://www.variety.com.

Kotcheff, Ted. *Director's Cut: My Life in Film.* Toronto and Ontario, Canada: ECW Press, 2017.

Krebs, Alvin. "Notes on People." *New York Times.* January 15, 1977. Retrieved April 3, 2017 from http://www.nytimes.com.

Kremer, Daniel. *Sidney J. Furie: Life and Films.* Lexington, KY: University Press of Kentucky, 2015.

Kung, Michelle. "The Hackman Connection: Talking with Gene." *The Harvard Crimson.* November 30, 2001. Retrieved October 4, 2017 from http://www.thecrimson.com.

Kunze, P. *The Films of Wes Anderson: Critical Essays on an Indiewood Icon.* New York: Palgrave Macmillan, 2014.

Leachman, Cloris, with Englund, George. *Cloris.* New York: Kensington, 2010.

Leigh, Wendy. *Patrick Swayze: One Last Dance.* New York: Simon & Schuster, 2009.

Lenburg, Jeff. *Dustin Hoffman: Hollywood's Antihero.* Lincoln, NE: IUniverse, 2001.

Lentz, Robert J. *Lee Marvin: His Films and Career.* Jefferson, NC: McFarland, 2006.

Leonelli, Elisa. "Mary Elizabeth Mastrantonio: a not so vulnerable beauty." *Venice.* 1991. Retrieved July 22, 2017 from http://veniceelisaleonelli.wordpress.com.

Leven, Russell. *Poughkeepsie Shuffle: Tracing The French Connection.* BBC, 2000.

Leydon, Joe. "Review: The Replacements." *Variety.* July 31, 2000. Retrieved September 6, 2017 from http://www.variety.com.

Levy, Shawn. *Paul Newman: A Life.* New York: Three Rivers Press, 2009.

Lew, Julie. "San Francisco Becomes a 'Class Action' Suitor." *New York Times.* February 25, 1990. Retrieved July 21, 2017 from http://www.nytimes.com.

Lewis, Jon. *Whom God Wishes to Destroy...: Francis Coppola and the New Hollywood.* Duke University Press Books, 1995.

Levy, Emanuel. "Review: The Chamber." *Variety.* October 7, 1996. Retrieved August 16, 2017 from http://www.variety.com.

———. "Review: 'Enemy of the State.'" *Variety.* November 15, 1998. Retrieved August 24, 2017 from http://www.variety.com.

Lindfield, Susan. "Film; First It Was Drugs, And Now It's Mother." *New York Times.* September 2, 1990. Retrieved July 21, 2017 from http://www.nytimes.com.

Lindsey, Robert. "All Hollywood Loves a Blockbuster—And Chips Off the Old Blockbuster." *New York Times.* May 30, 1976. Retrieved April 1, 2017 from http://www.nytimes.com.

———. "Striking Actors and Studios Still Far Apart." *New York Times.* July 23, 1980. Retrieved April 28, 2017 from http://www.nytimes.com.

———. "Oscars Make And Break Careers." *New York Times.* March 28, 1982. Retrieved April 30, 2017 from http://www.nytimes.com.

LoBianco, Lorraine. "Articles: Downhill Racer (1969)." *Turner Classic Movies.* Retrieved February 1, 2017 from http://www.tcm.com.

Logan, John. *I'll Eat You Last: A Chat with Sue Mengers.* London: Oberon Books, 2013.

Longsdorf, Amy. "For Gene Hackman, giving interview is like crossing enemy lines." *The Morning Call.* November 29, 2001. Retrieved October 1, 2017 from http://www.articles.mccalls.com.

Louman, Robert R. "Marseilles: Sailors, Girls, Forts, Fairs." *New York Times.* January 12, 1975. Retrieved March 16, 2017 from http://www.nytimes.com.

Lovell, Glenn. *Escape Artist: The Life and Films of John Sturges (Wisconsin Studies in Film).* Madison, WI: University of Wisconsin Press, 2008.

Lovenheim, Barbara. "Long Island Interview: Ralph Donnelly; A Movie Impresario Assays Changing Tastes." *New York Times.* January 1, 1989. Retrieved July 14, 2017 from http://www.nytimes.com.

Lyman, Rick. "At the Movies ... Jack Warden's Game." *New York Times.* August 4, 2000. Retrieved September 18, 2017 from http://www.nytimes.com.

———. "At the Movies; Interrogating The Detective." *New York Times.* September 15, 2000. Retrieved September 21, 2017 from http://www.nytimes.com.

———. "'A Beautiful Mind' Wins Four Golden Globes." *New York Times.* January 21, 2002. Retrieved October 7, 2017 from http://www.nytimes.com.

Lyons, Warren. "No More Crying the 'Blue Leaves' Blues. " *New York Times.* July 25, 1971. Retrieved February 4, 2017 from http://www.nytimes.com.

Lytellton, Oliver. "Wake Up, Time to Die: 5 Things You Might Not Know About 'Blade Runner.'" *IndieWire.* June 25, 2012. Retrieved October 22, 2017 from http://www.indiewire.com.

Mackey, Dale. *The Sky Divers.* MGM, 1969.

MacLaine, Shirley. *My Lucky Stars: A Hollywood Memoir.* New York: Bantam Books, 1995.

McCarthy, Todd. "Review: 'Unforgiven.'" *Variety.* July 31, 1992. Retrieved July 24, 2017 from http://www.variety.com.

———. "The Firm." *Variety.* June 28, 1993. Retrieved July 30, 2017 from http://www.variety.com.

———. "Review: 'Geronimo: An American Legend.'" *Variety.* December 5, 1993. Retrieved August 1, 2017 from http://www.variety.com.

———. "Review: 'Wyatt Earp.'" *Variety.* June 20, 1994. Retrieved August 2, 2017 from http://www.variety.com.

———. "Review: 'The Quick and the Dead.'" *Variety.* February 12, 1995. Retrieved August 4, 2017 from http://www.variety.com.

———. "Review: 'Crimson Tide.'" *Variety.* May 8, 1995. Retrieved August 7, 2017 from http://www.variety.com.

———. "Review: 'Get Shorty.'" *Variety.* October 6, 1995. Retrieved August 10, 2017 from http://www.variety.com.

———. "Review: 'The Birdcage.'" *Variety.* March 3, 1996. Retrieved August 12, 2017 from http://www.variety.com.

———. "Review: 'Absolute Power.'" *Variety.* February 6, 1997. Retrieved August 19, 2017 from http://www.variety.com.

———. "Review: 'Twilight.'" *Variety.* February 26, 1998. Retrieved August 22, 2017 from http://www.variety.com.

———. "Review: 'Antz.'" *Variety.* September 21, 1998. Retrieved August 27, 2017 from http://www.variety.com.

———. "Review: 'The Mexican.'" *Variety.* February 27, 2001. Retrieved September 11, 2017 from http://www.variety.com.

———. "Review: 'Heartbreakers.'" *Variety.* March 11, 2001. Retrieved September 13, 2017 from http://www.variety.com.

———. "Review: 'The Royal Tenenbaums.'" *Variety.* October 4, 2001. Retrieved September 22, 2017 from http://www.variety.com.

———. "Runaway Jury." *Variety.* October 9, 2003. Retrieved October 9, 2017 from http://www.variety.com.

———. "Welcome to Mooseport." *Variety.* February 15, 2004. Retrieved October 12, 2017 from http://www.variety.com.

McCarter, Jeremy. "The Disappearance of Gene Hackman." *Newsweek.* January 14, 2010. Retrieved November 7, 2017 from http://www.newsweek.com.

McDougal, Dennis. *Five Easy Decades: How Jack Nicholson Became the Biggest Movie Star in Modern Times.* Hoboken, NJ: John Wiley & Sons, 2008.

McGee, Scott. "Articles: Close Encounters of the Third Kind (1977). "*Turner Classic Movies.* Retrieved March 30, 2017 from http://www.tcm.com.

———. "Articles: Ordinary People (1980)." *Turner Classic Movies.* Retrieved April 18, 2017 from http://www.tcm.com.

McWeeny, Drew. "25 Years In LA Part 1: Gene Hackman, Eazy-E, and Albert Brooks defending a film." *Uproxx.* June 8, 2015. Retrieved October 25, 2017 from http://www.uproxx.com.

Macklin, Tony. "Plant Your Feet and Tell the Truth": An Interview with Clint Eastwood." *Bright Lights*

Film Journal. January 31, 2005. Retrieved July 26, 2017 from http://www.brightlightsfilm.com.

Mancini, Vince. "Gene Hackman told Wes Anderson 'Pull up your pants and act like a man.'" *Filmdrunk.* October 17, 2011. Retrieved September 25, 2017 from http://www.upprox.com/filmdrunk.

Mankiewicz, Tom, and Donner, Richard. Superman DVD Audio Commentary. Warner Bros., 2006.

Mantello, Joe. *I'll Eat You Last: A Chat with Sue Mengers.* The Shubert Organization, 2013.

Marchese, David. "On the 30th Anniversary of Hoosiers, the Movie's Director Recalls What a Pain Gene Hackman Was." *Vulture.* November 3, 2016. Retrieved May 30, 2017 from http://www.vulture.com.

Martin, Douglas. "Toronto Film Festival: Big and Getting Bigger." *New York Times.* September 14, 1985. Retrieved May 27, 2017 from http://www.nytimes.com.

_____. "Greg Goossen, Baseball Player Who Broke Mold, Dies at 65." *New York Times.* March 4, 2011. Retrieved December 4, 2017 from http://www.nytimes.com.

Martin, Pamela Sue, et al. *The Poseidon Adventure* Special Edition DVD Cast Audio Commentary. 20th Century Fox, 2006.

Martinez, Michael. "Boxing: Notebook; Barkley and Toney Try the Old Way." *New York Times.* February 12, 1993. Retrieved July 29, 2017 from http://www.nytimes.com.

Mashberg, Tom. "Sending Artworks Home, but to Whom?" *New York Times.* January 3, 2014. Retrieved October 27, 2017 from http://www.nytimes.com.

Maslin, Janet. "Movie Review: 'March or Die' Ambles Off to a Bloody Ending." *New York Times.* August 6, 1977. Retrieved April 4, 2017 from http://www.nytimes.com.

_____. "New Odd-Couple Movies Are Oddly Conventional." *New York Times.* April 3, 1981. Retrieved April 28, 2017 from http://www.nytimes.com.

_____. "'Superman II' Is Full of Tricks." *New York Times.* June 19, 1981. Retrieved April 15, 2017 from http://www.nytimes.com.

_____. "The Screen: Travolta In 'Two of Kind.'" *New York Times.* December 16, 1983. Retrieved May 8, 2017 from http://www.nytimes.com.

_____. "Film: 'Misunderstood.'" *New York Times.* March 30, 1984. Retrieved May 12, 2017 from http://nytimes.com.

_____. "Movie Review: 'Uncommon Value,' With Gene Hackman." *New York Times.* December 16, 1983. Retrieved May 14, 2017 from http://www.nytimes.com.

_____. "At the Movies." *New York Times.* June 21, 1985. Retrieved May 27, 2017 from http://www.nytimes.com.

_____. "Film: Tale of a Divorce, 'Twice In A Lifetime.'" *New York Times.* October 23, 1985. Retrieved May 19, 2017 from http://www.nytimes.com.

_____. "Film: Gene Hackman As a Coach in 'Hoosiers.'" *New York Times.* February 27, 1987. Retrieved May 29, 2017 from http://www.nytimes.com.

_____. "Movie: 'Superman IV: Quest for Peace.'" *New York Times.* July 25, 1987. Retrieved June 7, 2017 from http://www.nytimes.com.

_____. "Review/Film; A Nice Guy Shot Down in Vietnam." *New York Times.* October 21, 1988. Retrieved June 14, 2017 from http://www.nytimes.com.

_____. "Film View; For Some Heroes, Life Is Just Too Much." *New York Times.* September 23, 1990. Retrieved July 21, 2017 from http://www.nytimes.com.

_____. "Reviews/Film; A Revisionist Portrait Of an Apache Warrior." *New York Times.* December 10, 1993. Retrieved August 1, 2017 from http://www.nytimes.com.

_____. "Review/Film; Correcting the Correctors on a Politically Correct Campus." *New York Times.* April 29, 1994. Retrieved August 6, 2017 from http://www.nytimes.com.

_____. "Film Review; Sharon Stone as Taciturn Gunslinger." *New York Times.* February 10, 1995. Retrieved August 4, 2017 from http://www.nytimes.com.

_____. "Film Review: Crimson Tide; Deciding the World's Fate from the Ocean's Bottom." *New York Times.* May 12, 1995. Retrieved August 7, 2017 from http://www.nytimes.com.

_____. "Film Review; A Hollywood Innocent Who's Anything But." *New York Times.* October 20, 1995 from http://www.nytimes.com.

_____. "The Birdcage." *New York Times.* March 8, 1996. Retrieved August 12, 2017 from http://www.nytimes.com.

_____. "Film Review: Macabre Surprises in a Medical Plot." *New York Times.* September 27, 1996. Retrieved August 18, 2017 from http://www.nytimes.com.

_____. "Movie Review: A Racist and Killer Or Just Misunderstood?" *New York Times.* October 11, 1996. Retrieved August 16, 2017 from http://www.nytimes.com.

_____. "Movie Review: A Whole New Meaning For Executive Privilege." *New York Times.* February 14, 1997. Retrieved August 19, 2017 from http://www.nytimes.com.

_____. "Film Review; A Round of Championship Bantering, Senior Division." *New York Times.* March 6, 1998. Retrieved August 22, 2017 from http://www.nytimes.com.

_____. "'Antz': In a Workers' Paradise, This Ant Feels Insignificant." *New York Times.* October 2, 1998. Retrieved August 27, 2017 from http://www.nytimes.com.

_____. "Film Review; The Walls Have Ears, and Eyes and Cameras." *New York Times.* November 20, 1998. Retrieved August 24, 2017 from http://www.nytimes.com.

Mateas, Lisa. "Marooned (1969)." *Turner Classic Movies.* Retrieved February 2, 2017 from http://www.tcm.com.

Maynard, Micheline. "The Media Business: Advertising; Campaign for United Airlines uses animation and casts Robert Redford as the voice of reason." *New York Times*. March 4, 2004. Retrieved October 12, 2017 from http://www.nytimes.com.

Maysles, Albert, Wes Anderson, et al. *With the Filmmaker: Portraits by Albert Maysles*. The Independent Film Channel/Genco Film Company/Princes of Serendip, 2001.

Meadows, Michael. *The Making of the Replacements*. pattyson.meadows productions/HBO, 2000.

Mell, Eila. *Casting Might-Have-Beens: A Film-by-Film Directory of Actors Considered For Roles Given to Others*. Jefferson, NC: McFarland, 2005.

Meryman, Richard. "The Sixties. Before They Were Kings." *Vanity Fair*. August 15, 2013. Retrieved January 6, 2017 from http://www.vanityfair.com.

Meyer, Nicholas. *The View from the Bridge: Memories of Star Trek and a Life in Hollywood*. New York: Plume, 2010.

Miller, Bryan. "Diner's Journal." *New York Times*. November 15, 1991. Retrieved July 28, 2017 from http://www.nytimes.com.

Miller, Frank. "Articles: First to Flight (1967)." *Turner Classic Movies*. Retrieved January 20, 2017 from http://www.tcm.com.

_____. "Articles: Bonnie and Clyde (1967)." *Turner Classic Movies*. Retrieved January 25, 2017 from http://www.tcm.com.

_____, _____." Articles: A Bridge Too Far (1977)." *Turner Classic Movies*. Retrieved April 2, 2017 from http://www.tcm.com.

Miller, Stephen. *Kristofferson: The Wild American*. London: Omnibus Press, 2009.

Mirkin, David. heartBreakers Special Edition DVD Audio Commentary. MGM, 2001.

Mitchell, Elvis. "Cannes Journal; More Is Less (Or Is That Vice Versa?) At Film Fest." *New York Times*. May 16, 2000. Retrieved September 18, 2017 from http://www.nytimes.com.

_____. "Film Review: Aw, All They Want Is a Chance to Play." *New York Times*. August 11, 2000. Retrieved September 6, 2017 from http://www.nytimes.com.

_____. "Film Review; Nothing Is What It Seems. Or Is It?" *New York Times*. September 22, 2000. Retrieved September 1, 2017 from http://www.nytimes.com.

_____. "Film Review; Courtroom Confrontation with Lots of Star Power." *New York Times*. October 17, 2003. Retrieved October 9, 2017 from http://www.nytimes.com.

Monaco, James. *American Film Now: The People, the Power, the Money, the Movies*. New York: Oxford University Press, 1979.

Moore, John, and Smith, Paul Martin. Behind Enemy Lines DVD Audio Commentary. 20th Century Fox, 2002.

Morton, Andrew. *Tom Cruise: An Unauthorized Biography*. New York: St. Martin's Press, 2008.

Mottram, James. "Movies: Under Suspicion: Gene Hackman." *B.B.C.* October 28, 2014. Retrieved September 2, 2017 from http://www.bbc.co.uk.

_____. "Movies: Under Suspicion: Morgan Freeman." *B.B.C.* September 24, 2014. Retrieved September 2, 2017 from http://www.bbc.co.uk.

Muir, John Kenneth. "Lance Henriksen Interview on The Quick and The Dead (1995)." *John Kenneth Muir's Reflections on Cult Movies and Classic TV*. May 3, 2011. Retrieved August 4, 2017 from http://reflectionsonfilmandtelevision.blogspot.com.au.

_____, _____. *The Unseen Force: The Films of Sam Raimi*. New York: Applause Theatre & Cinema Books, 2004.

Munn, Michael. *Gene Hackman*. London: Robert Hale, 1997.

Murch, Walter. The Conversation DVD Audio Commentary. Paramount, 2000.

Neame, Ronald. *The Poseidon Adventure* Special Edition DVD Director's Audio Commentary. 20th Century Fox, 2006.

_____. with Cooper, Barbara Roisman. *Straight from the Horse's Mouth: Ronald Neame, an Autobiography*. United Kingdom: Scarecrow Press, 2003.

Neibaur, James L. *The Essential Jack Nicholson*. London: Rowman & Littlefield, 2016.

Newman, Nick. "Wild Script Details for Scorsese's 'Wall Street' Roll In, Hinting at the Possible Return of Gene Hackman." *The Film Stage*. August 23, 2012. Retrieved October 22, 2017 from http://www.thefilmstage.com.

Nickson, Chris. *Denzel Washington*. New York: St. Martin's Press, 1996.

_____. *Superhero: A Biography of Christopher Reeve*. New York: St. Martin's Press, 1998.

Nightingale, Benedict. "Theater; 'Death and the Maiden' Becomes a Tale of Two Cities." *New York Times*. May 10, 1992. Retrieved July 29, 2017 from http://www.nytimes.com.

Nixon, Rob. "Articles: Close Encounters of the Third Kind (1977)." *Turner Classic Movies*. Retrieved April 1, 2017 from http://www.tcm.com.

Norman, Michael. "Hollywood's Uncommon Everyman." *New York Times*. March 19, 1989. Retrieved July 12, 2017 from http://www.nytimes.com.

Norris, Sally. *Richard Attenborough: A Life in Film*. BBC/Events Production London, 2014.

O'Connell, Sean. "Interview: Tony Scott talks Denzel, Gene Hackman's retirement, and runaway trains for 'Unstoppable.'" *Hollywood News*. October 25, 2010. Retrieved October 18, 2017 from http://www.hollywoodnews.com.

Parish, James Robert. *It's Good to Be King: The Seriously Funny Life of Mel Brooks*. Hoboken, NJ: James Wiley & Sons, 2007.

Parker, Alan. Mississippi Burning DVD Audio Commentary. MGM (Video & DVD), 2001.

_____. Mississippi Burning. The Making Of The Film. Retrieved July 6, 2017 from http://www.alanparker.com.

Parker, John. *Michael Douglas: Acting on Instinct*. London: Headline Publishing, 1994.

Parker, Trey. South Park: "Krazy Kripples." Braniff, 2003.

Peary, Gerald. *For the Love of Movies: The Story of Film Criticism*. AG Films, 2009.

BIBLIOGRAPHY

Peden, Lauren David. "Film; Seen the One Where Arnold Sells Noodles?" *New York Times.* June 20, 1993. Retrieved August 1, 2017 from http://www.nytimes.com.

Pener, Degen. "Fewer Killer Dresses at the Oscars." *New York Times.* March 31, 1993. Retrieved July 31, 2017 from http://www.nytimes.com.

Petrie, Donald. Welcome to Mooseport DVD Audio Commentary. 20th Century–Fox, 2004.

Phillips, Gene D. *Godfather: The Intimate Francis Ford Coppola.* Lexington: University Press of Kentucky, 2013.

_____, _____ _____. with Hill, Rodney. *Francis Ford Coppola: Interviews (Conversations with Filmmakers).* University Press of Mississippi, 2004.

Phillips, Julia. *You'll Never Eat Lunch in This Town Again.* New York: Random House, 1991.

Piven, Jeremy. PCU DVD Audio Commentary. Starz/Anchor Bay, 2013.

Pomerance, Murray, and Palmer, R. Barton. *A Little Solitaire: John Frankenheimer and American Film.* Piscataway, NJ: Rutgers University Press, 2011.

Quirk, Lawrence J. *Paul Newman: A Life, Updated.* Lanham, MD: Taylor Trade Publications, 2009.

Radosta, John S. "Pole Won by Jones at Glen." *New York Times.* October 7, 1979. Retrieved April 18, 2017 from http://www.nytimes.com.

Reed, Rex. "'A Lotta Things I Wanted More and Didn't Get.'" *New York Times.* June 19, 1966. Retrieved January 17, 2017 from http://www.nytimes.com.

Reeve, Christopher. *Still Me.* London: Arrow Books, 1998.

Resnik, Muriel. *Son of Any Wednesday.* New York: Stein And Day, 1965.

Reynolds, Burt. *But Enough About Me.* London: Bonnier Publishing, 2015.

Rich, Frank. "Review/Theater; Close, Hackman and Dreyfuss In 'Death and the Maiden.'" *New York Times.* March 18, 1992. Retrieved July 25, 2017 from http://www.nytimes.com.

Richards, David. "'Maiden' Is a Thriller in Spite of Itself." *New York Times.* March 22, 1992. Retrieved July 28, 2017 from http://www.nytimes.com.

Riding, Alan. "A Mexican City Relives Nicaraguans' Rebellion." *New York Times.* October 10, 1982. Retrieved April 30, 2017 from http://www.nytimes.com.

Rigoulot, Leslie. "Hugh Grant on "Extreme Measures." *Film Scouts.* September 20, 1996. Retrieved August 18, 2017 from http://www.filmscouts.com.

Robb, Brian J. *Brad Pitt: The Rise to Stardom.* London: Plexus Publishing, 2002.

Roberts, Stephen V. "The 1972 Campaign." *New York Times.* April 17, 1972. Retrieved February 13, 2017 from http://www.nytimes.com.

Rohter, Larry. "Theater; Dorfman's 'Maiden' Cries Out." *New York Times.* March 8, 1992. Retrieved July 28, 2017 from http://www.nytimes.com.

Rooney, David. "Review: 'Heist.'" *Variety.* September 3, 2001. Retrieved September 19, 2017 from http://www.variety.com.

Rosen, Christopher. "Why Gene Hackman Was Reluctant To Do 'Royal Tenenbaums.'" *HuffPost.* August 10, 2013. Retrieved September 26, 2017 from http://www.huffingtonpost.com.

Rosen, Robert L., and Hackman, Gene. DVD Audio Commentary. The French Connection II. 20th Century Fox, 2002.

Rosenthal, Mark. Superman IV: The Quest for Peace DVD Audio Commentary. Warner Bros., 2006.

Rushfield, Richard. "Streamfix: From Popeye Doyle to Wes Anderson—6 Great Gene Hackman Performances." *Uproxx.* January 30, 2015. Retrieved October 25, 2017 from http://www.uproxx.com.

Ryzik, Melena. "Casting 'Nebraska' Via Radio and Other Producing Secrets." *New York Times.* January 20, 2014. Retrieved October 27, 2017 from http://www.nytimes.com.

Saland, Ronald. The Day of the Director. Professional Films/Robbins Nest Production/Warner Bros., Year Unknown.

Salkind, Ilya, and Spengler, Pierre. Superman—The Movie (Four-Disc Special Edition) DVD Audio Commentary. Warner Bros., 2006.

Sampson, Mike. "Could Gene Hackman come out of retirement for Alexander Payne's next movie?" *Joblo.* October 12, 2011. Retrieved October 20, 2017 from http://www.joblo.com.

Schechter, Scott. *The Liza Minnelli Scrapbook.* New York: Citadel, 2004.

Schickel, Richard. *Clint Eastwood: A Biography.* New York: Random House, 1996.

_____. *Eastwood and Co. Making Unforgiven.* Lorac Production/Warner Bros. Television, 1992.

_____. *Eastwood on Eastwood.* Lorac Production/TNT Productions, 1997.

_____. Unforgiven DVD Audio Commentary. Warner Bros., 2010.

Schmidlin, Charles. "Martin Scorsese's 'The Wolf of Wall Street' Script Calls For Gene Hackman Voice-Over, Dwarf Tossing & More." *IndieWire.* August 24, 2012. Retrieved October 22, 2017 from http://www.indiewire.com.

Schnakenberg, Robert. *The Big Bad Book of Bill Murray: A Critical Appreciation of the World's Finest Actor.* Philadelphia, PA: Quirk Books, 2015.

Schoell, William, and Quirk, Lawrence J. *The Sundance Kid: A Biography of Robert Redford.* Lanham, MD: Taylor Trade Publishing, 2006.

Schwartz, Sherwood, and Schwartz, Lloyd J. *Brady, Brady, Brady: The Complete Story of the Brady Bunch as Told by the Father/Son Team who Really Know.* Philadelphia, PA: Running Press, 2010.

Scivally, Bruce. *Superman on Film, Television, Radio and Broadway.* Jefferson, NC: McFarland, 2007.

Scott, A.O. "Film Review; It's Take Your Daughter to Work Day." *New York Times.* March 23, 2001. Retrieved September 13, 2017 from http://www.nytimes.com.

_____, _____. _____. "Film Festival Review; Brought Up to Be Prodigies, Three Siblings Share a Melancholy Oddness." *New York Times.* October 5, 2001. Retrieved September 22, 2017 from http://www.nytimes.com.

Bibliography

_____, _____. _____. "Film Review; Forget the Girl and Gold; Look for the Chemistry." *New York Times*. November 9, 2001. Retrieved September 19, 2017 from http://www.nytimes.com.

Scott, James. "Gene's Road Rage Fight." *The Free Library*. October 31, 2001. Retrieved October 4, 2017 from http://www.thefreelibrary.com.

Segaloff, Nat. *Arthur Penn: American Director (Screen Classics)*. Lexington, KY: University Press of Kentucky, 2011.

_____. *Hurricane Billy: The Stormy Life and Films of William Friedkin*. New York: William Morrow and Company, 1990.

Sella, Marshall. "Boyish Wonder." *New York Times*. December 2, 2001. Retrieved October 5, 2017 from http://www.nytimes.com.

Sellers, Robert. *What Fresh Lunacy is This?: The Authorized Biography of Oliver Reed*. London: Constable, 2014.

Senior, Jennifer. "Film; The 50-Year Hoffman-Hackman History." *New York Times*. October 12, 2003. Retrieved January 3, 2017 from http://www.nytimes.com.

Shepard, Richard. *I Knew It Was You: Rediscovering John Cazale*. Oscillscope Films/HBO Documentary Films/Rat Entertainment, 2009.

Sheward, David. *Rage and Glory: The Volatile Life and Career of George C. Scott*. Milwaukee, WI: Applause Theatre & Cinema Books, 2008.

Shone, Tom. "Another film, another hospital trip." *The Telegraph*. July 16, 2002. Retrieved August 10, 2017 from http://www.telegraph.co.uk.

Simon, Alex. "Waiting For Gene: A Visit to the set of Under Suspicion." *The Hollywood Interview*. @1999. Retrieved September 5, 2017 from http://www.thehollywoodinterview.blogspot.com.au.

_____. "Andrew Davis: The Hollywood Interview." *The Hollywood Interview*. November 29, 2012. Retrieved July 13, 2017 from http://www.thehollywoodinterview.blogspot.com.au.

Smith, Richard Harland. "Articles: Mad Dog Coll (1961)." *Turner Classic Movies*. Retrieved January 10, 2017 from http://www.tcm.com.

_____, _____. "Articles: The Hunting Party (1961). " *Turner Classic Movies*. Retrieved February 6, 2017 from http://www.tcm.com.

_____, _____ _____. "Articles: The Poseidon Adventure (1972)." *Turner Classic Movies*. Retrieved February 14, 2017 from http://www.tcm.com.

_____, _____ _____. "Articles: Night Moves (1975)." *Turner Classic Movies*. Retrieved March 11, 2017 from http://www.tcm.com.

Snider, Eric D. "12 Dusty Facts About Unforgiven." *Mental Floss*. August 29, 2015. Retrieved July 27, 2017 from http://www.mentalfloss.com.

Snyder, David. *The Silence of the Lambs: Page To Screen*. KPI/Bravo Original Productions, 2002.

Soderbergh, Steven and Lester, Richard. *Getting Away With It: Or: The Further Adventures of the Luckiest Bastard You Ever Saw*. London: Faber & Faber, 2011.

Spacek, Sissy, with Vollers, Maryanne. *My Extraordinary Ordinary Life*. New York: Hyperion, 2012.

Spada, James. *Streisand: In the Camera Eye (Barbra Streisand)*. New York: Harry N. Abrams, 2014.

Spengler, Pierre, and Salkind, Ilya. Superman II DVD Audio Commentary. Warner Home Entertainment, 2006.

Sragow, Michael. "Interview: Jan Troell." *Film Comment*. March 4, 2016. Retrieved February 24, 2017 from http://www.filmcomment.com.

Stafford, Jeff. "Articles: Bonnie and Clyde (1967)." *Turner Classic Movies*. Retrieved January 25, 2017 from http://www.tcm.com.

_____. "Articles: The Split (1968)." *Turner Classic Movies*. Retrieved January 26, 2017 from http://www.tcm.com.

_____. "Articles: The Conversation (1974)." *Turner Classic Movies*. Retrieved February 20, 2017 from http://www.tcm.com.

Steinberg, J. S. "Articles: I Never Sang for My Father (1970). " *Turner Classic Movies*. Retrieved February 4, 2017 from http://www.tcm.com.

_____. "Articles: Superman II (1981)." *Turner Classic Movies*. Retrieved April 15, 2017 from http://www.tcm.com.

Sterritt, David. *The Cinema of Clint Eastwood: Chronicles of America*. New York: Columbia University Press, 2014.

Stevens, Kyle. *Mike Nichols: Sex, Language, and the Reinvention of Psychological Realism*. New York: Oxford University Press, 2015.

Stirling, Richard. *Julie Andrews: An Intimate Biography*. New York: St. Martin's Griffin, 2009.

Susman, Gary. "Gene Hackman's fender bender leads to fisticuffs." *Entertainment Weekly*. November 1, 2001. Retrieved October 4, 2017 from http://www.ew.com.

Swayze, Patrick, and Niemi, Lisa. *The Time of My Life*. New York: Simon & Schuster, 2009.

Tatara, Paul. "Articles: The Gypsy Moths (1969)." *Turner Classic Movies*. Retrieved January 29, 2017 from http://www.tcm.com.

Taubman, Howard. "The Theater: Comedy by Irwin Shaw." *New York Times*. April 12, 1963. Retrieved January 12, 2017 from http://www.nytimes.com.

_____. "The Theater: 'Rainy Day.'" *New York Times*. October 23, 1963. Retrieved January 13, 2017 from http://www.nytimes.com.

_____. "The Theater: 'Any Wednesday' Opens. "*New York Times*. February 19, 1964. Retrieved January 15, 2017 from http://www.nytimes.com.

_____. "Theater: 'Poor Richard' Comedy by Jean Kerr at the Helen Hayes." *New York Times*. December 3, 1964. Retrieved January 16, 2017 from http://www.nytimes.com.

Terrill, Marshall. *Steve McQueen: The Life and Legend of a Hollywood Icon*. Chicago, IL: Triumph Books, 2010.

Terry, Clifford. "Robert Redford Goes Behind The Camera for a New Image." *New York Times*. July 27, 1980. Retrieved April 28, 2017 from http://www.nytimes.com.

Thames, Stephanie. "Articles: The French Connection (1971)." *Turner Classic Movies*. Retrieved February 7, 2017 from http://www.tcm.com.

BIBLIOGRAPHY

Thau, Michael. *The Magic Behind The Cape.* Warner Home Video, 2001.

_____. *Making Superman: Filming the Legend.* Warner Home Video, 2001.

_____. *Taking Flight: The Development of "Superman."* Warner Home Video, 2001.

Thomas, Robert McG., et al. "Scouting; Hucksters Head for Victory." *New York Times.* November 27, 1985. Retrieved June 4, 2017 from http://www.nytimes.com.

Thomas, Tony. *Gregory Peck. Pyramid Illustrated History of the Movies.* New York: Pyramid Publications, 1977.

_____, _____ and Solomon, Aubrey. *The Films of 20th Century Fox. A Pictorial History.* Secaucus, NJ: The Citadel Press, 1979.

Thompson, Douglas. *Clint Eastwood—The Biography of Cinema's Greatest Ever Star.* London: John Blake Publishing, 2007.

Thompson, Howard. "Movie Review: 'Underworld, U.S.A.' and 'Mad Dog Coll.'" *New York Times.* May 13, 1961. Retrieved January 10, 2017 from http://www.nytimes.com.

_____. "The Screen: Raquel Welch in 'Fathom,' an Adventure Feature:Thugs Chase Actress in Brisk Thriller." *New York Times.* December 14, 1967. Retrieved January 22, 2017 from http://www.nytimes.com.

_____. "... Contest for Place Close." *New York Times.* January 4, 1968. Retrieved January 22, 2017 from http://www.nytimes.com.

_____. "The Screen: 'Marooned,' Space Film, Opens the New Ziegfeld:Story Built on Perils of Planetary Trips." *New York Times.* December 19, 1969. Retrieved February 2, 2017 from http://www.nytimes.com.

_____. "Screen:Liv Ullmann, Hackman in 'Zandy's Bride.'" *New York Times.* May 20, 1974. Retrieved February 24, 2017 from http://www.nytimes.com.

Toner, Robin, and Weaver, Warren, Jr. "Briefing; Taken Aback." *New York Times.* June 23, 1987. Retrieved June 4, 2017 from http://www.nytimes.com.

Toole, Michael J., and Stafford, Jeff. "Articles: Bite the Bullet (1975)." *Turner Classic Movies.* Retrieved March 15, 2017 from http://www.tcm.com.

Tracey, Kathleen. *Morgan Freeman: A Biography.* Fort Lee, NJ: Barricade Books, 2006.

Travers, Peter. "Postcards from the Edge." *Rolling Stone.* September 12, 1990. Retrieved July 19, 2017 from http://www.rollingstone.com.

_____. "Class Action." *Rolling Stone.* March 15, 1991. Retrieved July 21, 2017 from http://www.rollingstone.com.

_____. "Unforgiven." *Rolling Stone.* August 6, 1992. Retrieved July 24, 2017 from http://www.rollingstone.com.

_____. "The Firm." *Rolling Stone.* June 30, 1993. Retrieved July 30, 2017 from http://www.rollingstone.com.

_____. "The Quick and the Dead." *Rolling Stone.* February 10, 1995. Retrieved August 4, 2017 from http://www.rollingstone.com.

_____. "Get Shorty." *Rolling Stone.* October 20, 1995. Retrieved August 10, 2017 from http://www.rollingstone.com.

_____. "Extreme Measures." *Rolling Stone.* September 27, 1996. Retrieved August 18, 2107 from http://www.rollingstone.com.

_____. "Absolute Power." *Rolling Stone.* February 14, 1997. Retrieved August 19, 2017 from http://www.rollingstone.com.

_____. "Twilight." *Rolling Stone.* March 6, 1998. Retrieved August 22, 2017 from http://www.rollingstone.com.

_____. "Antz." *Rolling Stone.* October 2, 1998. Retrieved August 27, 2017 from http://www.rollingstone.com.

_____. "Enemy of the State." *Rolling Stone.* November 20, 1998. Retrieved August 24, 2017 from http://www.rollingstone.com.

_____. "The Replacements." *Rolling Stone.* August 11, 2000. Retrieved September 6, 2017 from http://www.rollingstone.com.

_____. "Under Suspicion." *Rolling Stone.* September 24, 2000. Retrieved September 1, 2017 from http://www.rollingstone.com.

_____. "The Mexican." *Rolling Stone.* March 5, 2001. Retrieved September 11, 2017 from http://www.rollingstone.com.

_____. "Heartbreakers." *Rolling Stone.* March 15, 2001. Retrieved September 13, 2017 from http://www.rollingstone.com.

_____. "Heist." *Rolling Stone.* November 9, 2001. Retrieved September 19, 2017 from http://www.rollingstone.com.

_____. "The Royal Tenenbaums." *Rolling Stone.* December 13, 2001. Retrieved September 22, 2017 from http://www.rollingstone.com.

_____. "Runaway Jury." *Rolling Stone.* October 17, 2003. Retrieved October 9, 2017 from http://www.rollingstone.com.

_____. "Welcome to Mooseport." *Rolling Stone.* February 20, 2004. Retrieved October 12, 2017 from http://www.rollingstone.com.

Travers, Steven. *Coppola's Monster Film: The Making of Apocalypse Now.* Jefferson, NC: McFarland, 2016.

Tucker, Betty Jo. *Susan Sarandon: A True Maverick.* Tucson, AZ: Hats Off Books, 2004.

Ullmann, Liv. *Liv Ullmann: Interviews.* University Press of Mississippi, 2006.

Vagg, Stephen. *Rod Taylor: An Aussie in Hollywood.* Albany, GA: BearManor Media, 2015.

Van Gelder, Lawrence. "At The Movies." *New York Times.* June 23, 1989. Retrieved July 11, 2017 from http://www.nytimes.com.

_____ _____. "At The Movies." *New York Times.* December 15, 1989. Retrieved July 20, 2017 from http://www.nytimes.com.

_____ _____. "At The Movies." *New York Times.* September 28, 1990. Retrieved July 21, 2017 from http://www.nytimes.com.

Verbinski, Gore, et al. the mexican DVD Director's Commentary. Dreamworks Video, 2001.

Vincent, Alice. "12 things we learned from Robin Williams." *The Telegraph.* August 13, 2014. Re-

Bibliography

trieved August 12, 2017 from http://www.telegraph.co.uk.

Von Glinow, Kiki. "Gene Hackman Airlifted to Hospital." *Moviefone*. January 13, 2012. Retrieved October 21, 2017 from http://www.moveifone.com.

Warner, Jennifer. *The Fantastic Mr. Anderson: A Biography of Wes Anderson*. Bookcaps, 2013.

Warr, Philippa. "Hackman announces first solo novel." *Digital Spy*. September 30, 2010. Retrieved October 17, 2017 from http://www.digitalspy.com.

Weaver, Sigourney, et al. heartBreakers Special Edition DVD Audio Commentary. MGM, 2001.

Weiler, A.H. "A New Life for "Father.'" *New York Times*. January 5, 1969. Retrieved January 28, 2017 from http://www.nytimes.com.

_____. "...Selected Shorts." *New York Times*. October 3, 1971. Retrieved February 12, 2017 from http://www.nytimes.com.

_____. "Movies." *New York Times*. February 6, 1972. Retrieved February 12, 2017 from http://www.nytimes.com.

_____. "...Selected Shorts." *New York Times*. February 27, 1972. Retrieved February 12, 2017 from http://www.nytimes.com.

_____. "Movies." *New York Times*. March 12, 1972. Retrieved February 13, 2017 from http://www.nytimes.com.

_____. "Screen: 'Poseidon Adventure' Arrives: Liner Disaster Opens the National Theater Hackman, as Minister, Leads Group to Safety." *New York Times*. December 13, 1972. Retrieved February 14, 2017 from http://www.nytimes.com.

_____. "Gene Hackman, Snoop." *New York Times*. May 7, 1972. Retrieved February 15, 2017 from http://www.nytimes.com.

_____. "Movies: ... Going Their Way?" *New York Times*. June 11, 1972. Retrieved February 15, 2017 from http://www.nytimes.com.

_____. "Movies ... Hackman Goes Wild." *New York Times*. October 8, 1972. Retrieved February 15, 2017 from http://www.nytimes.com.

_____. "Movies ... Go, Gene, Go!" *New York Times*. October 15, 1972. Retrieved February 15, 2017 from http://www.nytimes.com.

_____. "... Selected Shorts." *New York Times*. April 29, 1973. Retrieved February 16, 2017 from http://www.nytimes.com.

Weinraub, Bernard. "All Is Glittery and a Bit Odd at Golden Globes." *New York Times*. January 25, 1993. Retrieved July 29, 2017 from http://www.nytimes.com.

_____. "Hollywood's Oscar Fever This Time Is Lukewarm." *New York Times*. March 18, 1993. Retrieved July 29, 2017 from http://www.nytimes.com.

_____. "Turning the Tables on Race Relations." *New York Times*. February 6, 1995. Retrieved August 9, 2017 from http://www.nytimes.com.

_____. "'Antz' Jumps the Gun on Disney's 'Bug's Life.'" *New York Times*. June 25, 1998. Retrieved August 26, 2017 from http://www.nytimes.com.

_____. "Television/Radio; A Vietnam War Film Takes On a Sudden Resonance." *New York Times*. December 9, 2001. Retrieved October 5, 2017 from http://www.nytimes.com.

Whale, James. *Bride of Frankenstein*. Universal Pictures, James Whale Production, 1935.

Whitehead, J. W. *Mike Nichols and the Cinema of Transformation*. Jefferson, NC: McFarland, 2014.

Wight, Douglas. *Leonardo DiCaprio—The Biography*. John Blake Publishing, 2013.

Witchel, Alex. "On Stage, and Off." *New York Times*. November 8, 1991. Retrieved July 25, 2017 from http://www.nytimes.com.

_____. "On Stage, and Off." *New York Times*. December 6, 1991. Retrieved July 28, 2017 from http://www.nytimes.com.

_____. "On Stage, and Off." *New York Times*. January 10, 1992. Retrieved July 28, 2017 from http://www.nytimes.com.

_____. "On Stage, and Off." *New York Times*. April 3, 1992. Retrieved July 29, 2017 from http://www.nytimes.com.

_____. "On Stage, and Off." *New York Times*. April 17, 1992. Retrieved July 29, 2017 from http://www.nytimes.com.

Wood, Robin, and Lippe, Richard. *Arthur Penn*. Detroit, MI: Wayne State University Press, 2014.

Wurtz, Jeff. *Inside the Actors Studio: Clint Eastwood*. The Actors Studio/Bravo/Belegeuse Productions/In The Moment Productions/NBC/Universal, 2003.

Wygant, Bobbie. Interviews Gene Hackman for Misunderstood 1984. Eric Clapp Films, 2011.

_____. Interviews Gene Hackman for Target 1985. Eric Clapp Films, 2012.

Yankee, Luke. *Just Outside the Spotlight: Growing Up with Eileen Heckart*. New York: Back Stage Books, 2006.

Yorkin, Bud, et al. Twice in a Lifetime DVD Audio Commentary. Warner Home Video. 2005.

Young, Stephen B. *John Frankenheimer: Interviews, Essays, and Profiles*. Plymouth, UK: Scarecrow Press, 2013.

Yule, Andrew. *Al Pacino: A Life on the Wire*. New York: SP Books, 1992.

Zoller Seitz, Matt. "How Wes Anderson Made *The Royal Tenenbaums*." *Vulture*. October 7, 2013. Retrieved September 25, 2017 from http://www.vulture.com.

Zolotow, Sam. "... Schisgal Has 3 New Plays." *New York Times*. June 23, 1966. Retrieved January 17, 2017 from http://www.nytimes.com.

_____. "... 'Any Wednesday.'" *New York Times*. October 17, 1963. Retrieved March 4, 2017 from http://www.nytimes.com.

_____. "... 'Natural Look' Opening Set." *New York Times*. January 30, 1967. Retrieved January 20, 2017 from http://www.nytimes.com.

Index

Numbers in ***bold italics*** indicate pages with illustrations

ABC News Nightline 109
Absolute Power 140
All Night Long 1, 77–***78***, 79, 166
Allen, Irwin 47, 48, 51, 64
Allen, Woody 102, 103, 142
America at the Movies 68
The American Film Institute Salute to Fred Astaire 79
American Masters: "Hitchcock, Selznick, and the End of Hollywood" 143
America[apost]s Game: The Superbowl Champions 163
Anderson, Wes 152, 154
Andrews, Julie 19, 20
Another Woman 102, 108
Anspaugh, David 90, 92, 93, 94
Antz 142–143
Apted, Michael 116, 139
Arakawa, Betsy 86, 110, 122, 166
Archer, Anne 113, 114, 115
Attenborough, Richard 67
Any Wednesday 15–16, 17–18, 19

Balaban, Burt 12
Banning 26–27
Barefoot in the Park 15
Baryshnikov, Mikhail 117, 118
*Bat*21* ***99***, 100, 108
Beatty, Ned 71, 72
Beatty, Warren 14, 22, 23, 24, 62, 63, 76, 77, 80, 106, 109, 110, 130, 154, 163
Behind Enemy Lines 156–157
Benton, Robert 22, 68, 140, 163
Bergen, Candice 35, 58
The Best of Hollywood 143
Best Shot see *Hoosiers*
The Birdcage 2, 134–***135***, 136, 162
Bite the Bullet 57–58, 64
Bonnie and Clyde 14, 22–***23***, 24–25, 26, 28, 29, 33, 39, 51, 57, 76, 137, 138, 156
Borgnine, Ernest 31, 46, 48
Boyle, Peter 38, 57
The Brady Bunch 34

Brando, Marlon 2, 6, 52, 69, 70, 72, 121, 148, 155
Brenner: "The Bluff" 11; "Laney's Boy" 18–19; "Unwritten Law" 19
Breslin, Jimmy 38, 39, 41
A Bridge Too Far 67, 74, 130
Bronson, Charles 39, 116
Brooks, Mel 56, 57
Brooks, Richard 57, 58
Brown, Jim 28, 30, 31
Bruckheimer, Jerry 131, 142
Burstyn, Ellen 27, 87, 155

Caan, James 10, 39, 116, 117
La Cage aux Folles 119, 134
Cagney, James 3, 39, 161
Caine, Michael 130, 154, 161
Cannes: Through the Eyes of the Hunter 150
Cassidy, Joanna 81, 82, 108
Cates, Gilbert 33
CBS Playhouse: "My Father and My Mother" 27–28
The Chamber 136–***137***, 138, 157
Chaparral 10
The Charlie Rose Show 145
Children from Their Games 13, 14
Cinema TV series 43
Cisco Pike 37, 84
Clark, Bob 106, 107
Class Action 116–117, 118, 133, 139
Close, Glenn 122, 123
Colors of Courage: Sons of New Mexico, Prisoners of Japan 160
Come to the Place of Sin 16
Community Shelter Planning 25
Company Business 117–118
Connery, Sean 136, 141, 159
The Conversation 52–***53***, 57, 64, 98, 99, 102, 111, 141
Coppola, Francis Ford 52, 53, 65, 108–109
Costner, Kevin 95, 96, 119, 127, 128
A Covenant with Death 25–26

Crimson Tide 130–132, 133, 142, 156
Crowe, Russell 128, 129
Cruise, Tom 123, 124, 130
The Curious Miss Caraway 7
Cusack, John 159, 160

Dafoe, Willem 104, 111
D'Antoni, Philip 38, 39, 44
Darnell, Eric 142, 143
The David Frost Show 34
Davis, Andrew 108, 109
Death and the Maiden (film) 123
Death and the Maiden (play) 122–123
The Defenders: "Judgment Eve" 13; "Quality of Mercy" 12
De Niro. Robert 109, 111, 156
Dennehy, Brian 79, 106
Dennis, Sandy 16, 17, 18
Deutch, Howard 147, 148
Dillon, Matt 88, 89
Diners, Drive-ins and Dives: "Big Breakfast" 163
Directions: "Marriage" 20
The Directors: The Films of Richard Donner 143
Doctor's Wives 34
The Domino Principle 65, ***66***, 67, 74
Donaldson, Roger 95
Donen, Stanley 62, 63, 64
Donner, Richard 70, 71, 72, 73, 116
Douglas, Kirk 6, 63
Douglas, Michael 63, 111, 116
Downhill Racer 31–32, 42, 140
Dreyfuss, Richard 64, 118, 122
Drury, David 100
Dunaway, Faye 137, 138
DuPont Show of the Week: "Ride with Terror" 16
Duvall, Robert 2, 8, 9–10, 52, 65, 91, 99, 111, 119, 127, 162

Earth and the American Dream 123

191

INDEX

East Side/West Side: "Creeps Live Here" 16
Eastwood, Clint 106, 116, 119, 120, 121, 125, 140, 164, 166
Eastwood Directs: The Untold Story 167
Egan, Eddie 39, 40, 41, 44, 60
Eichhorn, Lisa 77, 78, 79
Enemy of the State 141–142
Escape from Andersonville: A Novel of the Civil War 164
Eureka 80–81, 82
Extreme Measures 139

Farina, Dennis 133, 136
The F.B.I.: "The Courier" 25
50 Years: The Best of Hollywood see The Best of Hollywood
The Firm 123–124, 130, 133, 157
First to Flight 25
Fisher, Carrie 115, 116
Fisher, Frances 120, 121
Fleder, Gary 159, 160
Flemyng, Gordon 28
Flynn, Errol 3, 6, 39
Foley, James 136
Ford, Harrison 79, 116, 138
Formula 1—Febbre della velocità 75
Fox, Huckleberry 83, 84
Fragments 20, 27
Frankenheimer, John 28, 29, 35, 38, 55, 56, 59, 60, 103, 159
Freeman, Morgan 119, 121, 125, 132, 143, 144, 145
The French Connection 36–37, 38–42, 44, 48, 108, 148, 156, 161, 166
French Connection II 38, 59–61, 64, 99
Friedkin, William 37, 38, 39, 40, 41, 42, 44, 67
Full Moon in Blue Water 100, **101**, 102, 108
Furie, Sidney J. 97, 98

Gandolfini, James 131, 133
Garde à vue aka The Inquisitor 103, 143
Garr, Teri 52, 102, 125
Gere, Richard 89, 90
Geronimo: An American Legend 127, 133
Get Shorty 2, 133–134, 161
Goldman, William 67, 78, 136, 140
Goossen, Gregory B. 133, 137, 141, 144, 151, 152, 165
Gould, Elliott 10, 73, 118
The Graduate 24, 26
Grant, Cary 6, 70
Grisham, John 123, 136, 138, 159
Grosso, Sonny 39, 40
The Gypsy Moths 28–29, 55

Harris, Richard 120, 121
Harris, Thomas 103, 111
Hawaii 19–20, 121
Hawk: "Do Not Mutilate or Spindle" 20
Heartbreakers 2, 148–149, 157
Heist 151–**152**, 155
Heroes of Iwo Jima 155
Hershey, Barbara 91, 93
Herzfeld, John 83
Hidden City 161
Hill, George Roy 19
Hill, Walter 127
Hoffman, Dustin 1, 7, 8, 9–10, 26, 58, 69, 89, 99, 109, 111, 116, 119, 159, 160, 162
The Hollywood Greats 162
Hoosiers **90**–95, 99, 147, 156, 165
Hopkins, Anthony 136, 141
Hopkins, Stephen 144, 145
Hopper, Dennis 90, 91, 92, 93, 94, 130, 138
The Hunting Party 35, 79
Hurt, John 103, 111
Huston, Anjelica 152, 154, 155
Hyams, Peter 113, 114, 115

I Never Sang for My Father **32**–33, 39, 42, 43, 140
I Spy: "Happy Birthday Everybody" 28
Imaginary Witness: Hollywood and the Holocaust 162
Inside the Actors Studio 4, 23, 24, 44, 57, 58, 155–156
Insight: "Confrontation" 34
The Invaders: "The Spores" 27
Iron Horse: "Leopards Try, But Leopards Can't" 27
Island of Hope, Island of Tears 117

Jane, Thomas 143, 144, 145
Johnson, Lamont 25
Johnson, Tim 142, 143
Jones, Tommy Lee 108, 109, 116, 125, 131
Jordan, Glenn 20
Justice for None 162–163

Kasdan, Lawrence 127, 128
Kiley, Richard 12, 58
Kotcheff, Ted 84, 85
Kramer, Stanley 65
Kristofferson, Kris 37, 84
Kulik, Buzz 30

Lancaster, Burt 28, 29, 44, 47, 103
Lane, Nathan 134, 136
Larry King Live 163
Late Night with David Letterman 9, 51, 92, 95, 100, 107
Laugh-In 43, 44

Lenihan, Daniel 124, 145–146, 148, 150, 158, 162, 164
Lester, Richard 71, 72
Lilith 14, 22, 23
Logan, John 1, 166
A Look at Liv 76
Look Up and Live: "The End of the Story" 13
Loose Cannons 106–**107**, 133
Lucky Lady **61**–64, 74
Lumet, Sidney 75, 89, 90

MacLaine, Shirley 115, 116
Mad Dog Call 12
Maltese, Faye Philippa (aka Faye Hackman) 6, 7, 10, 11, 12, 17, 20, 35, 37, 45, 82
Mamet, David 151
Mankiewicz, Tom 68, 70
Mastrantonio, Mary Elizabeth 116, 117
March or Die 67–68, 74
Markle, Peter 100
Marooned 29–30, 31
Marvin, Lee 39, 42, 43, 56, 58
Masterson, Peter 100
McQueen, Steve 39, 63, 64
Medford, Don 12, 35
Mengers, Sue 1, 39, 63, 69, 75, 77, 78, 108, 166
The Mexican 148
Meyer, Nicholas 117, 118
Midler, Bette 133, 166
Minnelli, Liza 54, 62, 64
Mirkin, David 149
Mississippi Burning 104–**105**, 106, 109, 111
Misunderstood **83**–84
Moore, John 157
Moore, Simon 128, 129
Morrison, George 8–9, 16, 17, 44, 110

Naked City: "Prime of Life" 13
Narrow Margin 113–**114**, 115, 118
The Natural Look 26
Neame, Ronald 47, 48
Neighbors 20
Newland, John 16
Newman, Paul 2, 38, 62, 69, 86, 116, 117, 140, 141
Nichols, Mike 15, 17, 26, 115, 122, 134, 136
Nicholson, Jack 1, 2, 23, 63, 64, 91, 100, 165
Night Moves 55–**56**, 64
Night of 100 Stars II 89
No Way Out 95–96, 127
Norton, B.L. 37
Nyby, Christian 25

100 Years of the Hollywood Western 130
Open and Shut 82, 119

192

Index

Pacino, Al 1, 49, 51, 74, 109, 130, 131, 156
The Package 108–109, 110, 125, 133
Parker, Alan 104, 106
Parsons, Estelle 22, 23, 24
Payback at Morning Peak 165
PCU 130
PCU Pit Party see *PCU*
Peck, Gregory 35, 37
Penn, Arthur 22, 23, 24, 25, 55, 56, 87, 88, 89, 103, 110
Peoples, David Webb 119, 125
Petrie, Donald 162
Pitt, Brad 148, 163
Pizzo, Angelo 90, 92, 94
Politically Correct University see *PCU*
Pollack, Sydney 123
Poor Richard *17*, 19
The Poseidon Adventure 1, 45, 46–*47*, 48, 57
Postcards from the Edge 115–116, 118, 134
Power 89–90, 95
Prime Cut 42–43, 83
Pursuit 167

The Quick and the Dead 128–130, 133, 143

Raimi, Sam 128, 129, 130
A Rainy Day in Newark 15, 16
Redford, Robert 1, 10, 15, 31, 76, 89, 111, 163
Reds 76–77, 80, 110
Reed, Oliver 35, 79
Reeve, Christopher 69, 70, 71, 72, 74, 97, 98, 99, 141, 161
Reeves, Keanu 147, 148
The Replacements 147–148
Resnik, Muriel 15–16, 17
Rey, Fernando 37, 59, 60
Reynolds, Burt 20, 42, 62, 63, 64, 91, 136
Richards, Dick 67
Richter, W.D. 77, 78–79
Riot 29, 30–31
Ritchie, Michael 31, 32, 33, 42, 43
Roeg, Nicolas 80, 81
The Role That Changed My Life: "I Was an Underdog" 165
Romano, Ray 161, 162
Rosenthal, Mark 97, 98
Rossen, Robert 14
Route 66: "Who Will Cheer My Bonnie Bride" 15
The Royal Tenenbaums 152–*153*, 154–155, 159

Runaway Jury 159–160
Russo, Richard 140, 163

The Saintliness of Margery Kempe 10–11
Salkind, Ilya 71, 73
Sarafian, Richard C. 29, 35
Sarandon, Susan 140, 163
Scarecrow 49–*50*, 51, 53, 83, 95, 99, 163
Schaefer, George 28, 34
Schatzberg, Jerry 49, 50, 83, 84
Scheider, Roy 37, 38, 39, 40, 41, 42, 44, 57, 67, 75
Schiffer, Michael 130, 131
Schisgal, Murray 20, 23, 27, 58
Scott, George C. 47, 77, 161
Scott, Ridley 79
Scott, Tony 131, 132, 141, 142, 165
Seberg, Jean 14
The Secret World of Antz 142
Shadow on the Land 29
Shelton, Ron 81, 117
Shurtleff on Acting 132–133
Sikking, James B. 113, 114, 115
The Silence of the Lambs 103, 111–112
Smith, Will 141, 142
Sonnenfeld, Barry 133, 134
South Park: "Krazy Kripples" 161
Speed Fever see *Formula 1—Febbre della velocità*
Spengler, Pierre 71, 73
Spielberg, Steven 57, 64, 79
The Split 28, 29
Split Decisions 100
Spottiswoode, Roger 81, 82
Stone, Oliver 119, 136
Stone, Sharon 128, 129, 142, 143
Streep, Meryl 2, 115, 116, 123
Streisand, Barbra 1, 77, 78, 79
Strong Black Woman 163
Sturges, John 30, 68
Superman 68–*70*, 71, 74, 142, 161
Superman II 68, 71, *72*–73, 98, 167
Superman II: The Richard Donner Cut 71, 73
Superman IV: The Quest for Peace 72, 97–98

Tallahassee 7000: "The Fugitive" 12
Tarantino, Quentin 131, 132, 141
Target 87–89
That Was the Week That Was 16

Thomas, Henry 83, 84
The Tonight Show with Jay Leno 132
The Tonight Show with Johnny Carson 43, 46, 52, 57
Towne, Robert 123, 131
Tramont, Jean-Claude 77, 78, 79
Travolta, John 83, 133, 134
The Trials of O'Brien: "The Only Game in Town" 20
Tripplehorn, Jean 123, 130
Troell, Jan 53
Twice in a Lifetime 86–87
Twilight 140
Two of a Kind 83

Ullmann, Liv 54, 55
Uncommon Valor 84–85
Under Fire 81–82, 86, 108, 117
Under Suspicion 143–145, 149
Unforgiven 119–121, 125, *126*, 129, 130, 133, 144
The Unknown Flag Raiser of Iwo Jima 167
The United States Steel Hour: "Big Doc's Girl" 11; "Brandenburg Gate" 12; "Bride of the Fox" 12; "Far from the Shade Tree" 12–13; "The Little Tin God" 11; "The Pink Burro" 11

Vaccaro, Brenda 13, 26
Verbinski, Gore 148
A View from the Bridge 8
V.I.P.—Schaukel 75
Voight, Jon 10, 87, 116, 141, 148

Wake of the Perdido Star 145, 148, 155
Washington, Denzel 90, 131, 132
We, the Marines 167
Weaver, Sigourney 148, 149
Weisz, Rachel 159, 160
Welcome to Mooseport 161–162
Wilder, Gene 22, 56, 57, 154
Williams, Robin 134, 136, 161
Wilson, Owen 152, 156, 157
Winston, Ron 26
Winters, Shelley 46, 47, 48
Wogan 98–99
Wyatt Earp 127–128, 130, 133

Yorkin, Bud 87
Young Frankenstein 2, 56–57, 63, 78, 98

Zandy's Bride 54–55, 64

www.ingramcontent.com/pod-product-compliance
Ingram Content Group UK Ltd.
Pitfield, Milton Keynes, MK11 3LW, UK
UKHW050524150426
5217IPUK00026B/1787